CERI STONE

LE LOOP

HOW TO CYCLE THE
TOUR DE FRANCE

First published by Pitch Publishing, 2022

Pitch Publishing
A2 Yeoman Gate
Yeoman Way
Worthing
Sussex
BN13 3QZ
www.pitchpublishing.co.uk
info@pitchpublishing.co.uk

ISBN 978 1 80150 115 6

Typesetting and origination by Pitch Publishing
Printed and bound in India by Replika Press Pvt. Ltd.

Contents

For Taela, Kaster and Oliver

One day you will just be a memory.

Make it a good one.

Le Loop and Tour De France Route(s) 2019

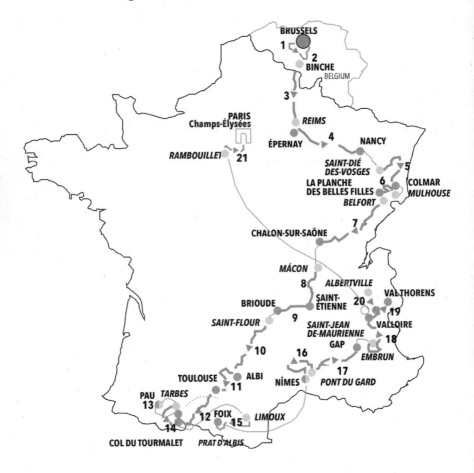

FALL SEVEN TIMES. GET UP EIGHT
– Japanese Proverb

Prologue

16 July 2019
Adversity

I COULD hear Fatima on the phone. She was a strong rider, great fun and not prone to the overdramatic. I was worried.

'THERE'S BEEN AN ACCIDENT.' There was panic in her voice.

'We need an ambulance. Ceri is out of the Tour.'

What? That brought me to my senses and rapidly cleared my lingering fog.

'Shut up Fatima. Fuck's sake I'm fine. I'm not stopping. Where is my Garmin? Will someone give me my bloody Garmin?'

I had no right to be so rude to Fatima she was just looking out for me. She was right, I had indeed had an accident. A bad one. I needed help and not just in finding my Garmin. There was a chance that I could be out of the Tour. All the lessons I had ever learned about resilience, overcoming adversity and never, ever giving up needed to be applied. Fast.

The 16th stage was, on paper, a straightforward parcours. We had endured some really tough days climbing in the Pyrenees, culminating in a very stressful stage 15, from Limoux to Foix, which included the Mur de Péguère with its climb of almost 3.5km and gradients of up to 20 per cent. We then transferred our aching limbs further east for a rest day, before starting over again with a run-of-the-mill stage. If there is such a thing in the Tour de France.

Stage 16 was an out-and-back, flat 177km route starting and finishing at our hotel in Nîmes. The greatest perils were some potential crosswinds and a lack of concentration, as we coaxed our legs back into a rhythm of churning the pedals over and over. We were lucky that the sun was shining, to the point of baking, and we seemed to avoid the worst of the mightily strong mistral breezes from the day before. It was stunning.

Nîmes is famous for its Roman monuments, such as the imposing amphitheatre Arena of Nîmes and the Maison Carrée, which is arguably the best-preserved Roman temple in the world. Not that we saw much of them on our rest day given our pressing need to eat, drink and refuel; launder kit; buy fresh supplies; tinker with bikes; receive massages and then eat, drink and refuel some more.

Early in the stage we did get to ride across the resplendent and iconic viaduct, Pont du Gard. The viaduct was less than a kilometre from feed stop one, which gave us time to fill up on cakes and energy drinks before the real riding started. As we left, we started to fall into our mini pelotons. I was due to be in a group which included my new-found friends Eric, Carmen, Andy and Stuart but as we moved out there was no sign of Carmen. I sent the others on and doubled back for her. It turned out she had punctured and had been left behind. Five minutes and a quick tube change later and we set off again, distanced at the back of a field of 100 or so riders with a lot of time to make up and plenty of kilometres to do it in.

This was a great day. The lead rider Emily had waited for us and I was fortunate to spend my time riding hard with two inspirational ladies. We were already 20 minutes adrift of the field and eager to make up for lost time. By lunch at feed stop three we had passed three groups of backmarkers and caught up with a team who would share the workload for the final 100km back into Nîmes. Carmen appreciated the support and camaraderie. I reflected as we glided over baking tarmac, with a warm summer haze wafting across our bikes, that you achieve far more working with a team compared to struggling on alone. I have long learned the value of teamwork and we were in unison for the day and rapidly made up lost time. The efforts of 16 days on the road were falling into place.

On the home stretch into Nîmes, we had the wind at our backs and a strong group of ten or so riding in perfect unison. We were strung out in formation with each taking a turn of 90 seconds on the front before drifting to the back of the group to draft in the wheels. The pace was rapid and the warm sun helped us glide along the smooth, almost empty roads through the tranquil fields of southern France.

The efficiency of the team was idyllic. We rode within inches of the rear wheel in front, hiding from the breeze, while Eric kept his eyes fervently peeled for somewhere to buy an ice cream. He was on a mission and we just had to maintain concentration and effort. I was in nirvana. The ease with which we were covering a vast terrain was almost euphoric. We were emulating the feats of our heroes who would be riding the Tour for real a week after us.

'Stopping!' the rider in front called out. He was six inches from my front wheel. He had punctured. He hit the brakes. I pulled back on mine. We were travelling at close to 30kph and I had nowhere to go. Riding on the right-hand side of the road I looked at swerving left but I was trapped inside him. As he stopped, he turned right and pulled into the side of the road. I hit the wing of his bike and went over the top of my mine.

I tried desperately to cling to my bike and keep it upright. I failed. I remember putting my hands out in a vain attempt to break my fall. I failed again. I hit my head. I smashed my right shoulder and right hip before my mate came to rest, landing on top of my left hip. The sound of my carbon frame scraping against concrete grated through me, but not as much as the impact of my helmet hitting the ground and smashing into my forehead. My Garmin computer went flying ahead of us and my prescription sunglasses shattered. My shorts were ripped to pieces and blood was on the concrete underneath our bikes.

I lay back and tried to feel my feet, my arms and my body. I dared not move my head. I was angry. I was frustrated. I was confused. I was embarrassed and above all I was frightened of failure. I had set out a year earlier with two big goals that I had set for myself, one of which was to cycle the Tour de France, and here I was, in pieces on some inanimate French concrete.

I heard Fatima tell the organisers I was out of the Tour.

FEEL THE FEAR AND DO IT
ANYWAY – Susan Jeffers

Chapter 1

Make Your Mind Up Time

I AM an unremarkable human being. I have no special skills, talents or abilities. I am an ordinary guy. I desperately wanted to do something remarkable, just once in this ordinary life.

I would love to state with great bluster and confidence that this book will change your life – if I am able to complete this book. If I can fulfil a goal and accomplish something worthy of note, it will prove wholeheartedly that you too can achieve whatever you put your mind to. Maybe then, your life could also change for the better.

While you read this book, you should start asking yourself what exactly it is that you want to do or want out of life. What would you like to be remembered for when your time is finally up? Do you want to climb a mountain? Start and run a successful business? Become a millionaire? Write a book? Whatever you dream of in life, I want to help you by first putting myself out there and trying to prove that I can achieve something that I had dreamed of, for a long, long while. If I fail then the odds are this book will not change your life because it will not be worthy of being published in the first place. But if you read on, let my deeds inspire you to reach for the stars. Or at the very least let my failings entertain you.

As I will frequently remind you, I am an ordinary guy. I am average height, average build, balding, pot-bellied, lazy and far from being an intellect. I do not possess one outstanding skill that sets me apart. I am not strong. I have no speed, power or any form of great athletic ability. Okay I am fit and relatively healthy. I have common sense and I guess some charm or charisma (you can be the judge of that), but I am not everyone's cup of tea.

My demeanour can be misconstrued as arrogance when in fact I am rather shy and masking a lack of confidence. I can polarise opinions. I have a generally positive outlook and see the best in everyone, but man do I like a good moan and woe betide the fool who crosses me. I have made many mistakes in my life and I have only learned from a handful of them.

I do not consider myself lucky, yet I am fortunate to have lived a great life and I have experienced some moderate successes as the years have passed by. I genuinely like myself (sorry all you pop psychologists) but I worry myself to sleep over what someone I don't know, or care about, thinks about me. If only you could like me as much as I do.

Where I am fortunate is that I have learned a great deal over the years. I have lived and worked with some amazing people and I have absorbed some very valuable lessons from all of them. I have read dozens upon dozens of self-help, success, goal-setting, sales, leadership and communication books and manuals. Some of them are nonsense. Some are plain common sense and there are others which hold nuggets of truth and encouragement that I have tried to remember over time. This is not one of those books.

I would not dare to devise some notion or ideal that I could market as my own. I do not possess the intellectual prowess for such a thing. I must also state that I am not a self-help guru, I am not a coach and I do not pretend to be Anthony Robbins or anyone of that ilk. I am not looking to sell out a huge seminar hall to tell my story. I do not wish to entice you to part with all of your savings on a critical training course which will change your life. You would be poorer for it and I suspect that is not the change you would have been looking for. I know who I am. I know my limitations. I am not greedy, but I do hope that just one person who reads these pages is motivated to cast off their shackles and give their lifelong dream a shot.

What I can do is take all of the finest gems of inspiration that have helped me down the years and apply these into a real-life scenario and prove that with the right motivation we are able to achieve anything we want.

Yes, we can achieve anything we want. Within reason. Swansea City keep telling me that at 52 I am too old to play for them. Seriously? I am exactly what they need right now.

Within this book you will find three key elements to help you in your quest for personal glory.

1. A very simple section of theory, based on what has worked for me over the years.

2. A practical application of that theory as I recount my tale and use all of those tools in my own personal challenge.
3. Some whimsical quotes that have amused and inspired me down the years.

As I mentioned, I am unremarkable. I wanted to do something remarkable and prove that any old fool can achieve something extraordinary. Are you with me?

If I am to recount my tale of eternal dream-chasing for your entertainment then this begs the following questions:

1. What is it that I want to do?
2. How can I achieve this dream?

Let's start with the second question first. Back to front I know but there is logic in my disorder and it creates a frisson of dramatic suspense.

How can I achieve success?

Let's get one thing straight from the start. There is no shortcut to success. This book will not provide an easy fix or a simple solution. It will not wave a magic wand where all of our dreams instantly materialise. I have tried that constantly and it has failed to deliver constantly. Success comes through hard work.

It needs dedication, commitment and resilience and it takes effort. This does not mean that it cannot be fun along the way because it should be. One simple thing I learned from a young age is that the journey is the destination. If you do not enjoy the training sessions you will not become a better player and you will not gain the satisfaction of performing at your peak in a match. But I digress. The aim of this book is to apply the lessons I have learned over the years, to put them into simple steps and prove that they do indeed work.

These are not inexhaustible but they are what work for me. I may not apply all of them throughout my journey but they form the gist of what it takes for me to succeed along the way.

If you were to do a quick search on the internet with the words 'Steps to Success' you would find hundreds of books, blogs, seminars, journals and even more training companies with websites, plus page upon page of straightforward lists, varying from three steps to success to 12 steps to success and more. The list of sources is endless and it is hard to know where to begin. Some titles claim to have a unique solution, others lay out common sense in a really logical way. Some provide a quick fix where others waffle without saying anything, in the hope of enticing us to sign up for a timeshare in the Balearics.

I have taken the best from all of these solutions, many ideas of which are repeated with varying headings down the years, and applied them to my own personal ambition. They are as follows:

Ceri's 7 (and a bit) rungs on the ladder to success

1. Dream Big and Commit
2. Preparation. Preparation. Preparation
3. Live and Love
4. Hard Work and Resilience

5. Motivation
    a. Focus on Success
    b. INIOP – My own personal motivating gimmick
    c. Love and Rage
6. Include and Inspire
7. Celebrate Hard

Again, I feel the overwhelming urge to insert the caveat that I am no expert in the field of life-coaching or motivating those in need. I have no science behind my theories and I have no qualifications in psychology or the life sciences. There have been no double-blind studies testing my logic so please understand that my seven (and a bit) steps are purely based on common sense and what has worked for me in the past.

I have a modicum of life experience to draw upon and I have tasted moderate success. I have successfully motivated and managed teams who have worked for me and I have achieved most dreams that I have chased. My goals have frequently been modest and not grand enough for what the human body and mind are capable of. I failed catastrophically as a young adult during one memorable period of my life, from which I learned more about myself than at any other stage since.

I learned that failure is inevitable and how you react to it is how you measure your character and achievements. I may one day confront this disaster or I may conveniently keep it buried in the dark recesses of the memory labelled 'Stupid Bloody Idiot Grow Up'. I have also never come to terms with the fact that Swansea City keep telling me that I am not good enough for them, even though my boots are in the back of my car for every game I go to watch.

If my logic is similar to anything else that you may have read or that has been published then I apologise. I have read countless books over the years and some of the greatness must have sunk in somewhere along the line. I have also learned from great people and taken on board every lesson they have taught. If I state the obvious, I apologise. This book is designed to be a 'proof is in the pudding' of all the encouragement I have received. In no way is it intended to be a plagiaristic homage to every coach who is out there. It is for this reason that my theory and definitions are kept deliberately succinct.

1. Dream Big and Commit

'Setting goals is the first step in turning the invisible into the visible.' – Tony Robbins

As Captain Sensible once sang in the early eighties, 'You've got to have a dream, if you don't have a dream, how you gonna make a dream come true?' Brilliant song 'Happy Talk' and the punk sell-out was correct. The first step to achieving any form of success or realising your goals is to have that goal in the first place.

So, dig deep and ask yourself what is it that you really want? What are your core values? What are you passionate about and what gets you out of bed in the morning? What do you love doing that helps others? If money wasn't an object, what would you do with your life? Spend some time looking at what it is that you really want and what you have an overwhelming passion for. Then make a decision.

The first rung on the ladder is making your mind up. Be passionate. Dream big and make a damned decision.

Once that goal is set, write it down. In fact, write it down and set a deadline. This means you cannot let the joy of procrastination overtake your progress. Then commit to it and commit to doing something daily that will help you win in the long term.

I will let you into a secret. As I write I am starting to re-evaluate my whole life and career so there is a chance I may go on a little journey within a journey. I have my great goal decided upon but that brings far more passion to my life than my current successful run-of-the-mill career. Let's see where this takes us.

Now that the decision is made and cast in stone, we need to work out how on earth we are going to complete the whole thing.

2. Preparation. Preparation. Preparation

'Our goals can be reached through a vehicle of a plan, in which we must fervently believe, and upon which we must vigorously act. There is no other route to success.' – Pablo Picasso

I love a good plan. And to paraphrase the A-Team I love it even more when a plan comes together.

The planning stage is the most essential aspect of attaining any form of success. Herein lie the building blocks and foundations for everything that will follow. There are many great quotes and lessons that will drive this point home and when you work in any form of corporate structure you will hear them all. They may be clichés but they are no less true and they certainly add value.

An old manager in my first career incarnation in insurance repeatedly told us: 'People don't plan to fail they fail to plan.' We heard this way too often but it has never left me, so thank you David 'Beaker' Goodman. I then achieved a dream of living and working overseas where we were repeatedly taught that the three keys to success are: Preparation. Preparation. Preparation. When you have to stand up and give a presentation to 300 angry tourists who have been overbooked, you need to know your stuff and that only comes with preparation.

The start of a good plan is to write it down. Take your overall goal and break it down into small daily, bite-sized chunks. Most people look at their grand dream and become overwhelmed at the sheer scale of it and they are defeated before they have begun. The way to make this easy and attainable is to 'Keep It Simple Stupid'. Another travel industry acronym.

A good example is something I used to do with my sales team when I worked in publishing. Each sales rep would have their individual pre-set target for the year. When you looked at a goal of generating a total of let's say £100k per annum, this could be overwhelming and borderline frightening at first glance. But if you break it down to the point that the average sale is £500 this means that the salesman has to make 200 individual sales per year, though that is still daunting and a long way off.

Let's say that he/she works for just 40 weeks of the year and takes an extended summer and Christmas break: this then equates to five sales per week, which in turn breaks down to one sale per day. If we say that on average the sales rep needs to attend two appointments to get one sale and has to make four phone calls to get one appointment, this means that the rep needs to make eight phone calls per day to get two appointments, which breaks down even further to making just one phone call per hour.

By breaking down the whole process and forming a daily plan, the sales rep could achieve their £100k target if they make just one phone call at 9am, each day. It is that simple.

Write your plan down. It could be a simple daily list or a detailed spreadsheet but simplify it into daily, easily achievable chunks. There are many great tools available, from training plans for a marathon to goal-setting journals which do exactly this.

Once your plan is written down, complete a journal or a log of what you have done each day. This not only helps you maintain some epic habits, it also serves as motivation when you have a wobble down the line. For instance, if you are training for a marathon over a period of four months and after ten weeks you feel that you are stalling in your progress and going nowhere, take a look at your log. As you look back you might just see that you have completed four sessions per week, or an average of 6–8 hours training per week; your average speed and distance will have increased gradually without you noticing and, overall, you will have covered more than 200 miles. That would already be some achievement in itself which means you can afford to pat yourself on the back and move on with the plan.

Break your goal down into daily epic habits. Write it down and keep a log of what you do. This allows you to live your dream.

3. Live and Love

'Do what you love. Love what you do.'

Ever since I started working overseas in the early nineties, I have had a poster on my wall which says 'The Journey is the Destination'. People frequently tend to get caught up in their end goal and it is easy to forget to stop and smell the roses along the way. Yes, commitment and dedication are a minimum to achieving any worthwhile goal but you need to enjoy the process to allow you to live it to the best of your ability. Living and loving the process is essential to prevailing in whatever you do. If you take a half-hearted approach, you will only achieve half of what you want. That to me is failure, whereas living a life filled with passion is success.

To live your dream, you need to adopt what I refer to as 'epic habits'. Every moment of every day, make your dream your focus and make decisions based around or including your end goal. Granted, daily life and careers will no doubt be a priority, so they either need to be included or worked around.

Success is never easy; it takes a special kind of dedication. When making decisions ask yourself does this benefit your goal? If not, then why are you doing it? Or what can you alter to make it beneficial?

In 2013 I ran my first Ironman race (yes, I have run more than one, which I will no doubt brag about down the line) and this transformed my life for the better. I started going to bed one hour earlier each night because the rest was beneficial to me. I went swimming before work and I overhauled my diet and made sure I ate at consistent times during the day. If I was at a function for work, I would choose the healthy meal options. If I was on the road for a couple of days, I would always book a hotel with either a gym, a pool or one near to a park where I could go for a run. My shower at home takes one minute to heat up so every morning I would do a plank for 60 seconds to make the best use of that time while I was waiting. When brushing my teeth, I would do it standing on one foot to strengthen my core muscles.

> *'If you want to change the world,*
> *start off by making your bed.'* –
> William H. McRaven

Like this awe-inspiring Navy SEAL, every day I started by making my bed. I adopted lots of small epic habits and made every decision include the process of training for an Ironman. I also trained for 15 hours per week as part of my training plan. All part of my epic habits.

Invest in yourself. This is supposed to be enjoyable and rewarding, it is not meant to be a thankless and soulless slog. You need to look after yourself and continually see improvement to be able to stay committed.

Reward yourself for small victories. Sit back and savour your achievements or growth so far and look after your health and well-being. If you are passionate about your goal then this will come naturally.

Believe in what you are doing, both overall and on a daily basis and act as if you have already achieved your goal. If you are a salesman, act as if you own the company and take responsibility for everything. If you want to run a marathon, train as if you are racing to compete with Mo Farah. If you want to write a book, write as if your book is already on the shelves. What the mind can perceive to believe it will achieve. Another gem from my insurance days. I learned so much from a career I hated.

Tell people about your goal. Get friends, family and like-minded people onside and involved in what you are doing. Before long they will start helping you and providing support, especially if you act as if this is happening. You will attract like-minded people or those with a similar interest and this provides a support network and further opportunities for learning.

Keep learning and improving. Maintain those epic habits and look for every opportunity to improve your knowledge, processes and outcome. Sir Dave Brailsford constantly talks about the aggregation of marginal gains. This is simply making small improvements of 1 per cent here and half a per cent there, which added together could make a 5 per cent difference, which in cycling terms is huge. Keep looking at your process and be flexible as you maintain great daily routines.

Another cycling legend, Sir Chris Hoy, frequently refers to the process when he talks on TV. I have tried to apply this in my daily life and it makes so much sense. Focus on the process on a daily basis and prioritise the process over the outcome. Make the process an epic habit. Live for it, love it and keep on learning.

If you focus on the process and ensure that you give complete attention to your training plan, your product knowledge, your target audience or sales technique, then the art of crossing that finish line, or getting people to sign on the dotted line, becomes automatic. Focus on, and love, the process, and the outcome will take care of itself.

If you live it and love it you will succeed. This in turn allows you to work hard towards this success.

4. Hard Work and Resilience

'Success is one per cent inspiration and ninety-nine per cent perspiration.' – Thomas Edison

There is no shortcut to success. If you want financial gain it has to be earned and worked for and there is always a price to pay. Warranted, you could win the National Lottery, but what are the odds on that? One in 60 million? One in 100 million? Those are your odds of success with no discernible effort. Jarvis Cocker once remarked that his band Pulp were an overnight success; it just took ten years of hard graft to get there. This applies to any goal or ambition.

There is no easy way to say this but if you want to achieve anything in life you need to put in the effort. Once you have set your goal, be prepared to work harder than anyone else in the room and if you think that preparation, training and effort is hard, try failing.

Something I learned whilst working overseas in the travel industry is that it is very easy to sit back, soak up the sun and live the easy life. But remember this: suntans fade, success lasts forever.

As well as the determination to put in the hours, you need the ability to pick yourself up when things go against you. Which they will. Life is not straightforward. Other people get in the way and complicate it and you will suffer setbacks along the way. This is when you need to develop a thick skin and resilience.

There is an old Japanese proverb which a good friend of mind, Masao Matsumoto, quoted to me over a beer: 'Fall seven times and stand up eight.' This in a nutshell is resilience.

Accept that failure is inevitable and realise that successful people are the ones who respond to this the best. My friend Masao is a good example and he is a great motivating presence for me. He has what I would define as the spirit of an Ironman.

Masao loves Ironman. He has competed in almost 50 of them. He particularly loves Ironman Wales in Tenby and Tenby loves him. Masao is a very busy man who lives in Tokyo. He has a successful career; this is his focus and he has a great life. He gets to travel and he competes in three Ironman races every year. The issue for him is that he does not have much time to train hard for Ironman and where he lives in Tokyo there is little or no opportunity for him to practise cycling up hills. In Ironman Wales there are a lot of hills. Steep ones. On both laps of the bike. And the run. Ironman Wales is regarded as one of the toughest on the circuit but it does have the greatest atmosphere, which embraces its latest sons like Masao. We love his spirit.

In 2011 Masao completed the first Ironman that was raced in Tenby and he made a lot of friends along the way with his humility, cheerful demeanour and generosity of spirit. He returned the following year and did not finish. He did not finish again in the next six years for one reason or another. In 2014 there were the most horrendous two-metre swells in the sea swim. In 2013 it was freezing cold and wet, making the bike route treacherous. In other years the course was just too much.

But Masao kept picking himself up. He returned year after year, having made more and more friends and in 2018 he made the bike cut-off with seven minutes to spare. He finished the whole race with roughly 20 minutes left available.

This was testament to his indomitable spirit, his drive to succeed and the ability to deal with minor failure and keep moving forward until he succeeded once more. His outlook makes him an inspiration and his resilience ensures he is a hero and a success. I owe a lot to him.

Masao's story is not dissimilar to that of basketball great Michael Jordan, whose greatness can be summed up in this one brilliant statement:

'I've missed more than 9,000 shots in my career. I've lost almost 300 games; 26 times I've been trusted to take the game-winning shot and missed. I've failed over and over and over again in my life. And that is why I succeed.'

Find that inner strength. Find the reason to go on and develop your resilience in all aspects of life because this is what will define you. If you can work out what motivates you in your quest, you too can be a bit more Masao.

5. Motivate Yourself

'The man on top of the mountain didn't fall there.' – Vince Lombardi

Motivation is key. Desire is what helps you on your way but motivation is what makes you succeed. Motivation makes you get out of bed every morning. It is what helps you decide on your goal in the first instance. It makes you resilient. It allows you to maintain your epic habits on a daily basis. It picks you up when you are down. It allows you to work hard. Harder than the rest. It makes you resilient and it helps you succeed.

The interesting factor with motivation is that some people have a natural innate drive that constantly fuels their fire, but for others it has to be nurtured and developed. From a personal perspective, I find it hard to start a project or piece of work and I find procrastination to be a constant companion. Once I make a decision and commit myself to a target and a routine, I find that I have a seemingly endless determination. But I need that push to get me out of bed in the morning and I find that I need to find ways to motivate myself to get going. However, I have learned how to find that desire and I have learned to push on when others sit by the roadside taking the easy way out. Whatever it is that fuels your inner drive, you need to discover it and nurture it. Personally, I find there are three categories which get me off my posterior (or on it in the case of writing a report for work).

a. Focus on the glory

This relates to the Captain Sensible song again, in that you have got to have a dream if you are going to achieve it, but it takes it a step further in that you need to focus on what that glory looks like.

Everyone loves success. We all love adulation and basking in the warmth of a job well done being recognised, but not everyone can see it. When I embark on chasing a dream, I picture myself succeeding.

There are many theories on visualisation techniques which are utilised time and again by top-class athletes and these can be easily filtered through online. At the beginning of a challenge, I believe in spending just ten minutes in a quiet space picturing myself succeeding. I act out the motions of completing a job. I focus on the smell of the environment; the noise from adoring crowds, the rounds of applause and cheering; how I will react to it; I dream of the emotions involved; be it heart-swelling pride, gloating over the vanquished, the emotion that brings you to tears or to roaring with delight. Add in as much detail as possible. Make it simple and then keep it with you.

I have used this to very simple effect with every marathon I have run, each Ironman I have completed and within the workplace with every award I have celebrated with my company. Focus on the success and tailor every action to that exact moment of glory.

b. INIOP

'Don't be distracted by criticism. The only taste of success some people get is to take a bite out of you.' – Zig Ziglar

This is my own personal motivating gimmick. These five letters are written on my forearm in every photo you will see of me crossing the finish line of each of my five Ironman successes. This mantra evolved because of the type of person I am and the way that I am frequently perceived.

As I have stated, I am an unremarkable human being but I have achieved almost every goal I have set out to do. At first glance I do not create an awe-inspiring impression and I am regularly underestimated. I do not possess one striking quality of genius, apart from my desire to see a job through to the very end. This inner fire is not instantly visible and it has been nurtured through experience.

It is a very British trait that we like to build up our heroes and then bring them back down to earth. We do not like our winners becoming too big for their boots or celebrating their achievements.

There are many people in this world who have failed in life before they have left school and these people will spend their entire lives bringing the rest of us down to their level. Think about it. Every family has that one person who tells you their own truth at every familial gathering. I have faced this frequently in life and I have learned to use this as a spur to make me a better person. My solution is very simple:

*Ignore Negative Influences
of Other People.*

Surround yourself with people who believe in you and make you feel great about yourself. When you are confronted by naysayers, ignore them. Do not allow them the time of day to influence your thinking and, if you do use them, use them as fuel to make you work that bit harder to be that better person.

c. Love and Rage – Passion

Love and hate are the two most powerful forms of motivation. Everything can be simplified into one form or the other and then channelled into an energy for the positive. I must stipulate that I prefer the word 'rage' over 'hate'. This is simply because I do not carry hatred with me, but I do have moments of rage and I have learned how to use this energy for my own greater good.

Love and rage are two incredibly powerful energies and filled with either you can climb mountains. This means that on occasion you have to be able to summon the energy from one or the other to fuel your desire. I do believe that you need to both include and inspire other people to use as a motivational tool but I will deal with this separately; however, there is considerable crossover in these steps of mine.

We have all heard tales of how love can inspire the meekest of people to superhuman feats of strength. Stories of how young boys have lifted cars off their fathers who have been trapped; tales of parents running into burning buildings to save children without thought of consequence to themselves; or people throwing themselves in front of loved ones at the first sight of danger. These are all a natural consequence of love and a simmering strength inside us all. If we can tap into this energy, we will develop the superhuman in us. The trick is to find the love that fires your spirit and makes you a better human being.

My personal motivating loves are twofold. Firstly, I should point out that I do not have a family of my own but I have a niece and two nephews who are my world and parents who are my everything. I love my brother's and sister's kids as if they are my own, so much so they have the dual power to make me superhuman and render me lifeless. One smile from them and I am Superman, but in the same token they are my Kryptonite and a disappointed glare can bring me to my knees. Tapping into their energy encourages me to be the best person I can be and their smiles could light up a thousand cities. That is something worth fighting for.

I desperately want the best for my niece and nephews and I want to create a better world for them. The best way that I can achieve this is to show them that anything is possible and if they put their minds to it they can have everything they want. In times of darkness or when extra effort is needed, I picture their young faces looking up at me and I am prepared to hurt far more for their gain than for mine.

My second area of love is my own ego. I love myself and I am not bashful to admit that I take a great deal of pride in my achievements. This is something that I use as a motivating tool because whenever I set a goal I am chasing it for myself. I simply love meeting people and seeing their faces when I say that I have finished an Ironman or that my company has won another award. This is all about satisfying my own ego and it is an important tool in my own motivation.

As a contrast I am driven by the fear of having to admit failure. I have a very positive outlook and it causes me great pain if I fail in an endeavour. If I flip it upside down, I take huge satisfaction from being able to boast about any form of success. Ironically, when I do achieve a truly significant goal, I am less likely to feel the need to brag. Deep inside I know that I have been great, which helps me feel very comfortable in my own skin, because my ego has been fed and satiated. This allows me to stride that little bit taller. As opposed to the shameful walk of failure.

In the same token rage can be just as powerful a gift when harnessed. Find that action, deed, misspoken word, decision or misjudgement that angers you and control it so that it energises your own actions moving forward. My favourite exponent of this was John McEnroe, who was able to combine the deftest touch with a tennis racquet with the rage that gave him a laser-like focus. I have used this regularly through the years, varying from anger at a refereeing decision in football to righting an injustice in the workplace. I have it well worked out now to the extent that I can tap into it in a triathlon.

I am not a strong swimmer so will struggle to be competitive in races but I have produced some decent splits on the bike and run, on occasion. As soon as I mount the bike, I lock into the rider immediately in front of me and focus on something I don't like.

This is usually inane and trivial but I can spend minutes screaming inside my head, 'Come on blue shorts, I've got you blue shorts, you are history,' and I focus on defeating the enemy in the blue shorts. Once I pull level I can switch off, smile and shout something encouraging to them – 'Good job buddy. You've got this.' I then target the next person who may have fat calves or a yellow bike and has the misfortune of being next in line.

Learn to find that rage. Don't make it personal and do not let it linger. A positive energy can very quickly become a negative when you focus all your energy on defeating one individual or action, which just happens to be a small cog in the grand plan.

Rage and love are two of the biggest sources of energy and your love can be enhanced further if you are inspiring greatness in others.

6. Include and Inspire

'The act of succeeding with a team makes an individual stronger.' – Arsène Wenger

'Include and Inspire' is an extension of finding your own motivation. Where your own desire gets you going and drives you forward, the act of inclusion and inspiring gives you a reason to succeed and in turn makes you a more rounded human being. This may not be top of your list of goal-getting strategies but it is important to my mindset of prevailing with character.

Including other people brings so many benefits. It allows other people to buy into your goal and help you out along the way. It provides motivation because your success may well impact on the well-being of others, particularly if you harbour a team-focused or industry-related goal. No one achieves greatness on their own and the support of others can be crucial. Yes, you have to take responsibility for your own actions but the assistance of others will only serve to make you stronger, quicker or wiser.

I can personally attest to this with so many examples but the greatest that stands out for me was the industry recognition and commercial gain I achieved with my last company. I was the managing director for an educational supplies business and we had a team of roughly ten people plus a board of directors based overseas.

During my decade of working with them we achieved some great commercial success by more than trebling the business income in our first three years of my tenure. We achieved some form of industry recognition or award every year that I was involved in the business. This came from our peers, the industry as a whole and our customers (not one written complaint in a decade meant we were doing something right). At each of these award ceremonies I was the figurehead for the business and I collected the trophies and I was the one in all of the photographs, press cuttings and industry articles.

I can safely state that I was good at my job. I set the targets and business plan for the year for our team to achieve and I was instrumental in a lot of the income that was generated. But here is the thing. I was not responsible for our success; I just took the glory. I worked with a team who were superb on a daily basis. Each one of them had a goal and a plan for the year. Each one of them dealt with problems and personal issues, yet each one of them was driven and resilient and working for the greater good of the team. We achieved great things because every team member was integral to our future and well-being.

I like to think that I was good at including the whole team in our business goals and how we would achieve them and I helped foster a wonderful team spirit. I was no greater than the sum of their collective parts and the team I worked with were superb every single day. This means that by being part of a team and including everyone in the team I had a successful career and achieved a huge amount because of them. Including others in your dreams is essential to the outcome.

The same can be said for the goal of inspiration, but this works in two ways. Firstly, you should look to inspire other people to greatness. I believe behaviour breeds behaviour and if you inspire those less fortunate you will receive greatness that exceeds your own individual targets. Secondly, you should look to see what inspires you and makes you want to be a more rounded individual by contributing to the lives of others.

The greatest example of this can be seen every year in April at the London Marathon. Countless runners cross that finish line with the thought of not letting their charity down. Inspiring those less fortunate spurs them on.

This was the first marathon I entered and finished in 2011 and I was running to make my four-year-old niece proud of me and to raise funds for a charity that was close to my heart at the time. I was able to generate just short of £5,000 for disadvantaged and disabled children and in so doing improve the lives of those who are not able to take part in an event like this. By inspiring and being inspired I was on the road to greater things.

> *'Try not to be a man of success.*
> *Rather become a man of value.'* –
> Albert Einstein

I know this quote contradicts some of my earlier points but I happen to love it. If you become a man of value, you will inspire others around you and you will gain motivation in return. This in turn allows you to celebrate your victories with gusto.

7. Celebrate Hard

'If you don't celebrate success, it won't celebrate you.' – Julian Hall

This is frequently overlooked but is crucial. I don't just mean celebrating the overall fulfilment of a goal but also celebrating milestones as you head down that path. If you don't celebrate success, you will feel less inclined to reach your goals the next time around and there is a danger that you will not recognise success in the future.

This is really straightforward and does not need labouring: simply set aside time to enjoy the rewards of your success and pat yourself on the back. If you have put the work in you will have deserved it.

My favourite example of this is back in 2013 when I completed my first Ironman race. I had set myself the goal of completing the race and I was not aiming for a specific time because I was still learning the event. Finishing was the ultimate goal for me. I succeeded and I indulged heavily. Not the way you are thinking.

I had promised myself that I would buy myself a tailor-made cashmere wool suit if I finished and that is exactly what I ordered a week after finishing. The beauty of this is that every time I put this suit on, not only do I revel in its timeless splendour and quality, but more importantly I am reminded of the fact that I achieved something epic.

I dreamed big. I worked hard. I was resilient, inspirational, determined and motivated and I achieved what I had set out to do a year earlier. I celebrated hard with some fine tailoring. That celebration constantly reminds me that I am capable of anything I put my mind to. I just need to apply what I have learned, and preached, to something that is even bigger in my heart.

This brings me back to the first question which I had conveniently skipped over: With the tedious theory of success element out of the way, what is it that I want to achieve?

This one particular goal had stirred in me during the mid-eighties when I was transfixed by the Channel 4 coverage of Greg LeMond's epic battle with his own team-mate Bernard Hinault for the Tour de France. As the drama grew and played out, I was in awe of these superhuman beings. Back then I was a very young and skinny kid and thought that such feats were way beyond my underdeveloped teenage reach. Any thought of doing something on that scale was deemed impossible or at best improbable, so I was happy to play football, be great at work and travel the world.

I would drift back to this dream from time to time but life would get in the way. Isn't that what happens when you are making plans? But then one fortuitous day in July 2018 I took the bull by the horns, briefly cast off my many and considerable shackles and insecurities and took one of the biggest risks of my life.

This was my commitment to myself.

> My name is Ceri Stone. I promise myself that I will achieve my lifelong dream of cycling the route of the Tour de France. Without the aid of performance-enhancing drugs.
>
> I also promise that I will publish a book detailing my experience which will become wildly successful.

That is step one. I have dreamed big and my goals are written down.

I suspect you noticed that I have two intertwining goals, not one? I hope this doesn't complicate matters? This is my journey, the story of how I reached for the stars, crashed very hard back down to concrete and hopefully inspired just one person that follows to chase their own unattainable rainbow. All because of an impulsive moment in 2018.

Enjoy the ride.

IF YOU ARE NOT LIVING
LIFE ON THE EDGE, YOU ARE
TAKING UP TOO MUCH SPACE –
Morgan Freeman

Chapter 2

July 2018
Dream Big (1)

I BELIEVED I had a window of three hours and in that moment, I despised Geraint Thomas. Yes, that soon-to-be Yellow Jersey-winning Welshman of the Tour de France 2018. Damned Geraint Thomas and his incredible achievements and superhuman exploits. Damned Geraint Thomas proving that nice guys do win; that hard work, determination and effort does pay off; that great things are achievable from the boy next door.

Damn that Geraint Thomas for proving to be an inspiration and forcing me to be a better human being. Damn him for teaching me that anything is possible and in the euphoria of his three-week tour de force encouraging me, albeit unwittingly from afar, to believe in myself and take on a challenge that was far beyond my wildest dreams.

Three hours I had. A small window. Sweat was dripping off my brow, my heart was racing at 140 beats per minute and my tongue was dry with nerves. I was edgy, exhausted and riddled with tension. How could this be? What I was about to do couldn't be that hard? I had done this dozens of times before with other events and my training over the previous few years meant that exact moment in time should have been routine. But I paused, caught my breath, questioned my motives for the umpteenth time and forced myself to push on. I refused to look back.

I rose out of my seat. It was still only 9.14am on Thursday, 26 July and the day was fresh but I had been preparing for this exact moment for the previous 12 months. Ever since a friend pointed me in the direction of an innocuous web page about some interesting bike ride. At that stage I had already signed up to cycle the three-day Dragon Tour in the mountains of the Brecon Beacons in June 2018 (I use the word mountains liberally for dramatic effect). Knowing of my love for a challenge, she thought this would be interesting. I loved and hated the Dragon Tour in equal measure.

I am not exactly an athlete and can be described as more of an honest trier. I am competitive with myself and for some reason there is a part of my DNA that doesn't like to be told that I am not allowed to do something. My sister thought that at 51 years of age I was only just becoming as grown up and mature as her seven-year-old son; so identical were we in outlook we were very easy to manipulate. Tell us we are not allowed something we enjoy and watch us do the exact opposite. You'll never run a marathon. You will never be able to swim 1,000m. You can't have those chips. You'll never finish a triathlon. That girl will be trouble. You will find it impossible to run an Ironman. No more beer for you. All statements, mistakes or challenges laid at my feet over the previous decade and all accomplished or regretted with a bit of hard work, training, hunger, effort, heartbreak, luck and thirst. By me, not my nephew. He doesn't drink yet.

But this moment was out of my comfort zone. This was too hard and too much to take on. How could I push through and find the will to see the journey right to the very end? Three weeks is a long time to be spent in the saddle for an amateur plodder like me, and 3,500km over 21 days is way too far for my ageing, creaking body to hold out.

To start with it would mean three weeks off work and making sure the team could cope without me. That was not taking into account the training of five days a week, at almost 20 hours a week on top of a busy working schedule, before I could even contemplate the long steep climbs in the Alps and the Pyrenees. They would surely prove to be too much for a skinny, beer-bellied, middle-aged man in Lycra like me. Would I have the reserves, the strength of character, the physical capabilities and the moral fortitude to carry on?

I needed to dig deep. I needed to make my mind up and decide if continuing was for me or not. I had a dream. Could I commit to it?

Decision made, I was out of my seat. I moved forward with a sluggish, unathletic gait, the propulsion coming not from my racing core but from a nervous beating heart. I was up, out and beyond the confines of the small, closeted, professional vacuum that was my office and shouted out to the workforce:

'Does anyone have any objections to me taking three weeks' holiday next July? You have 60 seconds to let me know.'

The staff looked on nonplussed, probably expecting me to generously offer a third cup of tea already for that morning. One asked why I would want so long. I explained that I wanted a sporting holiday where I would take on a huge challenge. They appeared disinterested, more concerned at dealing with a customer with great care in the way that I had tried to teach them over the years. They were a great bunch and the sum of their parts ran the company without me needing to be in the MD's chair, but that was for another day and another challenge I would need to confront. Their daily lives were far more important than my comfortable concerns over whether I should have a glass of red or white wine with my dinner that evening.

'Course you can boss,' one of the ladies generously replied.

Mumbling my nervous thanks, I ambled back into my office, relieved that one last barrier was ticked off my list. I regained my seat, composed myself, put my hand on the mouse and clicked the box that said 'Enter'.

A couple of grand lighter, I had signed up to cycle the route of the 2019 Tour de France over three weeks the following July. It would finish on my 52nd birthday in Paris. A very happy coincidence.

It turned out that the window to enter was only 17 minutes compared to the three hours permitted the previous year. I had used up every second of it and became the last to join the group. If the staff in the office had objected, I would have missed my slot. If I had procrastinated further and made that third cup of tea or taken a last-minute, pre-button-pushing, toilet break, I would have missed my slot. But something inside urged me on, something drew me towards those intoxicating mountains and I completed the very straightforward task of clicking a mouse on a box that said 'Enter'.

Five simple letters in a random order that had me committed to the greatest challenge of my small and comfortable life. How hard was that?

And what the hell had I done?

Damn you Geraint Thomas. You had a lot to answer for.

*THE MAN ON TOP OF THE
MOUNTAIN DIDN'T JUST FALL
THERE* – Vince Lombardi

Chapter 3

Preparation. Preparation. Preparation (a)

ONCE I'D booked Le Loop, I spent the rest of the day asking myself 'what have I done?' My heart rate didn't really drop while I was in the office and the nerves would have taken hold for a while longer, until I remembered that I had to put in two hours' worth of gentle swim training at a lake near Reading that night. I was in the final stages of my training plan for Ironman Tallinn, in Estonia, which was taking place a couple of weeks later.

That event took my mind off Le Loop because I would face adversity in that race on a scale that I could never have imagined. It was even worse than Ironman Nice the year before. At the time I couldn't believe what was happening to me but looking back I see that those events had taken me out of my comfort zone and had inadvertently supplied great preparation for what was to come. Both of them took some recovering from and I use these tribulations as an example of what the human body can tolerate.

After I'd returned back to the UK in mid-August, to a career which was becoming mundane in comparison to the challenge that lay ahead, the recovery took a couple of months. I was back doing moderate exercise by November, in time for my training to start in earnest the following January. It left me six full months to prepare to cycle the route of the Tour de France in 2019.

Not just to cycle Le Loop but to do it clean and without the aid of any performance-enhancing substances. This was very important to me, because at the end of my journey I wanted to stick two fingers up to the drugs cheats from cycling's murky past and say 'Up Yours Lance'.

I have read pretty much every book and watched most films relating to the drug cheats of cycling's recent history. I do not judge these people but I do abhor them for destroying a most magnificent sport. Cycling is exhilarating, both to ride and to watch the greatest athletes competing at their very best. I love it.

I have had an on-off love affair with cycling, depending on where I am in the world and the TV coverage that has been available. In the days before the internet, I was reliant on the brilliant Channel 4 footage with the most enthralling commentary from Phil Liggett. The battles of Hinault and LeMond, closely followed by the eight-second Tour with LeMond and Fignon in 1989, brought a swashbuckling, knights-at-ten-paces sense of bravado and romance to my young and impressionable mind. The eighties were a boom of technicolour, advertising and greed. The Tour made me feel invincible and that anything was achievable in life. I was hooked.

As the following decade unfolded and the drug abuse crept into the peloton, I drifted away from the sport and knew very little of its racers and characters. It didn't help that my first-ever road bike, my beloved Vindec Ventura, was stolen from outside my parents' house in the late eighties and it took 25 years for me to get around to replacing it.

Where once I would cycle everywhere, I was now consumed with different priorities in life, from holding down a rubbish job, to paying rent, learning how to take rejection from pretty ladies and stealing the odd bit of romance with others. I lived in Gloucester, Bristol and then Cheltenham and football was my overall sporting priority. Cycling had gone on to the back burner but I never lost the admiration for the characters of the sport.

I have always had a fascination with what makes people successful and what drives them to excellence, while others settle for being comfortable and happy. As I developed into a manager and leader, I looked into this even further to see how I could get the best out of people and more importantly out of myself. I was intrigued by what would make someone push themselves to the limit for five hours or so in a day, struggle up a steep mountain for 90 minutes and then sprint at the end. They would then get up and repeat the whole process, not just the next day, but for up to 20 days afterwards.

At this stage I didn't understand the nuances of race tactics and roles in the team but I could see what these titans went through to be a professional in their sport, let alone the very best. What I have never tolerated is the need to cheat and take shortcuts and this added further fuel to my motivation to be able to ride the Tour clean. I think I have two absolute reasons why this is the case. Both involved a bit of introspection and self-honesty.

As I have developed leadership skills over the years, I have learned a lot about people and human behaviour. I had the benefit of working in education supplies and more specifically the publishing and product development aspect. One area of focus for the business was in learning difficulties and I developed a very basic layman's understanding of special needs. This is pretty dangerous because it is so easy to label an employee with ADHD or autism because of an individual character trait or flaw.

I have no expertise, but I have learned that I have certain traits of Asperger's syndrome (a form of autism) that I have been able to manipulate to my advantage. I have a tremendous sense of right and wrong, although the contradiction in my personality is that I like to get up to mischief. I like things to be neat and orderly and in their place. When I eat I do so symmetrically, to the extent that if I have a meal of steak, potatoes, carrot and broccoli, at the end of the meal I will have one small mouthful of each portion left to eat in turn. If someone sends me a message with eight points, I have to answer (or at least acknowledge) all of the eight points before I can move on, much to the infuriation of some ex-girlfriends who just wanted me to listen.

A great asset is that it is very difficult for me to tell a lie or be dishonest, and this caught up with me on many occasions as a fledgling adult. Even worse, I hate it when I know that other people are lying and I have a good instinct for it. I have learned to brush this aside but it causes an irritation that I find hard to dismiss.

Incidentally, with my layman's knowledge of learning difficulties and Asperger's syndrome I would always employ someone with this condition. I guarantee they will never, ever let you down. The syndrome will not allow it. Aspies rule. But I digress.

I also cannot tolerate being accused of lying when I am being honest. This is a rare circumstance that will induce rage. I cannot stand dishonesty or being cheated and like everyone else I have been the victim of cheats. It hurts. It rankles and it causes a sense of frustration that is hard to let go. To this very day. Really hard.

I was failed once by a PE teacher in my school days. I wasn't his only victim because he had a poor reputation, but the memory still lingers and has helped shape some of my attitudes to life since.

The single incident occurred roughly 37 years ago and it still rankles. It is like a boil on the posterior that continually pops up to remind me that life is unfair. There have been many instances since that have hurt, many of which were on the football field and especially when I have watched Swansea City conned out of points by Premier League divas falling over as Jose Mourinho brushes past the TV set. I have lost out on promotions and pay rises because I have been honest and refused to lie and dish the dirt on colleagues. I have also witnessed layabouts brazenly taking shortcuts in marathons and other endurance events, as I suffer on for another hour or two while they saunter across the finish line. I know these people are only cheating themselves and in the long run they never prosper, but it still rankles.

This teacher was commonly regarded throughout the county as a cheat and I learned nothing from him. In the early eighties he gave a decision against me in a house rugby match, which was so blatant and incorrect he made Tyler Hamilton look like Mother Theresa.

Defending in our own half I had chased after a long kick over the top of our back line. The ball had crossed the try line and, unopposed, I touched it down for a dropout on the 22-metre line. As I turned to pick the ball up and walk back to the 22, one of the opposition ran up and theatrically fell on the ball. A try was awarded. I was incandescent with rage. I was ten yards ahead of the guy and had clearly made the ball safe. This learned educator laughed and we lost the match by two solitary points. His cheating had made the difference to the end result and our house finished as runners-up in that year's competition.

This was the example I was being set by a middle-aged man who was employed and entrusted to mould young minds. I learned a lot, for all the wrong reasons, and the lesson has remained ever since. That PE teacher was a dick. Don't be a dick, Ceri. In my own sporting utopia, there is no room for cheats. That was the only valuable lesson I learned from Mr N.

The other aspect of my dislike for cheating is that it is never worth it in the long run and I learned this lesson the hard way. When I was a young adult, I cheated consistently for a year and I paid the price.

I mentioned that I failed in a calamitous fashion once and this too has shaped my outlook on life. It may not seem like much these days, to an advanced businessman in his fifties, because I have had a lot of experiences in life since that render that moment in time trivial in comparison, but to a childish 18-year-old it was catastrophic. In 1986 I failed my first year at college.

I was taking a computer science HND and I screwed up. This was the biggest learning curve of my life. I spent the entire year learning how to live, date, play football, drink and socialise and I forgot that I was there to study and pass a course. It didn't help that I was/am wholly unsuited to computer science and to this day I am still a bit of a technophobe. But that would be making feeble excuses for my mistakes and errors in judgement.

I have since come to learn that I was wrong and I made some big mistakes. Those mistakes were cataclysmic to me and life-altering, because I had to pick myself up and start all over again. At that time, I was fortunate that I had my whole life ahead of me. I was even more fortunate that I could rebuild my life almost immediately by being accepted on to a more suitable business studies course.

Quite frankly, when I was doing the computer science course, I didn't do the work. I cheated and copied course work. I cheated on assignments and I barely studied for my exams. I chose instead to lie in the arms of a soon-to-be ex-girlfriend who was giving up the course to return to her fiancé. When the end-of-year exams came around, I wasn't prepared for them or intellectually capable of succeeding. I took shortcuts the whole year and never once put the work in that was required for my virginal young mind to succeed.

I have some mitigating circumstances for my actions, but they only gloss over the bare facts of my incessant ineptitude at that time. I have never forgiven myself for being lazy and taking so many shortcuts. It hurts to this day and I use that year as a motivating tool, because I never, ever want to visit the darkness of failure again.

I cannot make excuses for, or justify, my consistent errors of judgement over the course of those three turbulent terms. At that stage of my life, I was making poor decisions and I was idle. I was 18 going on 12, both in physical looks and immaturity. Many times that year I was a blatant cheat. I cheated myself. I cheated my family who had supported me through that year and I cheated the college who had invested in me. I failed miserably and I was kicked off the course. I am not sure I will ever come to terms with the dirty stain of maladroit performance from that period that lives in the dark recesses of my mind. I let myself down. I let my family down. I was, and still am, ashamed.

However, I knew I had something to offer in this world so I vowed that I would never ever take the easy option again. I vowed that I would never ever fail again, but if I did it would not be for a lack of effort or professionalism. I vowed that I would never take any shortcuts moving forward and that I would set myself a higher set of values to live by.

I have fallen short many times over the years, but not through inertia. I eventually learned from this disaster and I developed a strong sense of injustice, similar to how ex-smokers become the most vehement members of the antitobacco brigade. I started my redemption by gaining an HND in business and finance two years after that failure.

Lazy choices don't pave the way in the long run and cheats never prosper. I promised that I would stand up for right over wrong moving forward. Failure on that scale was a lot to take on board as a young child but it has inadvertently served me well. If I was to cycle the Tour, I would do it clean, without so much as an Ibuprofen. No shortcuts.

I was very young at 18. I genuinely looked like a 12-year-old. My maturity was not much better. This served to provide me with a drive for the rest of my years and something which I have been able to tap into. To put it bluntly I have an element of small-man syndrome.

Once I eventually grew up and became an adult in my mid-twenties, I realised that I was no longer small, but by that stage I had become accustomed to being the small man. I am not a small man but an average guy. Then again, a small man would say that wouldn't he?

I am naturally young-looking, but during your school years this is a distinct disadvantage. Couple that with the fact that I am a July baby, I had to learn to compete with kids who were up to ten months older than me. I was the shortest, skinniest and youngest-looking kid in the year. To compensate (very much the right word) for being the smallest I learned to stand up for myself. I learned to speak on a level way above my age and intellect and I harnessed a fire in my belly. For this I am grateful but I still needed to grow up and learn. A lot. This energy has frequently helped me professionally, socially and in harnessing my moderate sporting aspirations.

Cycling isn't my first sport of choice. My heart was stolen by football and it still has me captured to this very day. I grew up wanting to play for Swansea City and Wales and I was obsessed. I played at every possible moment. I watched every bit of TV coverage available (I am grateful that we didn't have the blanket saturation of the game that we do nowadays with satellite TV because I would never have left the house) and I read every available article, book and comic on the game.

I lived for football. I wasn't bad either. I had a decent touch, read the game well, scored and created goals and never gave less than 100 per cent in both training and matches. But I was always small for my age, both in height and stature and I never had any natural power or speed. At a lower level you could compensate for this with intelligence, technique and sharpness, but when I reached a dubious semi-professional level with Endsleigh Insurance in the early nineties, I found that no amount of training right, healthy living and studying the game could help me. I wasn't good enough and there were no shortcuts for me to take. I wouldn't allow myself to take them if they were available but this turned out to be a blessing in disguise.

Realising that I had reached the peak of my limited sporting prowess at the age of 24 and being stuck in an insurance career I hated, I was able to free myself to live my life. For a decade I lived it to the absolute limit by moving overseas to work in the travel industry. I travelled. I worked very hard and was great at a job I loved. I partied even harder.

I have a sense of adventure and I pushed this to the extreme. I wore myself out. My word it was worth it. I experienced more in a decade than most people would in five lifetimes. I learned huge amounts both professionally and personally. I had the absolute privilege of meeting some incredible people, some of whom I worked with, some became friends, others had a major influence on my life and others I fell in love with. I learned from them all.

I lived through a military coup in the Gambia and the massacre in Luxor; I had two people die in my arms and saved the lives of three others; I nearly drowned while scuba diving in the Maldives; I had a knife pulled on me in Greece by a car rental agent; I had a gun pulled on me by a policeman at a gig in the Gambia and again by a bar owner in Goa. Not wanting to sound boastful, this scratches the surface of the best days of my life, and some of it is covered in my first book *Indian Summer*. I wouldn't bother wasting three hours of your life reading it because you will never get them back; send me the 30p royalty instead. And through all of this I lost most of my fitness.

This all took place during the nineties when Swansea City barely reached the giddy heights of the third tier of professional football and drug abuse was rife in the cycling peloton. Very convenient for a decade of living overseas, without a TV to my name to witness the misery on both fronts. Football still has my soul and I am committed to my annual season ticket at the Swansea.com Stadium.

When I was restarting my life back in the UK 15 years ago, I found that I was struggling on the football pitch and couldn't keep up with the younger lads around me. In my late thirties, with work taking over from sport, I unconsciously hung up my boots and started to put on a few pounds as good food and cheap beer took their toll on a sedentary lifestyle. This continued into my early forties until one horrendous week I had a very big wake-up call.

Gout. I wouldn't wish it on my worst enemy. It crept up on me out of nowhere and was punishment for too many years of a very rich diet, lack of exercise, stress as I worked too hard and celebrated harder. My chosen vices were beer and red wine. The doctor gave me some antibiotics for pain relief and gave me a choice: I could have medication daily for the rest of my days or I could improve my diet, lifestyle and exercise regime to keep it under control. I am not a fan of drugs at the best of times (another reason for me wanting to stick the proverbial two fingers up to Lance and his cohorts). I don't like the side effects and what they do to me. I get a much bigger high from being energised and clear-headed.

Needing to rid myself of this excruciating pain and ensure that it never returned I took a long hard look at my life and how I could improve it. Seriously, the pain is like nothing I have experienced. It is like taking large crystals, wrapping them around your joints and then pressing down hard on them with your skin. When you think you can't take any more pain you then set them on fire. To recover you need rest but sleep is impossible because the pain is seemingly endless. The more tired and stressed you become the greater the pain and the longer it will last. It feels like a never-ending catch-22 of agony.

The first attack lasted for about five days and I was aware of its effects for weeks afterwards. I have had a couple of attacks in the dozen or so years since and they have been equally traumatic but have usually cleared up within two or three days. I have learned to listen to the warning signs my body provides and I find that if I drink plenty of water, cut out alcohol, take some painkillers and do some exercise, my system will reward me with peace and pain-free extremities. I chose not to have a lifetime of medication and opted to regain my healthy lifestyle from two decades before, back when I considered myself a budding athlete.

I overhauled my diet and cut back on red meat, starchy food, fish and asparagus, which all seem to act as triggers for me. I cut back on my drinking and every year I abstain for at least a month, which is a great habit I picked up in Tunisia in 1995, thanks to a bet with a friend I was working with who gave up smoking for the month. I had the better end of that deal.

I needed to start exercising again. My problem with exercise is that I am competitive, particularly with myself, and I need a goal and a deadline to keep me motivated. Simply going jogging or taking out a gym membership was never going to be enough for me. I crave attention and glory and love to be appreciated. I needed something to aim for and thus began my journey to Ironman triathlons and Le Loop with a 10k run in Swansea. From small acorns do great oak trees grow and this one simple race transformed my life.

I set myself a moderate goal. I set a deadline and I formulated a training plan and healthy regime to achieve it. I worked hard, prepared well and saw the plan all the way through to the end and finished the race in 46mins. Slower than I wanted or expected but still a small achievement. Hooked again.

Following on from this I decided to go big and enter the London Marathon. I followed my rules for success and in 2011 I crossed the finish line in 4hrs 22mins and was disappointed.

I had achieved my goal but I had not performed to the level I had aimed for. There was a good reason for this and something that pushed me even further in my quest for athletic adventure.

My training for the London Marathon had been progressing really well and I felt invincible. With two months to go I had finished a half marathon comfortably in under 1hr 40mins and I was very confident of a sub four-hour marathon, so I decided to up my training schedule and push myself even harder.

I veered off course from my training plan, which had been worked out in detail to include the mileage, speed work and especially rest that my creaking limbs needed. I overdid it. In one week, I completed a 22-mile long run on the Sunday, then followed that up with a 16-mile easy run the following day, an 18-mile fartlek run on the Tuesday, an additional 20-mile long run on the Wednesday, rested on the Thursday and had an easy 10-mile run on the Friday. This was way too much for a middle-aged plodder who had partied hard for a decade before and I paid the price. I hadn't paid enough attention to the process and the outcome was taking care of itself. It wasn't the one I wanted.

Starting out on the Friday run, I couldn't push off on my left leg and started to feel a dull pain in my shin. I pushed myself through the agony and made matters worse. I had shin splints and it felt like running on a broken leg. With only seven weeks left to the marathon I was now unable to run at all and I was in pain when I walked. I had to find some way to keep my fitness up and hope that I made the start line.

By coincidence, 2011 was the first year that Ironman Wales was being held in Tenby. It is where I went to school as I grew up and lived a mere five miles away. I had always had a fascination with Ironman, having watched a documentary in the early eighties with my dad. It was about a 60-year-old man who had had a heart bypass operation, and his preparation for the race. I remember sitting there transfixed and flabbergasted at the distances involved and thought this was all from another world.

At school the next day we discussed this amongst friends and no one could believe that such a feat was possible, let alone that it could be completed in under 17 hours. The seeds were sown in my early teens and little did I know that they would resurface 30 years later.

With the injury I could barely walk, let alone run and I needed to keep my cardio fitness up. I love the water but could hardly swim a couple of lengths so I was left with one choice. I splashed out £500 on an aluminium frame road bike from a local store. I had no idea what I was doing, looking for, or needed, but I was desperate and bought the first bike I saw. And it was pretty. I then embarked on replicating my running regime on my shiny new toy.

I had no idea about fit, position, cadence or how to use the gears but, in a way, this helped me train hard and I learned as I went along. As I headed out for my second or third training ride I was overcome with jubilation as I revelled in the childlike joy of the wind howling in my face and my legs spinning like a cartwheel. I had no idea if what I was doing was effective but I was taken back to my childhood of riding my Vindec Ventura, which had been my pride and joy. I had worked in a chip shop every summer from the age of 13 and I spent one of those summers saving the £100 to buy my first brand-new bike. I would race around the country lanes with friends and struggle up 17 per cent hills around the county. I often came last in our races because I never learned how to use the gears properly and my scrawny frame generated very little power. As I howled with delight flying along an open country road 30 years later, it hit me. In my desperation to be fit for the London Marathon I had a realisation (epiphany would be too strong a word). I would one day become an Ironman.

After an injury-affected disappointing finish in the London Marathon, I repeated the feat later in the same year in the Chicago Marathon. I still had not recovered from the shin splint injury and my time suffered as a result, but I finished and became addicted to the sense of achievement.

I loved the camaraderie amongst racers and the tall tales of international derring-do and I was desperate to improve. In all I have completed 19 marathons and in autumn 2013 I eventually ran a race fit and healthy and, with the years of dedicated training and practice, I managed a time of 3hrs 34mins on a blustery, cold and lumpy Dublin course. But now I was including cycling in my training plan and looking to go longer. So, the natural progression was to leap across the finish line in Ironman Wales 2013.

In booking Ironman Wales this was the first time that I started to really formulate and put into practice all of the success theories that I had read about over the years. I seemed to stumble across a formula that worked for me and the basis of this is what I would take into Le Loop. I had to try it out in a pretty extreme event first.

By entering this race, I had 12 months to get myself ready, thus committing to something big and setting myself a deadline. Something I couldn't back out of, unless I wanted to lose my £400 entry fee and receive a slap in the face of my fragile ego. I formulated a detailed training plan which came with the most excellent book, *Ironman Start to Finish: 24 Weeks to an Endurance Triathlon*. This book was superb and I still use it today and base all of my training principles around what I learned in it.

It taught me the basis of training, how to plan it correctly and incorporate elements like rest, diet, weight training and technique. Best of all it had a detailed day-by-day and week-by-week training schedule over 24 weeks to get me ready for a race in September.

This meant that my training plan did not have to start in earnest until the first week in February and I needed to maintain a base level of fitness up until Christmas. I entered two ultra-trail marathons in the autumn of 2012 with the second being a 36-mile run around the Gower coastline at the end of November. It was very hilly, wet, windy, cold, muddy and dangerous and I struggled round in six-and-a-half hours. It was brutal and I did not enjoy it. I have not entered an ultra-marathon since but off the back of the race I knew for the first time that I could endure and suffer for more than six hours at a time. Not once did I consider quitting and heading for a warm soup and a hot shower. This was something to build on.

I started the 24-week plan in the January and factored in two full weeks of rest during the eight months leading up to Ironman. This meant that I could overdo some weeks but recover well enough to keep up a heavy schedule. I took swimming lessons, which helped a little, but not a lot, because I was as good as starting from scratch, with a very poor technique. The only thing I was good at was breathing, otherwise everything was wrong and my whole front crawl had to be broken down and rebuilt. This was by far my weakest area and still is to this day.

I followed the run and the bike elements of the training plan to the letter and I had a head start with the endurance fitness from the ultra-marathon only a couple of months previous. I was so far ahead in this area that in April 2013 I ran a marathon in Llanelli as a training exercise and posted a time of 3hrs 46mins without even pushing the pace. I knew that I was halfway there. That was a small milestone that warranted celebration. A handful of marathons leading up to 2013 had been great preparation for the big one.

Not long after that marathon, just after the bank holiday weekend, I met my baby. She eventually gained the nickname of Trigger, for reasons that would unfold over the years, but it was love at first sight. The moment I saw her I knew we would be one. Although I have looked at others since, I have always tried to be faithful to her. I walked into a local shop and there she was. Glowing. Sleek, black, dynamic and so beautiful. My Giant TCR SL was displayed on a wall and I had to have her. With her lightweight carbon frame, she was speedy, quick to respond, great going uphill and handled like a dream and after only a couple of rides I felt like she was an extension of my own body.

I opted against a time-trial bike because Ironman Wales is notoriously hilly with some very steep climbs reaching up to 17 per cent, which Trigger would handle better than an out-and-out speedster. Plus, comfort is essential on a bike when you are looking at spending seven hours or so in the saddle. Trigger and I were inseparable right up until 16 July 2019.

I prepared well. I lived for the training and I loved it. I learned a lot about myself and how I am driven and motivated and I have been able to harness this ever since. Throughout all of my training I focused on success. I had a mental image of how I would cross that finish line by leaping high into the air and punching my fist, a bit like my old goalscoring celebration from the days with Endsleigh. There would be nothing modest or understated with this achievement and that applied to the reward that I had promised myself.

Work was going very well and as MD of a business I had helped grow from a £1.4m turnover to a profitable £4.5m entity in under three years, I wanted something that allowed me to acknowledge that success. That was where the idea for my first-ever tailor-made three-piece suit came from. My own ego was driving me on and providing the love, and with a now six-year-old niece to impress I wasn't going to let her down either. I had to implement my own personal mantra of INIOP thanks to my sister.

'You will never finish Ironman. It will kill you. It will literally kill you.'

'Funny way to say happy birthday,' I replied without a hint of sarcasm.

For my birthday in July 2012, I had gone to watch a sprint triathlon with my brother to see what was involved and we came away energised and utterly sold. I had already made up my mind that Ironman was on my bucket list and this was the final piece in my ambitious jigsaw. It wasn't so well received by my sister though.

I love her to bits but she can be a bit impulsive and dramatic. I owe her a huge thanks because those words stayed with me. Every dark moment, every difficult training session when there was nothing in my legs and every time the sofa begged me to drink beer instead of heading out into the cold to train some more, I was able to draw on either her words or the ingrained image of me flying over the finish line. Thank you, Piglet, for your unorthodox support.

I worked at it and I had to develop new levels of resilience as I encountered bike problems, waning motivation, fear and injury niggles. But I learned to get angry quickly followed by a big sulk and then rational thought would prevail and I would always find a solution to any given problem or lack of motivation.

I included my family in my preparation and my brother came out on some long bike rides to keep me company and help measure my progress. On 9 September 2013 I leaped across the finish line as I had promised in a time of 14hrs 34mins 40secs. I was 962 out of 2,200 registered, where realistically 1,800 started, and I was equally ecstatic and disappointed. I was over the moon (I love a good football cliché) to have finished the race but I knew I could go faster. I chose to focus on the positive for the following month or so before the finish time started to niggle at me and I entered again for the following year, seeking improvement. But in the moment, the suit I ordered was splendid.

I had taken the theories of success from so many manuals, guidebooks, mentors and video tutorials, etc. and I had effectively put them into practice into this life-altering achievement. I wanted more and to see how far I could push myself. The first priority was to get better at Ironman and the following year I improved my time by almost an hour, which is pretty significant.

In 2016 I cheated on Trigger and bought myself a mistress in the form of a time-trial bike. Together we crossed the finish line on a fast Copenhagen course in sweltering conditions in a time of 11hrs 38mins 14secs. Everything came together for this event and I put in close to an ideal performance, considering my abilities, and my finish time would have been good enough to have won the first Ironman ever raced. That was good enough for me as a plodding 50-year-old.

I naively thought I had put together all of my teachings to develop a winning formula, then life taught me even more valuable lessons. I had to develop my skills of resilience and overcome adversity on a hefty scale in Ironman Nice and especially Ironman Tallinn in 2018. The other thing that Nice taught me was that I had a love for cycling in the hills and I wanted to sample more of them. This eventually led me on to internet searches for cycling stages of the Tour de France.

I never dreamed in a million years that I would be able to do the whole thing but 12 months later I found myself elatedly signing up for the biggest challenge of my life. I was booked into cycle the whole of the Tour route in 2019 with the most glorious and worthwhile event ever in Le Loop.

By this stage of my fledgling endurance sojourn, I was accustomed to putting together a plan that would work for me. It would need to fit around my work schedule, be detailed enough for me to stick to it absolutely, but then flexible enough for me to work around it. Overall, it needed to prepare me for spending up to ten hours a day in the saddle, every day for three weeks, cycling up to 244km at a time. (For us Brits please note that in cycling terms the Europeans rule the sport and all distances are metric.)

From my Ironman experience I knew that I could tolerate five or six days a week of intense sessions where needed. With this in mind, I worked out a plan of training for six days a week, with one of those days being an optional cross-training day depending on what my body was telling me. Unfortunately, my body usually tells me to sit down and have a kebab and a beer, so I had to ignore it a lot of the time. Each of these training weeks was part of a five-week block. I would increase the intensity and mileage over weeks one to four and then have an easier recovery period in week five.

I entered a number of events which would prepare me better for the summer. I especially had to learn how to ride with groups at high speed as opposed to the non-drafting competitions I was used to, and I needed to improve my technique and bike-handling skills.

My average week would pan out as follows:

- Monday: 30 minutes with heavy weights to build power in legs and core; one-hour easy swim
- Tuesday: 60–90 minute-tempo (turbo) bike sessions. High intensity designed to improve speed, cadence or climbing and putting my heart rate into high levels for sustained periods
- Wednesday: Another version of Tuesday. One week would be speed work and the next climbing. I chose back-to-back sessions to prepare for what would come
- Thursday: Optional cross-training day. Usually a 90-minute fartlek (tempo) run. Finish with 30 minutes on light weights for injury prevention
- Friday: Rest day
- Saturday: Long bike ride, measured by time rather than distance and always with a low heart rate
- Sunday: Repeat Saturday but with a different route

I would build up my mileage and time on the bike on my long rides as follows:

- Week 1: Two-hour ride and approximately 60–75km (depending on terrain)
- Week 2: Two hours 30 minutes ride and approximately 70–90km
- Week 3: Three hours 30 minutes ride and approximately 90–120km
- Week 4: Four-hour ride and approximately 110–140km
- Week 5: Two-hour gentle ride

I would then build up the next block and start with a three-hour ride moving up to back-to-back five-hour rides.

This would continue so that I would be able to comfortably do back-to-back eight-hour rides by the beginning of June when I had entered the Dragon Tour in south Wales. This was a mere four weeks from the start of the Tour. I planned into the schedule the fact that I may only be able to do one long ride on the weekend and, if this was the case, I would do 1.5 times the scheduled double rides; i.e., if I was due to do two two-hour rides, instead I would do just the one three-hour ride. There were many reasons why this might happen, based around weather, work, Swansea City, health and family commitments.

I kept a diary of every training session I did, as I have done since my first marathon, which meant I could keep a track of my weekly and monthly distance covered and time spent training. I thought I had a pretty straightforward plan to work with. From experience I knew that my speed, strength and endurance would build gradually and I would be able to achieve this with a bit of effort and management.

IT'S NEVER TOO LATE TO BE THE
PERSON YOU WERE MEANT TO BE
– George Eliot

Chapter 4

July 2018
Inspiration

IT'S NOT enough to set myself a challenge. If I am going to commit to something pretty epic then it has to have meaning. It has to be worthwhile. It needs to make a difference in this world (even if that is inspiring just one other person to get off their arse and be a better person). It has to be something that aligns with my core values.

I can be naughty and push boundaries, plus I am prone to some very insightful sarcasm; however, my values are based on honesty, integrity and kindness. I want to be happy and I want everyone around me to be happy as well. I have empathy for others and I am a nice guy, just don't ever confuse nice with weak because I have a devilish streak which I keep locked away for special occasions. I want to leave the world in a better position than I found it. I have a desire to tackle challenges that are extraordinary and beyond most rational thinking. I want to set the best example possible for my niece and nephews. Lofty ambitions, but isn't that the purpose of this tome?

I struggle for motivation at work if the ethos of the business is not ethical or not aligned to my set of values. Of course, I want great wealth and to live a life of luxury, but at what cost to my soul? I have always had these values; I have only been able to verbalise them in the past decade or so.

I have had two jobs in my life where the focus was solely on making the sale. We were not allowed to improve people's lives. We were not allowed to look at a long-term sale or necessarily provide advice that was best for the customer. We were expected to sell and sell hard. I enjoyed some of the trappings that came with these positions but I lasted less than a year in both, because to my mind what we were doing was not entirely humane. It did not add value to the world.

I have provided training on this point for sales teams, where the focus of the sale is based on your core values. It is why my most recent role was so successful, because our core values were aimed at making learning fun. We wanted children to enjoy their education and we designed incredible resources which helped improve children's learning outcomes and made teachers' lives that little bit easier. We made money and a small profit. Our overriding priority for a long time was to have a positive impact in the primary school classroom and most profits were put back into the development of even greater resources. Essentially 90 per cent of the sale was based around our core values and the remaining 10 per cent was the mere details of which resources to buy. This was a constant soft sell and a permanent message which was based around what was best for the customer.

Everyone in my team bought into these values and it is a key reason for our long-term success. I bought into this ethos and I thrived. In the last couple of years, the board shifted their focus to cutting costs in an effort to generate more profit and this impacted on the quality of both our offering and service. I had been on a decent package and had a good lifestyle, even if it was entirely work-centric, but with the shift in focus from above I was in need of something more worthwhile to sink my teeth into. For me to get out of bed each day my life needs meaning.

As fortune would have it, Le Loop provided me with both the epic challenge I craved and some significance to my life by raising funds for the William Wates Memorial Trust. This event and charity were to change my life on a scale that I could never envisage.

The Challenge

Le Loop is an event that has been running for a decade and it is the main source of fundraising for the William Wates Memorial Trust (WWMT). It is straightforward: exactly one week before the Tour de France takes place, we cycle the entire route of the race.

We usually stay in the same hotels and we have a great support team and organisation to back it up. The professionalism is on another level and for a group of mixed ability athletes, we are treated like the pros who will follow us seven days later. It needs to be experienced to be believed.

There are different 'Loops' that can be tackled, varying from two stages of the Tour to whet your appetite to cycling the whole of the Tour de France in the Grand Loop. Most days there are approximately 100 riders setting off at the beginning of a stage. Out of those, 40 to 50 will be Grand Loopers, hoping to complete the full thing. This is not for the faint-hearted.

I had signed up for the Grand Loop. I wanted to experience the full thing and push myself to places I could never have envisaged, growing up. I wanted to cycle the whole of the Tour de France.

Warranted I would not actually be cycling the Tour de France. I was never that talented an athlete, even in my wildest of dreams, but we would cycle the exact same route and we would experience what it would be like to cycle the Tour. Just a little bit slower than Geraint Thomas and the rest of the peloton. Le Loop is not a race either, it is a tour and no time limits are placed on participants. It means that if you have a healthy level of fitness and have completed a competitive level of training, you can tackle the same route the modern-day swashbucklers on two wheels do.

Digressing a little, but this is a beautiful aspect of cycling that I adore. Not only is it a sport for all shapes and sizes, as anyone can ride a bike, no matter their physique, it also affords us fans an opportunity to 'walk in the footsteps of Geraints' (pun intended. Sorry). It genuinely is inclusive and cares not a jot about colour of skin, gender, learning difficulties, body image or religion. Cycling is open to everyone.

I have never had the opportunity to play football at Wembley, to play rugby at the Principality Stadium, cricket at Lords or tennis at Wimbledon. It is just not allowed. Plus, Swansea City have banned me from going near the grass on matchday and the training pitches during the week. However, cycling (and triathlon) allows us to ride the exact same routes that superhumans tackle in the toughest races in the world each year. For a brief three weeks I would metaphorically rub shoulders with heroes such as Hinault, Merckx, LeMond, Fignon, Alaphilippe and Thomas. I desperately wanted to see how I would fare.

As the Le Loop website says, we cycle the same roads, often staying in the same hotels, with feed stops, luggage transfers and a team of mechanics, medics and physios to keep bike, body and mind together. During my three-week sojourn I would come to rely heavily on all the amenities that were on offer, plus some emotional support on top.

The organisation that is involved in running an event like this is of the highest order and Sarah, who is with us throughout the Tour, is meticulous. She runs a tight ship and we would get our money's worth and beyond. I would come to be in awe of the whole operation.

On top of being a well-run ship, it is also a very happy place to live. The atmosphere and camaraderie are superb and everyone involved is very supportive, from the staff to fellow riders. The ship may not always run smoothly, especially if we literally hit a bump in the road, but there is a network of friendly faces, cheap jokes and physical and mechanical back-up to provide riders with the greatest opportunities to realise dreams. Like the sport itself, Le Loop is inclusive and it has a place for everyone – assuming you have done your training and reached your fundraising target.

Compared to a lot of one-day events, it doesn't cost that much either. In relative terms it works out at a very cost-effective three-week holiday, albeit an exhausting one.

In July Le Loop releases the first 100 places for the following year. These are all of the 40 Grand Loop spots plus 60 guaranteed Loop places. More spots will become available in the autumn when the route is announced. A non-refundable deposit of £500 was required to secure my place.

Once the Tour route is released in October it is divided into Loops. The basic cost for a Loop is £165 per night which covers food, accommodation, transport on tour and a small admin fee. The overall cost for the full experience will usually amount to somewhere in the region of £4,000. Entrants need to cover the cost of getting to the start and home from the finish, plus incidentals such as extra nights in Paris, bike transport and excess luggage, etc. We spent very little cash during the Tour itself and this was usually on massages, bike repairs, beer and ice creams.

The cost compared to entering a triathlon or a marathon is phenomenal, but for this you get the following:

- Accommodation (mostly twin share; single supplements are available to buy in January)
- All food: breakfast, evening meal and four feed stops during the ride
- Fully signed route, the stuff of legend
- Mechanical, medical and moral support
- Luggage transfers

- Coach transfers to the next stage start when the stages aren't contiguous
- Optional massage at the end of each stage
- Professional lead cyclist to support the riders every day
- Free training advice
- Weekend training rides
- Discounted entry into the Tour of Wessex, which is great preparation for Le Loop
- Discounts from other charity partners such as insurance, training kit, bike service and purchase

As I was to find out, seasoned professionals would regularly offer support to inexperienced riders like me, be it with technique, bike technical or morale. They very rightly state on their website that the camaraderie is the stuff of legend and it is right up there with the professionalism from the organisers. This is not a fly-by-night jolly. This a serious undertaking and the attention to detail is meticulous whilst making every member of staff and entrant feel like family.

Riders on the Grand Loop are expected to raise a minimum of £3,000 for the WWMT. At the time of booking, I thought, 'This shouldn't be too difficult if I put in the effort,' and it created a loyalty and kinship with the charity, which would remain long after my challenge was over. I was lucky. I surpassed my fundraising target by the end of March, which was one less thing to worry about.

The Meaning
The William Wates Memorial Trust was founded in 1998 to commemorate the life of William Wates, who had an

incredible sense of adventure. I didn't know him, but from talking to the trustees he was an inspirational human being and his life is still touching others 20 years on from his passing. The Trust supports projects that offer young people opportunities, otherwise unavailable to them, to fulfil their potential and stay away from a life of crime. The WWMT would provide a greater depth to my narcissistic ambitions.

The objective of the Trust is to support projects that encourage young people experiencing severe disadvantage to keep away from antisocial behaviour and criminal activity, enabling them to fulfil their potential. The type of projects they work with are usually involved with sports, the arts, theatre and youth groups, etc. Charities in the south-east and throughout the UK benefit from their work. This was good. This was a cause I could buy into.

I loved the fact that every penny raised for the Trust would go to worthy causes. I also loved the charities that we would be riding to support. I wanted to put something back into this world and the William Wates Memorial Trust aligned with my values. If I completed my challenge not only would I be able to inspire a few others to dare to walk where only fools tread, but I might just be having a positive impact on other people's lives in the process.

I am fortunate in that I come from a loving home and a solid background. Great misfortune has not been a companion of mine and I have been lucky to have a great start in life. Any cock-ups along the way have been entirely my own doing. I am fully aware that not everyone in this life is as lucky as I am. By cycling Le Loop, I could help to redress that balance a little.

I fell into the career of educational publishing by accident but over the course of two decades I became passionate about improving the opportunities for young people. The WWMT had parallels with this passion and ticked a lot of boxes. I am obviously obsessed with sports and I have benefited so much from competitive exercise and involvement. I could see the value of using sporting opportunities and the arts to improve the lives of young people at risk. If I succeeded, I could positively impact the lives of, and provide opportunities for, those that haven't had the start in life that I did. It was an honour to support a cause so worthwhile. I bought into the aims of the Trust and this would fuel my desire in the months to come.

In the build-up to the Tour we had the opportunity to visit a couple of the Trust's charity days, seeing youth groups in action at places like Crystal Palace FC. During the Tour, representatives from the charities came to join us. Some of them would cycle one or two stages, others would help at feed stops and on one lucky day we had a budding photographer capturing us in action. These would prove to be inspirational, selfless individuals striving to make the world a better place. They put my trivial concerns about profit margins, pay rises and what the hell I would do once the Tour was over into context. It was very easy for me to go all-in.

IF YOU THINK TRAINING IS
HARD, TRY FAILING – Anon

Chapter 5

January 2019
Preparation. Preparation. Preparation (b)

THE FIRST quarter of 2019 started poorly and went backwards from there. I had in place a definitive training plan and I put in place and maintained some epic habits that were designed to help me along the way. However, every time I took a step forward it felt like I was taking two steps backward. In hindsight I can see that I was developing resilience and tenacity, but at the time it felt like the sporting gods were not in my favour.

I had conflicting moods in that I was both excited and healthily terrified at the prospect of cycling 3,500km over 21 days. This was the fuel that was driving me forward, but on the flip side I was largely dissatisfied at work and becoming increasingly disillusioned with where I was going in life.

Oh man, this reeks of a mid-life crisis. Running away from a normal job to ride a bike? I promise you it isn't. I am just trying to be a better man and move forward in this world. It doesn't look good though, does it? But the more I fell in love with the prospect of attempting to crack the Tour, the more I grew as an individual and discovered new and great things about myself. As this happened, I became more and more dissatisfied with my professional and living environment.

I was provided with an apartment above the office in Hungerford, where I was able to stay during the week when I was not on the road. The advantage of this is that it was an apartment above the office. The disadvantage of this is that it was an apartment above the office.

While I was at work I would focus solely on work and training, and I did not need to worry about everyday tasks in my home in Wales, like cleaning the bathroom, or mowing the lawn, or painting the exterior walls, or politicians turning up unannounced canvassing votes. I threw myself into the training and tried to implement some epic habits.

I gave up alcohol and reverted to a healthy diet. I gave up sweets and snacks completely and for breakfast I usually had a pint of fruit smoothie, plus an occasional bowl of muesli, then I would have my main meal of the day for lunch, which would be a balance of protein, carbohydrates and greens (grilled chicken, broccoli and rice would be a favourite and to be naughty I would allow myself some tomato ketchup. A boy has got to live, right?). In the evening I would eat after training and would have something along the lines of homemade vegetable soup or a good old classic like beans on toast. This would often be washed down with a protein shake. Once a week, usually on my rest day, I was allowed to cheat. I frequently opted for a burger or kebab.

I was able to maintain the diet through most of the training period. But I was feeble-willed and started drinking again after six weeks.

Each morning I had to wait a minute for the shower to heat up so I would do a plank to strengthen my core. I would stand on one leg while I brushed my teeth for two minutes for the same reason. I installed a pull-up bar in one of the doorways in the apartment with the intention of doing ten quick chin-lifts every time I walked past. I quickly discovered that I am weak and I never really developed any extra upper-body muscle. I started going to bed one hour earlier each night to get some extra rest, but like the booze ban this didn't last that long because it turns out that I am a bit of a night owl.

I looked at what else I could do to help my performance in the long run. I addressed bike issues as spring approached and they would turn out to be expensive. I did one of those commercial blood analysis tests with the aim of checking my health and blood values to see if they could improve my performance or highlight areas of weakness. I didn't learn a great deal. I discovered that I probably suffer from seasonal affective disorder (having spent half of my life in sunny climes, I am not surprised that a cheery British winter softens my mood) and that I need more vitamin D in my life. Given the lack of sunshine in the UK, I took supplements for three months until the weather improved, which it never really did. The blood test also told me that, approaching 52, I had to watch my cholesterol and a greater balance of fish in my diet was suggested. I don't like seafood but had to find a way to suck that up.

What the results did not really show or help with was my red and white blood cell counts, which are average (notice a running theme about me as a whole?), and advice on how to improve them. I was specifically hoping for a reading on my haematocrit level, which is the indicator that professional athletes use to measure their suitability for endurance sports. It is also the area where they cheat by increasing their blood values. I learned nothing new and opted to maintain my status quo. I chose to concentrate on putting in the miles and raising funds for the WWMT.

The fundraising didn't start in earnest until March, but the training got underway on 2 January with an indoor tempo bike session. A gentle introduction to get my legs used to the workload they would be put under in the months to come. Mother nature doesn't believe in gentle and the weather that started the year was awful.

That first weekend I planned to do a long ride with my brother. He lives 20 miles away from my home in south Wales so the plan was to cycle to him early in the morning, ride together for an hour and then I would ride home at an easy pace. It pissed down with ice-cold rain while 30mph freezing winds swirled around me, as I struggled to complete part one of the day. I had on my winter jacket and thermal boot covers, plus a couple of extra layers, but a Pembrokeshire winter finds a way right into your bones. An autumn of inertia, a Christmas of extreme overindulgence and the remnants of a chest infection took their toll. By the time I reached my brother's home I couldn't feel my hands or feet. I bailed. I don't like the cold and to my mind I was supposed to be training for the heat not a blizzard. I made my brother run a hot bath for me and I quit on my first test of the year, while he managed 45 minutes outside before easing my fragile ego and returning earlier than planned himself. At the first test of my strength and resilience I had failed. It turns out I am not as strong as I had hoped. Not a good omen.

It didn't get much better. The weather continued to hamper my schedule and I struggled to put in the long rides. The following week brought similar conditions and I managed a 55km ride on an undulating route, but returned home exhausted because I was suffering from the hunger knock (rather inappropriately known as 'bonking' in cycling vernacular). Entirely my fault after I had experimented with homemade rice cakes, instead of my usual energy bars, and they failed to do the job I needed. As Dad used to say, 'Sometimes you win and sometimes you learn.' He also used to say, 'Don't learn from your mistakes, let others make the mistakes and learn from them'. At this stage I was doing a lot of learning and not much winning. All the mistakes were mine.

The weather seemed to continue in this vein for most of the first half of the year, being very cold, very wet and very windy with intermittent spells of sunshine. For a fair-weather soul my spirits were damp, like the weather, and they took a long while to warm up. My training continued to be hampered up until May, when I was less than two months away from Le Grand Depart.

I was grateful for the small victories I was amassing with the indoor tempo sessions on the bike. These had been as regular as clockwork and the midweek training was pretty much going to plan. I was starting to feel some of the benefits from these workouts as my speed and strength gradually started to show some signs of progress. But these were 80-minute routines and nowhere near the eight hours I would be looking for on a daily basis on the Continent.

By mid-February I had only managed three long rides worthy of the name and not one weekend of back-to-back rides. The saving grace was that the one decent ride I managed to get in was longer than four hours and I had broken the 100km barrier for the first time. My progress was tedious and frustrating to manage. Training was nowhere near on schedule. Professionally, my enthusiasm was waning and this was affecting my overall joie de vivre, but at least I was maintaining some very good daily habits. Then I went to New York for a weekend.

The trip to NYC was work-related but taken as a poorly timed holiday. I went to visit the Annual Toy Fair for the company with a view to finding another distributor to promote our resources in the States. The issue with this scenario is that my board of directors didn't actively encourage me to make this trip so I took it as part of my annual leave.

I booked and paid for flights, hotel, entry into the show and all other sundry expenses myself. Was I committed to the cause or looking for a way out by arranging meetings with contacts interested in my services? The year before, my New Year's resolution had been to make the owners money whether they liked it or not. I did very well, but I was getting tired of making other people wealthy at my expense.

The Toy Fair generated some interesting leads and the potential for market growth, but my heart wasn't in it. I had two dinners with business partners, but instead of talking business I could only think about the three weeks in France that were six months off. Live it and love it, and the Tour had captured my soul, possibly at the expense of my career.

Despite the backward steps in training, my mind was focused on the task ahead. I maintained some epic habits in New York by refusing to take taxis or public transport and I walked for almost eight hours every day, clocking up some serious gentle mileage (kilometrage doesn't sound right). I ruined all that good work by stumbling off the self-imposed wagon and drank heavily for each of the four days. One of those nights on the sauce was with a business rival who offered me a job. I am not sure if my head was turned, but my mind was made up on that trip and I had another challenge to confront.

Arriving back in the UK I had missed a good bank of training and I missed a further week through a mixture of jet lag and flu symptoms. I was gearing up for the biggest challenge of my life and I was the one creating the adversity which I had to overcome. I wasn't sure how many more backward steps I could take so I had to clear my mind and concentrate on the task at hand.

A week after landing back in the UK I had a late-night conversation with my board of directors, who happened to be based in New Zealand where the company was founded. I resigned my position and gave them 12 months' notice. Pretty generous, but it was in my contract to allow them that time to find a successor. I don't think they were that upset to see me go because we had long held conflicting views on how the business should develop and what our overall strategy should be. I guess I was embarking on more than just the one journey.

I immediately started to question my rationale and what I would do with the rest of my life, but I knew that the job was not making me happy and I was no longer inspired by anyone in the business. We had outgrown each other. In the space of ten days, I had put myself back to square one in my preparation; I was soon to be jobless, but I now had a new laser-like focus. I swear this isn't a mid-life crisis. The job hunt could wait until after Le Loop. New York was epic.

With a clear mind I was able to put together my first two weekends of back-to-back long rides. I found that a combination of the tempo bike sessions and the long walks in New York had surprisingly built up a small bank of endurance fitness. I was clear-headed and nothing was going to stop me in my quest now. Apart from myself.

In the middle of March 2019, the Le Loop team had organised a training weekend in Cheltenham. This was great for more than one reason. Firstly, the weekend involved two relatively easy long rides and my fitness was at a level to cope with them comfortably. The Saturday would be for everyone signed up for the coming year's Tour, which gave us a chance to meet new friends who we would be sharing memories with in the summer. The Sunday ride would be alongside previous Le Loop alumni, otherwise known as Loopers. This would allow us to pick their brains, gather some useful hints and tips and gain an insight into what lay ahead.

The second reason is that I had lived in Cheltenham for a couple of years in the early nineties and had the most amazing time there. I still have a few friends in the town so this was a good opportunity to catch up after the training and talk about the glory days from my footballing-led insurance past. It should have been a very useful weekend of training.

As luck would have it, that same weekend I was due to attend the Education Resources Awards on the Friday night. These are a celebration of everything that is great amongst the suppliers of resources into the education sector. In 2019 we were up for two awards. The first was for one of our products, a set of board games, and the second was for Supplier of the Year. The latter is a highly sought-after award. It does not generate any more business, this isn't the Oscars, but it does provide confidence, prestige and a huge boost to the ego. As you may have gathered, love of self is a constant theme in my personal motivation levels.

The evening takes place at the motorcycle museum in Birmingham. It is a black-tie affair, complete with a celebrity comedian as compere and a great after-party at the venue and beyond. It is always very well attended and I have a lot of friends within the industry, so realistically I knew that I may indulge a little bit. My plan was to go to the awards, stay the night in Birmingham and then drive to Cheltenham during the Saturday to spend the night there and join in with the Sunday ride. I knew deep down that I wouldn't be able to make it in time for the Saturday ride and if I did I would be in no fit state to join in.

We won both awards. I celebrated hard. I was on a table of eight with some great friends in the industry. We represented four companies and every one of us won an honour of some form. This was great closure for me. It proved that I was doing something right professionally and it was great to be able to sign off my career on a high note.

This wasn't the first award we had ever won but it was one of the most satisfying for me personally. I was the glory-taking face of a great team who had delivered repeatedly over the years, but after a decade of positive achievement I could bow out on a high.

In that moment of rare glory on the Friday night, champagne was in order. Given that I was due to cycle through the Moët et Chandon region on stage three of the Tour, we drank that. A lot of it. I didn't get to bed until 6am. I missed the whole of the training weekend and managed a six-mile jog on Sunday evening which barely assuaged my huge levels of guilt.

The awards had the double whammy of helping me achieve the bulk of my fundraising target for the William Wates Memorial Trust. The ERAs raise funds every year for a chosen charity and at the beginning of the year I had won a vote for our trade association the BESA (British Educational Suppliers Association) to adopt WWMT as their nominated charity for 2019. As providence would have it, the BESA organises the ERAs and all profits from a collection that evening went to the WWMT. I provided a brief video presentation at the beginning of the evening; I was introduced and my challenge was explained to the gathered businesspeople. Guests were then expected to make a generous donation.

Given that I had stumped up the first £500 out of my own pocket I knew that whatever we raised at these awards would take me very close to my fundraising limit. I should point out that if ever I raise money for a charity, I always put my hands into my own pocket first. I am of the opinion that if a cause is worthwhile, I should put my money where my mouth is and set the example for others to follow. I find it distasteful and frustrating when I see others asking for funds on social media because they are taking part in an event, when they donate nothing themselves. If the cause is worthwhile, you will contribute and this raises confidence with all other potential donors. The WWMT had become close to my heart and the £500 on top of my entry fee was more than worth it. It was a very successful evening in so many ways for me, but again my progress had been put back.

I would like to say that the following week I was back on track, but come the Saturday I suffered an unbearable gout attack. I spent three days unable to move. I couldn't put socks or shoes on. I couldn't rest because the pain was excruciating and I couldn't put any weight on my foot to let me walk, let alone run or ride a bike. It passed as quickly as it had flared up, but the damage had been done. Close to three months into my training and it was still one step forward and two steps back. I needed to raise the bar. If I thought that training was going to get harder, I should try failing.

The only way I could improve things would be with a sustained period of training and winding up my long rides on the weekends. Although I was still partial to a beer at the end of a week, I was able to maintain some of my epic habits. My diet was healthy. I was on top of work and my little daily routines, and I was getting plenty of sleep. I was in a good place with the shorter midweek sessions which focused on speed, power and sustained high tempo, and these had stood me in good stead. As we moved into April and through Easter, I was able to put in a few decent back-to-back sessions on the weekends and the muscle memory from the previous years' Ironman races woke up and helped me push through.

I had managed a couple of six-hour and 160km rides, which is a pretty impressive 100 miles. This was still 80km short of what we would expect to do on a daily basis in the event, but I felt some form coming to my legs, just as the sun started to make an appearance for the first time in months.

The weather during the first part of the year had been tough. It was constantly cold, wet and windy and for a fair-weather guy like me, soul destroying. It was difficult to find the motivation to get out of bed some days let alone don my kit and ride a bike into freezing winds. Because I was so far behind, I forced myself out regularly, knowing full well that once I was on the road I would be dabbling in my drug of choice. Out in the fresh air, doing any form of exercise or sport is my happy place and it is a healthy addiction. I was finding my rhythm and a tiny bit of strength on the hills. As Easter came around, I took four days of leave and planned on spending at least seven of the resulting ten days off (two weekends and two bank holidays) on my bike doing mixed multi-day rides. I needed to decide, once and for all, which bike I would be taking to the Tour.

I owned two bikes. One was a time-trial Ceepo Katana for triathlons and not suitable for a long tour. To start with the time-trial bars and geometry did not make it conducive for riding in groups and, secondly, it was awful going up hills, as I found out in Ironman Nice two years previously. It was torturous on a long hot climb.

My road bike was my beloved Giant TCR which I bought six years previous and had shared some exhilarating adventures with. She was nicknamed Trigger but her real name was Trigger's Broom. This was because I had replaced the wheels, rear derailleur, brakes, gear cables, cassette, chains, pedals, pedal rings, handlebars and saddle over the years. But she was still the same old beauty who had served me well.

She wasn't the best carbon fibre bike, but she was like a second skin to me and we had learned to handle each other well. I knew how to ride her down hills and she glided up them, the steeper the better. She was responsive on the flat and although not the most aerodynamic bike she didn't let me down when I put my foot on the pedals. Over a long flat course, the TT bike would easily outperform Trigger, but Trigger was much more comfortable to ride and she was much stronger on the hills, which were the great challenges on the Tour ahead.

The big downside with Trigger, apart from starting to show her age, was that she only had ten gears on the cassette and this meant that I could only go as high as 28 teeth on the largest cog on the rear cassette. Ideally, I needed a minimum of an 11-32 cassette and even better an 11-34. This is often referred to as a granny gear but would make it easier to spin up those steep ascents and would mean a little less effort. I know that I can guts it out for one hard day in the hills, but I needed to be planning for multiple days of effort. I needed to make up my mind on whether or not I was going to keep

Trigger and upgrade the gear selection and buy a new set of wheels for her, or bite the bullet, break off our relationship and treat myself to a new bike.

Over the Easter period I spent a couple of days looking at other bikes and took test rides on a new Giant, a Specialized S-Works and a Bianchi. I was tempted by all of them but not one of the store owners seemed to want to make the effort to sell me a bike. None of them made me feel special. Then, as I embarked on a pre-planned block of Easter training rides my mind was made up for me.

On Tuesday, 16 April I headed out from my home in Kilgetty on what was my third training ride of the week. I had ridden 113km on the previous Sunday on a beautiful out-and-back route. I left Kilgetty on an initially easy hill ride before leaving the quaint market town of Narberth and plodded up through the rolling hills of the Preseli mountains. These were often part of my Ironman training routes because they offered everything: long, gradual ascents to the very top of the mountain range, the occasional steep drag, open fields with blustery winds from all directions and very unpredictable weather conditions. Plus, striking windswept, rural views of a moss-filled hill range over the county. My legs were starting to wake up and I was keen to add to the mileage during the rest of the week.

After an easy short and sharp ride on the Monday I set off for another long ride on the Tuesday. This time I followed the coast from Tenby into a headwind all the way out to the peninsula of Angle, which is part of lap one on Ironman Wales. From there I headed north to Haverfordwest and then east for 35-odd miles to Carmarthen before heading back home in a rolling circuitous route.

My plan was to get another 160km ride under my belt but I fell agonisingly short. I was about 12km from home when Trigger stopped abruptly. I could feel something wasn't quite right in the hour or so leading up to this, but I couldn't put my finger on what it exactly was. An instinct told me to pull over and inspect her but at the same time my determination to hit the big 160 was driving me on. I had a lot of hours of missed training to catch up on.

As I pushed through the gears up the steady incline of Llandowror hill (which happens to be my favourite spot for measuring improvement through a training cycle) I heard a couple of sharp clinks and then metal scraping on tarmac. Pretty much simultaneously a spoke had snapped in my front wheel and the rear derailleur had snapped in half. Not for the first time in my athletic life I had to phone a member of the family and ask them to come and rescue me.

This is a source of amusement for the family because at least once a year they will get the phone call, and someone will ask, 'Where is he this time?' I am a little mishap-prone and I have had chains fly off on steep descents in the Preseli mountains; I have had tyres shredded on the Tenby Road bypass outside Carmarthen from discarded glass and I have suffered multiple punctures over the years when I only carry one spare tube with me. I am accustomed to a quick tube and tyre change nowadays. But with a rear derailleur and old wheels failing it was time to take decisive action.

I made the call to have Trigger rebuilt and it wasn't cheap. I bought a new set of slightly deeper rim wheels, hand built from Kinetic-one and I chose to completely replace the gear system to an 11-speed bike. This meant installing both a front and rear derailleur and buying two new cassettes for the wheels to give me greater choice on the hills. My new set-up was a Shimano Ultegra 11-speed drive-train and in the months that followed I would become very grateful for the 11-34 spare cassette that I ordered. I had no shame about using the granny gears.

The total cost of a full service, where Trigger was stripped and rebuilt, was roughly £750 and the new set of wheels were in the same ballpark. I should probably have splashed out on a newer and better bike, but I wasn't ready to end my journey with Trigger just yet. The other rather significant cost to the new set-up was that it took a week to carry out. I had lost another bank of training right when I was finding my rhythm. I was able to get out for some shorter TT speed rides and kept up the running, but it wasn't the same as haring out for hilly sojourns on my baby.

Once I got Trigger back, I was able to get into the routine of back-to-back rides over a weekend at last and I finally managed to get one great ride in on 4 May. This was a bank holiday weekend and I had three big back-to-back rides planned. I set out on the Saturday to ride around Berkshire on a circuit from Hungerford up to Lechlade-on-Thames, across to Cirencester before riding south to Bath and then heading back to Hungerford and the flat above the office.

The weather was warm and breezy, the roads were heaving and the route was flat compared to Pembrokeshire conditions. A great day out ruined only by the usual poor quality of British roads. They were so uneven and lumpy that towards the end of my ride two of the screws had fallen out of my cleats. Guess what? That's right, I didn't have spares and shops were shut on the Sunday, so training was brilliant and then held up once again. A pattern was emerging. One step forward and two steps backwards.

I was getting nervous at this stage, not just for Le Loop but also for the Tour of Wessex at the end of May and the Dragon Ride in the beginning of June. These would be the acid test for me of whether, or not, I would be able to complete the route of the Tour de France. I had a mediocre bank of training under my belt and I was showing signs of progress.

I knew I could complete one stage of Le Loop but at this stage in my preparation I was nowhere near being able to face the full thing and I was less than two months away from the Grand Depart. I knew I had it in me to come through this and I knew I could overcome adversity. I had to be able to deal with what life threw at me and there was no way that I would ever face adversity on a scale that I had in Ironman Tallinn.

SUCCESS IS NOT FINAL. FAILURE IS NOT FATAL. IT IS THE COURAGE TO CONTINUE THAT COUNTS –
Winston Churchill

Chapter 6

August 2018
Resilience

I LEARNED a lot about myself during Ironman Tallinn. What could go wrong, did go wrong and I had to find a way to overcome it. As I look back now it is with a lot of pride, but at the time I thought I was cursed and I could easily have given up. But to paraphrase a Texan drug cheat, Des and Sylvia didn't raise no quitter.

I had encountered my fair share of adversity during Ironman Nice the previous year and it was like the Ironman gods were sending me a message: maybe this isn't the sport for me. In Copenhagen in 2016 I had put together my best ever race and for a 50-year-old I had finished in a very respectable time. Everything seemed to be coming together with experience and I believed that I had a really solid foundation to build upon. The following year I threw myself into training for Nice and in hindsight I think I overdid it.

The hardest thing to prepare for in the south of France was the heat. For 2017 only, the race was taking place on 22 July as opposed to 16 June. This was because, after a terrorist attack in 2016, the French government had imposed a moratorium on all events on the Promenade for 12 months, which finished in July 2017. It is very hard to replicate the kind of warmth I would encounter there in the UK.

My solution was to push myself harder in training, but unlike pro-athletes I don't get to rest after a long hard training session. I had to work a 60-hour week. I would also spend another 15 hours or so driving the motorways of the UK to earn the living that subsidised my yearning for travel and adventure. I pushed too hard right throughout my training. If I was supposed to do a one-hour run, I would do 90 minutes. If I was supposed to a five-hour bike ride on the flat, I would do six hours on hills. I never really let my body recover after any of the sessions and I was plagued with sore throats, cold symptoms and little niggles throughout. I forced myself to push through and I didn't listen to my body.

A month before the race I entered an Ironman-distance bike race around the gentle roads of the Cotswolds. I raced hard when I should have been using this as a gentle long ride with a low heart rate. I kept my tempo up throughout and finished a 180km ride in 5hrs 20mins. This showed that I was more than ready for a race but it burned up too many matches.

Burning matches is a great way of explaining how you use up your energy in a race. Imagine if your energy is a full box of matches. Every time you exert yourself, you burn one or two matches depending on the effort involved. Ideally you want to finish a race burning the final match as you cross the finish line. You don't need to have used up half of the box before you even make the start line.

A week after that ride I picked up a throat infection which lingered persistently right up to the day before the Ironman. This included man-flu-like symptoms and my three-week taper (easing up of effort) before the race was ruined by almost zero training. My body was forcing me to listen to it and after a six-month slog I was ordered to obey.

I arrived in Nice and the temperatures were above 30°C and rising. I had no energy and only adrenaline kept my morale from sapping. The course in Nice is amazing, but the atmosphere is a bit flat. There is so much going on in the city that it is just another event and not cherished the way it was in Copenhagen, or especially Tenby, where it is the highlight of the calendar.

The swim is in the sea and it is warm and salty. Ideal for a fast time. The ride takes you into the hills surrounding the city and they are long, Tour de France-like drags. Roughly 60km are spent cycling uphill and then descending down the other side. The temperature on the tarmac is close to 40°C. The marathon consists of four laps of an out-and-back, pan-flat route taking you to the airport and back to the Promenade on solid concrete. I suffered.

The swim was a wetsuit-legal swim but the pros were not allowed to wear theirs. In retrospect it was too hot for wetsuits and this started a series of problems that would snowball. I had one of my best swim-times ever. The sea was dead calm and the extreme saltiness provided extra buoyancy which played into the hands of a heavy leg sinker like me. One hour and 12 minutes later and I was getting changed for a long bike ride. The problem was that I was baking hot. I had lost too much weight through sweat and I was unable to recognise this and didn't realise I had to handle it so early on in the race.

I headed out on the bike and wondered why all the French riders had bandanas flowing from the back of their helmets and were wearing short-sleeve tri-tops as opposed to the usual vests. They knew something that I didn't. The heat would take its toll.

I guess I suffered from some form of heat stroke. At the top of the second, long 20km drag, cycling up what felt like a stifling oven, I pulled over to get some water at a feed stop. I gulped it down and then threw up. Repeatedly.

It didn't help that my gears had been slipping on my bike. I was in effect left with two gears, which meant that I had to struggle up the hill in too high a ratio. This in turn sapped my energy and burned up all of my matches. A medic told me to withdraw from the race and showed me where the first aid tent was. It was littered with exhausted bodies, caked in sweat and giddy from the suffering. I agreed. As he turned his back to show me to the tent I jumped on my bike and rode off into the distance. Foolhardy is a word that could be used.

I found a second wind on the second half of the ride and overtook a lot of bodies that were sat on shady verges, seeking respite from the heat. This was no longer about posting a decent time; this had now become a war of attrition against myself. At least I had a flat marathon to look forward to.

The marathon was soul-destroying and one of the most uncomfortable I have ever run. A straight course meant that there were no landmarks to break up the route. The concrete pavement was hard on the feet and joints and it reflected the unrelenting sun. The locals were so dismissive of the runners that there was little to no encouragement. I was lucky that I had a good mate cheering me on and providing daft insults throughout the route.

What should have been a four-hour marathon became a five-and-a-half-hour slog. At the end my body was broken. My time was mediocre. I finished. I did not once contemplate giving up. I found some inner resolve and was determined not to put all of my training to waste.

The old expression is that quitters never win and winners never quit. I am proud to say that in extreme conditions I did not quit. I was nowhere near winning either, but baby steps, which ironically were what I was taking on the marathon. Plenty to learn from and to take into the next event where surely things would be better.

I had learned from my mistakes by the time I reached Ironman Tallinn a year later. I knew that weather would be an issue in more ways than one, although not quite on the scale that we eventually encountered. The gods tested us in this challenge. But this time my preparation had been almost ideal and I was confident of posting a decent time and maybe being competitive in my age group.

Tallinn is a beautiful city in Estonia. It is right on the Baltic Sea and is popular with Scandinavian tourists, especially the Finnish. The old walled town provided a perfect backdrop for the whole of the event and it was mostly sensational. The swim was in the harbour facing out to the ocean and was one straightforward lap. The bike course was fast and flat in the open fields, out in the surrounding countryside. It was like taking a trip back in time to a bygone mediaeval world and was incredibly quaint. The run comprised four laps around the old town and down to the harbour and back and was a mixture of flat and awful short, steep hills. There were four on each lap plus a revolting temporary bridge to cross the road, which pounded your hamstrings. Potentially this was a fast course. I didn't do as well as I hoped.

I would like to blame the rampant cheating that took place in the race, but this did not affect my performance. A strong Eastern European contingent had entered in the age group categories hoping to gain qualification for the World Championships at Ironman Kona. Rumours were rife that their abilities were not naturally driven, but were of a more synthetic nature. I have no evidence of this, only constant gossip from clean athletes, but some performances were staggering and beyond comprehension. The marshalling on the bike course was pretty lackadaisical and large pelotons formed where groups were able to work together and draft in the wind. I refused to entertain this and my performance suffered in comparison. But these were the least of my concerns. My tribulations were caused by an airline.

To get to Tallinn on the day I wanted, to allow myself time to acclimatise, I had to fly via Berlin. I flew with a British airline and then changed planes to a Polish carrier for the final leg to Estonia. Between the two of them they lost my luggage. When I checked in, I had an uneasy feeling. I barely made my connection at the German airport because we had a ten-minute window to catch the connecting flight and there were no instructions as to where to go for this transition. I could very easily have been left wandering around Berlin airport looking for absent luggage. As it transpired, I was the last person on to the plane and I was eventually left wandering around Tallinn airport looking for absent luggage. It was no consolation that the same fate had befallen a couple of other travellers on the same flight.

I went through the routine of notifying the airline of my missing luggage and received a report number. There was a whole tedious process during my week in Tallinn where I constantly chased the lost luggage, but the short version is that it did not show up at all. It was properly lost and not just left lying around at a terminal waiting to be reclaimed.

This caused a lot of stress and needless worry when I should have been concentrating on my race and a few days' holiday afterwards. The greatest concern was that all of my race kit was in my luggage. I had two things in my favour. The first was that I had my TT bike delivered separately, so at least I could guarantee that I would be able to race. The second was that the people of Tallinn and the organisers of Ironman were superb. But my race was severely compromised.

One of the biggest rules of any form of competition is: nothing new on race day. Stick to what you are familiar and comfortable with. Everything was going to be new for me and would take some getting used to. You don't buy a pair of trainers and run a marathon without breaking them in.

For the whole of my stay, I existed with the clothes that I wore on the flight out and some spare shorts, underwear and T-shirts that I bought in Tallinn. I splashed out on new race kit which cost me over £700. Outside of the race I felt like a nomad, wandering around in cheap and dirty clothes that I would discard by the end of the trip.

During the race I was permanently uncomfortable and irritated. I had to buy a new wetsuit, goggles, running shoes, socks, cycle shoes, helmet, water bottles, unfamiliar energy bars and a host of other little odds and ends. The organisers were great and said that if the wetsuit was not damaged after the race, they would refund me 80 per cent of the sale price. The flipside is that I was limited to what stock they had left and had to choose a suit that was marginally too loose and pretty uncomfortable. My racing wetsuit is like a second skin and this one felt like an uneven straightjacket. Nothing new on race day.

I had to buy a pair of trainers and cycle shoes that were both brands I was not familiar with and again they were good but not ideal. The other issue with the cycle shoes was that they did not come with cleats attached and this meant that I had to cycle ten kilometres out of town to a bike shop to buy the last pair of cleats in stock. Turns out I wasn't their only customer that day.

This additional stress and unnecessary exercise hampered my preparation. I should have been sitting with my feet up 24 hours before the most important day of my year. The anxiety was amplified further that evening. Following a final carbohydrate-laden meal on the Friday night I went to bed early. I had zero hours sleep. I struggle to sleep the night before a race at the best of times and as I was drifting off around midnight a group in the room next door decided to hold a drunken party. A hotel full of athletes and we had the room next door to a college dorm.

I had a mate who had come out to join me and he was a godsend because he took so much of the pressure off me. He helped me find kit when I needed it, kept me calm when I became anxious and he knocked on the door and calmed the party down in the early hours before the race. He also took the mickey out of me on the marathon and made friends with some rather interesting Irish ladies, who we would celebrate with during our stay.

An hour after he asked the students to quieten down, they were at it again. This time the hotel reception silenced them but the damage was done. I was going into a 13-hour race with zero sleep. The only option was to grab my early breakfast from the hotel and prepare for the start. The hotel chef picked this morning to drink too much vodka and sleep through his alarm. There were some pretty uptight athletes in the hotel lobby demanding a breakfast that had been confirmed repeatedly, but none was forthcoming. There was a sandwich fridge in the lobby and I grabbed one of the last meals from the day before and an apple. Final meal before an endurance race and I was chomping on a stale cucumber and cottage cheese roll, which I would later throw up during the swim.

If my luggage had been with me, I would have had a bowl of porridge, a protein bar, a banana and an isotonic energy drink. But by now my mind was focused and locked in on the race. To quote a very good friend of mine, I had to pull myself together and Get Shit Done. I was able to block out the negative distractions and grabbed a taxi to the start of the race and the coldest swim of my life.

The Baltic Sea is freezing. Even in August it is brass bleeding monkeys. It was so cold that the following year they moved the swim to a lake, because it was so dangerous in 2018. It was so cold I came out of the water with blue feet and a tingling in my fingers. I saw people being covered with blankets and given warm soup, it had that drastic an effect on some competitors. I struggled and was glad to get out of the water. My strategy in an Ironman is to survive the swim and don't drown, ride the bike without crashing and pick up time on the run. This swim was survival of the fittest.

The loop took us around an industrial harbour and we battled the elements just to get out and on to the bike. Did I mention that it was cold? Officially the organisers said that the water temperature was a race legal 15°C. Unofficially the locals confirmed that it never gets above 8° in the height of summer. Not safe for racing in. There was a stench of diesel in the water, wafting from the great container ships, and the weaker triathletes were throwing up, which is where I saw the cottage cheese and cucumber again. It was a relief to get out of the water, take off the wetsuit for the final time and put on a strange race kit for a fast bike leg.

The bike leg was indeed quick. Where my swim was completed in a disappointing 1hr 28 mins (16 minutes slower than Nice the year before), my bike split was a decent 5hrs 46mins. It set me up nicely for the run and could have been marginally quicker, if it wasn't for three key reasons. The first was that I rather piously refused to join any of the pelotons and benefit from drafting. There were some large groups and a lot of competitors had inaccurate times and would have been disqualified at most other events. I am only a little bit bitter, but I can look myself in the mirror and be proud of my achievement. Plus, I was never going to trouble the podium in this race, not when 50-year-old Russians were finishing in under ten hours. Phenomenal standard I was up against.

The second was that my new bike shoes were rubbing and forming excruciating blisters. This is something that is easily managed because pain is temporary and the glory lasts forever if you succeed. The third reason came about through another shift in the weather and this time it was of biblical proportions.

Halfway through the bike split, the gentle warmth from the sun seemed to fade away and allow dark clouds to make their presence felt. These were not in the forecast. With about 50km left to go on the course the heavens opened. The professional athletes were already on the marathon by this stage but the rest of us mortals had a tricky bike ride home. The heavens didn't just open; they poured down bucketsful of water; they brought in a roaring thunder which was deafening and lightning that was eerily close to the road ahead.

The route quickly filled with little rivers that moved our bikes as we negotiated the highway. Water was almost six inches deep and the mask on my helmet was pelted with torrential rain. I needed windscreen wipers and could barely see.

This sounds dramatic, but I saw plenty of riders take shelter in bus stops and what spectators there were completely disappeared. I foolishly carried on and decided I had come too far and through too much to stop getting my shit done. I am not sure where this willpower came from because the sensible option would have been to take cover, but I found an inner reserve I didn't know existed and finished in a very respectable time for me. Without drafting.

No sooner was I finishing the cycle leg than steam started to come up from the tarmac. The storms disappeared almost as quickly as they had arrived and we were left with hot and humid conditions to run a marathon. This was Nice all over again. Only this time my stomach was growling with the lack of proper diet leading up to the race, the strange energy bars and drinks that it was not used to and the extreme fluctuation in temperatures. The marathon route was breathtaking in many ways. It took us through a park which surrounded the old walled city, on the cobbled streets lined with sandy-coloured stone walls, with temples and spires looming above us and plenty of crowds offering generous encouragement. I didn't notice a single bit of it. I was in agony from the second lap onwards.

Again, this poor workman is going to blame his tools. The trainers I had hastily bought the day before were a good fit, but they were too tight to run a marathon in. From the word go they started rubbing and I ran the entire race with my toes clenched. A month later I would lose four toenails from the damage caused. My running gait was uncomfortable and far from relaxed.

By the second lap the stomach cramps had caught up with me, the intense heat causing me to lose too many salts. I jumped into a cubicle and suffered an horrendous bout of diarrhoea. Where the temperature was mid-30s outside, it was a good 10° hotter inside the plastic cocoon and I lost even more salts through perspiration. This ruined my race as I had to visit the boys' sweaty cubicle three more times and finished a run with chafing shorts in five hours, when I should have been one hour quicker. Once again, I was underwhelmed by my overall time, a respectable 12hrs 28mins 24secs, but I was delighted to have prevailed. I learned a lot about myself and I learned even more about motivation.

In both of these races I faced adversity and I regard them as part of my overall training plan for Le Loop. In the first instance the trials were of my own making and I had to quickly learn from them. On the second occasion none of it was my fault, it was the risk you take when putting yourself out there in the knowledge that real life, human frailty and simple bad luck can trip you up. It is in these moments that you learn the most about your character and you develop more as a human being.

I had to find a way to accept the misfortune and then I had to find a way to deal with it and complete my goal to the best of my ability. Through experience I have learned to become more pragmatic when it comes to dealing with disaster. We have to accept that failure and bad luck will strike us. It is a fact of life and instead of bemoaning the misfortune, which is the easy option, we have to accept and proceed. There is always a way to succeed. We just have to find it.

I have broken this down to the simplest of terms for me to handle. When misfortune strikes, I have developed my own method for resilience. Unfortunately, this has too often happened through experience. I get angry quickly. I let off steam. I sulk briefly and then I take stock of the facts. Once I know the bare, cold facts I formulate a plan. The greater your preparation and the more practiced your process is, the easier it is to find a route to success and the required plan becomes clear. If your training has been solid then the process will matter far more than the outcome. A positive outcome is always as a result of a great process. If disaster strikes and you have covered all possible scenarios then it is not your fault. You may not achieve the complete result that you had been seeking, but so long as you had committed yourself completely and given your very best you will have succeeded. Failure comes when you do not put yourself out there and do not try to achieve your greatest dreams. From failure comes success. Learn the lessons and keep creating those chances.

My luggage was returned to me six weeks after I arrived back home. It had travelled round most of Europe. The airline refused compensation.

A RIVER CUTS THROUGH ROCK,
NOT THROUGH ITS POWER, BUT
THROUGH ITS PERSISTENCE –
James N. Watkins

Chapter 7

May 2019
Preparation. Preparation. Preparation (c)

AS I moved into May I was behind on my training schedule. On a positive note, I did have a solid bank of midweek work behind me and I had comfortably managed a couple of decent long rides in the previous six weeks. I knew from experience with Ironman that you do not reach race distances and race speed in your first week of training, they are gradually developed over a period of six months and you notice small breakthroughs and wins along the way.

My power and speed were increasing steadily and I could sustain these efforts for longer periods. On the flip side I was only two months away from the greatest challenge of my life. I still needed to put in a really serious bank of effort and there was no longer any room for shortcuts. In my mind it was touch and go if I would be ready in time.

My plan for the remaining weeks was broken down into two blocks of three weeks, followed by a third block of tapering my efforts. The first block was intense training, which had to be fitted around my work schedule. The second block was an intense period of competition where I was entered into two separate three-day tours or sportives. And block three was aimed at keeping my legs turning over but allowing for a bit of rest to ensure that I was fresh for the Grand Depart at the end of June. Squeaky bum time.

To complicate matters with block one, work was becoming a little hectic and bordering on stressful. After I had handed in my notice the board had asked me to make a couple of staff redundant and this impacted the efforts of everyone in the company. We were a small team and I couldn't have been prouder of the work the gang were putting in. But everyone's workload had increased and we all had to be capable of filling in for other members of staff. We had always been efficient but this cost-cutting was causing some tension.

To compound matters, at the beginning of May our financial controller suffered what we thought was a heart attack, but in the end turned out to be an anxiety attack. This would impact on her right up until the day I would leave and in turn this increased the pressure on the other office staff. Le Loop was at the wrong time of the year for the business because our financial year-end was 30 June. This means that we have to do the annual stocktake, check the accounts, deal with any discrepancies or amendments and close off the financial year. This year we would be doing it without a financial controller and without the managing director, because I would be in Brussels riding a bike for fun.

As if this wasn't difficult enough, we had the matter of switching over to a new accounts package at the beginning of July. The government had introduced Making Tax Digital and our current package was not compatible with their system. Our systems had to be updated at a hefty cost, and training for all the company was required. To compound matters, this also happened to be one of our peak periods of trading.

I had to ask myself some difficult questions. Should I give up on a lifelong dream and do the sensible thing and stay at work?

On the one hand, it could be construed as irresponsible to leave a business and team I had built up for over a decade, at a crucial period, and jet off for three weeks of dubious pleasure. I was a decent leader and my team had been loyal and performed magnificently for me over the years. Did I want my legacy to be that of someone who abandoned them at a difficult hour? I had come through repeatedly and was not comfortable with letting them down right now.

On the other hand, I had an opportunity to fulfil a lifelong dream and I had raised almost £5,000 for the charity. I had clocked up a lot of hours of intense training and I would lose my entry fee and other related costs. I had set myself a challenge and was pouring my heart and soul into it and now I was on the verge of giving it all up – but I was not sure if I would be able to live with myself if I did.

I spoke to the board in New Zealand and explained the position and we devised a solution. To my mind there were two deciding factors. The first was that the board made it clear that they did not think I was responsible for a lot of the success we had earned in my decade of guidance and that my role was disposable. That was a kick in the teeth and freed me from any misguided loyalty to them.

The second, and more crucial factor, was that they asked me if I thought the staff were reliable and could they cope without me after I left the business. I told them the team were brilliant, emphatically so, and that they would succeed.

That made the decision easy. We put in place a contingency plan for the financial year-end. We would employ a temp to cover the bookkeeping, we delayed the implementation of the new accounts package to September, we gave extra authority to the team to learn how to make decisions without referring to me and I would walk back into a mountain of work at the end of July, when I would be exhausted after a long tour. Well worth it. I was going to ride Le Loop.

I just needed to be ready for it.

Block One

As the fear of the Grand Depart started to overwhelm me, I changed my training routine and made slight alterations to my diet. I cut out caffeine and fizzy drinks and all snacks disappeared. Caffeine and a sugar-based drink can give you a great energy boost in the middle of a ride when you are struggling. By cutting them out six weeks before an event I knew I would feel the full benefits when I needed them. Many guys on the Tour would have coffee all the time, but I felt like I would be better off rationing my intake. Nothing scientific here, it is merely something that had served me well with triathlons in the past couple of years.

I concentrated mostly on bike work from here on in. I cut out the swim and run training. I increased the effort with the weight training and I did three tempo bike sessions during the week and back-to-back rides on the weekends. The tempo bike sessions were key.

I have always used my own homemade, and unscientific, VO2 max test which measures where I am in my progress. I do this on a regular exercise bike seen in every gym up and down the country. These bikes usually have difficulty levels from 1 to 25, with 1 being ridiculously easy and a very fast spin and 25 being exceptionally tough and comparable to cycling up a hill with a 20 per cent gradient.

I would start at a very easy level 6 and spin the bike at 90 revolutions per minute (the machines are all digital and show the stats). I would keep this up for as long as possible and after every minute I would click the machine up one difficulty rating, with the aim of measuring how long I could sustain the effort. The idea is that as my endurance and power builds during the programme I should be able to sustain the effort for longer.

Back in my unfit January state I was able to hold 90 revolutions up to level 14. At the beginning of May I was able to sustain it to level 17 and by the time I reached the Tour I wanted to be between 18 and 19. It is quite rudimentary, but it works for me and allows me to measure my progress. I was actually on track with this most basic of tests.

The tempo sessions now incorporated much more hill work and I would do 20 to 30-minute bursts all in the difficulty levels of 18 to 25 when I went to the gym, which is the equivalent of cycling hills from a 10 per cent gradient up to 20 per cent. When I was able to do similar sessions outdoors on the road, I was lucky that only nine miles away from my apartment I had two hills, not far apart, to practise on. Both were approximately one kilometre in length and had gradients of 8 per cent up to 16 per cent.

I would repeat time trials up each of these ascents, pushing myself to exhaustion with the aim of going quicker each time. My logic on both of these sessions was to condition my legs for the mountains that I would face in France. I needed to be able to cope with some monstrously steep ascents taking us up to an uncategorised 25 per cent gradient on La Planche des Belles Filles (a stage I had targeted right from the moment the Tour route was announced).

I needed to be able to sustain some of these efforts for up to two hours on the very long climbing days, particularly with famed mountains such as the Col du Tourmalet, the Galibier and the newly introduced ski station summit of Val Thorens which finished the Tour off with a 30km climb.

I was becoming quite anxious thinking about the mountains. I was used to hills, but short, sharp shocks and not the long, extended beatings that lay in store. I knuckled down and threw myself into both my work and my training. Nothing was half-hearted and I saw some glimmers of hope leading up to the Tour of Wessex at the tail end of May.

Block Two

To help in my preparation I had entered two three-day events in May and at the beginning of June. The idea was to get used to riding for more than two days in succession, without having the stresses of work to worry about in between them. I would develop the skills of riding in a group and I needed to learn the etiquette of doing so. I had only ever ridden in one multi-day event before and I knew I had a lot to learn. Both events were known to have some steep and long, by UK standards, climbs and this would stand me in good stead.

The first of the two events was the Tour of Wessex, which is recommended by the Le Loop organising team. We received a discounted entry and there would be a healthy contingent of Loopers in attendance. This would give me a chance to meet some of the people that I would be riding with in France and to pick the brains of the alumni. I endeavoured to harvest as many useful tips as possible. This was a good habit I would maintain throughout the Tour.

The Tour of Wessex was three days with a total of 330 miles of riding, or 531km, and we would exceed 100 miles on each of the three days. This would be a first and a significant achievement for me. This was a steep learning curve.

Racing in triathlons, marathons and Ironman, I have learned to pace myself to ensure that I go as fast as I can for as long as I can. There is no thought about rest, recovery or the next day. The focus is to make sure that my last match has been burned as I cross the finish line. If I manage it correctly, I know that I will have given my best and I will have posted a decent time.

The difference with a multi-day sportive is that it is not a race, although there is still a lot of sporting bravado and competition. We can't help it. With the Tour I had to learn how to manage the workload over three days and pace myself accordingly. I learned the hard way.

Day one I couldn't contain myself. I had been told that Cheddar Gorge was the most significant hill on the route, and it was early in the stage. I breezed up its gentle 7 per cent slope and thought that was the worst segment of the day over with. It turns out there were a few more shocks in store and I really should have done my homework properly. Preparation. Preparation. Preparation.

Every hill afterwards I attacked with gusto and false bravado, only to come close to bonking (I know) on one significant climb. Midway through the stage we had a two-kilometre climb which reached a purported 20 per cent (according to the more expensive Garmin computers of those I overtook). Some riders were walking the hill, others were weaving across the uneven road and midway through the ascent I felt like I had hit a brick wall.

I have never ever walked on a hill in my life and I wasn't going to start that bad habit on that one. I reminded myself of the adage about success being 99 per cent perspiration and I dug in. It took every ounce of effort to reach the top at a ridiculously slow crawl and I became an embarrassing weaver. I made it, but I was spent. I still had another 65km to go.

After some water and an energy bar I recovered a little and caught up with some of the Loop alumni. I wanted to impress them and prove to myself that I was capable of riding at this level. The issue for me was that these guys were/are very talented riders and I was left blowing out of my arse for 30km before I drifted off the back and was left to ride into a strong headwind on my own.

A couple of times a group would pass me and I would desperately try to cling on to them, but I had nothing left. I ambled back to the finish in six hours and in the middle of the field. Moderately respectable but not the level I had been hoping for. Lesson learned.

As a result of day one, the next day was a 190km slog. It took us down to the south coast and back on a busy bank holiday Sunday. Traffic conditions were horrendous and British drivers proved that they still don't have any patience for bike riders. It wasn't quite as hilly a day as the Saturday, but the winds were strong and permanently against us.

I relented halfway through and had a can of coke to see me through to the end of the day. I found it difficult to get into any pelotons, or groups of riders, and had to ride solo for most of the day, making my effort even tougher.

This is a funny thing about sportives. In theory you should be riding in groups or pelotons all day long and this should make the riding easier by reducing your workload when you sit in the wind. It has been my experience that this doesn't happen despite there being hundreds of cyclists alongside you.

Groups who enter together tend to stick together and they are reluctant to let an outsider join their gang. Individuals who have entered aren't generally used to riding in groups and it makes it harder to get a small peloton going and comfortably working together. On this day I would have liked to have ridden with some more Loopers, but I didn't have it in my legs to keep up with them. I burned more matches than necessary and left myself a lot to do on the final day. It was all money in the training bank, I guess.

I started the bank holiday Monday feeling empty inside and latched on to a very big group for the first 40km or so. The route took us to the north coast of Somerset through Minehead and Allerford over a very lumpy 179km. We experienced a long 7 per cent drag out by the coast, which was a shortened version of many of the mountains we would face in Le Loop and there were a couple of stinging 20 per cent-plus climbs that sapped everything out of the legs. I met up with a few Loopers and was able to share the pace with them, particularly into a strong headwind out to the coast. It was so strong that the feed station's tents were blown over and rendered useless. This was eight hours of a long hard plod, but then something decent happened.

As we turned around, the wind was in our favour and I made friends with Andy who would be doing the full Tour with me. Andy can talk even more than me. Occasionally we can be irritating but in that moment in time we took our minds off the pain with inane chat about Swansea City and Tranmere Rovers and I picked up even more tips for the summer. Without knowing it we had breezed our way back to the finish and had left quite a few riders in our wake. My legs had adapted to the multi-day extended effort and I had found some semblance of form. The Tour of Wessex wasn't comfortable, but I had benefited from it immensely.

During the Tour I had met many of the team who would be riding Le Loop in the summer and made some new friends. My legs had suffered for three days on a tough route and they had not let me down. They proved to be strong if not powerful and I found that I could recover fairly well. I also took on board a crash-course of things I needed to learn for cycling the Tour de France.

I learned how to pace myself and not to go too silly early on; I learned about the need for epic habits on a daily basis, the importance of cleanliness, being organised, how to ride in a group and not do daft things like brake suddenly; I was given advice on equipment, gear ratios, feed strategies and so much more and I now had a group of friends on Strava who would provide community and advice over the coming weeks.

I realised that I should rest a little before attacking the three-day Dragon Tour, which followed two weeks later. First a couple of beers that evening to reward myself for a half-decent job to be ticked off the preparation list.

I took the lessons from Wessex into the Dragon Tour and had a good experience, apart from the weather and more specifically the forecasts. Every day they predicted temperatures to be roughly 16°C, with slightly overcast skies and the occasional shower. I wore kit accordingly and carried with me a light rain jacket.

The temperatures never exceeded 12°C and with the wind-chill factor up in the mountains it was considerably colder, plus it pissed down. Not just an occasional shower. Constantly. My kit stank out my hotel room at the end of each day and I used a hairdryer in my shoes to dry them out, only for them to be soaked again the following day. It was farcical.

That aside, the Dragon Tour was three days of slightly shorter but much steeper riding than Wessex. It is organised by Human Race and day three is one of the most popular single day sportives on the UK calendar. Close to 15,000 people ride this day on routes varying from 99km to 300km. I had taken part in the event the year before and knew what to expect. Apart from the downpours. But something happened on day two that caught me by surprise.

The stage was a relatively short 101km in comparison to what I was used to, and the route comfortably undulated through the countryside surrounding the Brecon Beacons near Abergavenny, until we reached The Tumble.

This is a hill which Geraint Thomas purportedly trained on as he developed his immense talent (I'm coming after you G) and is six kilometres with an average ramp of 10 per cent. This would be a good test for what was to follow in July. Having suffered on the Tour of Wessex and emptied my box of matches too soon into the whole event, I set off steadily, bordering on over-cautious. I dropped into my lowest granny gear and tried to ease my way into the hill. I found a rhythm and concentrated on maintaining the effort without overexerting myself. And then it happened.

I started picking off riders. Cyclists who had been dropping me on the flat looked like they were riding backwards in treacle compared to my effort. Six months of specific hill tempo training was finally starting to fall into place and not a moment too soon. I was feeling strong and borderline athletic, although I don't think Geraint Thomas would have been losing any sleep over my talents.

I counted 31 people that I passed going up that hill and not one overtook me. At the top, an experienced club rider caught up with me and said, 'That was impressive. What club do you ride for?'

That was one of the greatest compliments of my life. For the first time that year I genuinely started to believe that I was a cyclist and that I could succeed in France. I floated all the way back to the finish line. I was still giddy as I was drying out my shoes and shorts that evening in the hotel bathroom. Oh, the glamour of amateur sport.

I am not sure why I bothered to dry out my shoes and put clean kit on for day three. By the time I had made it to the start line I was soaked to the bone and shivering. Large crowds on the roads meant I had some company, but my spirits were as damp as the weather. I struggled for form until we reached the Devil's Elbow.

On the final day the climbing begins within 15km of the start and it is up and down all day long. The climbs are pretty impressive and provide a useful challenge, but the biggest test would be the Elbow. I guess it is all in the name. The Brecon Beacons are famed for a handful of ascents like this: 2.5km with an incline of up to 20 per cent in places. Steep, punishing and littered with more feeble bodies along the side of the road.

It was here that I woke up and my body came to life. I had been struggling with the conditions, but as we approached the Devil's Elbow a little ray of sun cracked through the dense, dark skies and this summed up my day.

Proving that the lessons were eventually sinking in, I once again started cautiously and, before I knew it, I was picking off riders one by one. I comfortably breezed through the finish line at the top of the hill. If nothing else I had found my climber's legs. I needed to be able to suffer a long day on the flat, which for me provides the biggest mental challenge. But I could do something about that before the Tour started.

Block Three

Exactly six days after the Dragon Tour had passed and 14 days before Le Loop would start, I set off on one last epic ride in my final preparation for the Tour. For the remaining fortnight I would taper down and would maintain some gentle spins and the odd tempo session to ensure I was fresh for the Grand Depart. Over the course of the preceding six months, I had lost almost one stone in weight. I had reached the level of ratio 19 on my home-designed VO2 max test and my speed and power had improved dramatically. I was strong in the hills, albeit short steep ones, but I didn't know if I had the distance in my legs for the longest of days in the saddle. There was only one way to find out.

I set off from my home in south Wales at 7am and headed out along the coast to the peninsula of Angle. The weather was cool with a gentle breeze. Nothing too difficult and bordering on ideal. At that time of year there are a lot of people out training on the Ironman Wales route and this meant I had company early in the day. My legs were raring to go.

From Angle I headed back and then followed the coast northbound up to the town of Cardigan. There is no such thing as a flat route in Pembrokeshire and this was especially lumpy, including a nice steep climb leading out from Fishguard and its historic little port. Echoes of Dylan Thomas spurring me on from *Under Milk Wood*.

I doubled back at Cardigan and rode up and over the top of the Preseli mountains, then down to the market town of Narberth where I turned east. I travelled as far as the county town of Carmarthen where my brother joined me for the last 35km home, braving a busy dual carriageway on a Saturday afternoon.

This was a flat, fast and windy section of road for 12 miles and it was a little hairy to say the least. We worked well and he was a big help in getting me back to where I started eight hours earlier and in one piece. I took a little detour and made sure that in one, mostly solo, ride I had covered 250km. This was the furthest I had ever cycled in my life and the first time I had ever exceeded 150 miles. The longest day on the Tour was due to be 244km.

With two weeks left until the Grand Depart in Brussels, I had finished my training. I had the taper period, which I would use to keep myself fresh and free from injury and ill-health. I had a lot of last-minute shopping to finalise and I had to ensure that my bike was delivered for shipping.

To all intents and purposes, I was ready. Or as ready as I would ever be. I knew that I could complete every single stage that the Tour de France could throw at me, the big question now would be whether I could finish them all over 21 days. Ordinarily I would have had a congratulatory beer that night, but I was now teetotal as part of my preparation. Bring it on.

*LIFE ONLY COMES AROUND ONCE.
DO WHATEVER MAKES YOU HAPPY
AND BE WITH WHOEVER MAKES
YOU SMILE* – Anon

Chapter 8

29 June 2019, Brussels
Live It and Love It

THE WELCOME briefing on the Friday night set the tone. It laid out all our instructions and epic habits we would need for the next 23 days. I was like a child in Willy Wonka's factory. Excited beyond belief and nervous as hell. But when I checked in to the hotel, it was nearly all over before it had begun.

The final two-week taper had been straightforward and I was as ready as I would ever be. I would have preferred to have got some more productive training under my belt in the first three months of the year, but this was no time for regrets. I had a very solid preparation behind me. Not perfect but solid and I had come on strong in the last two months. Now was a time to look forward and live in the moment. As much as you can enjoy spending up to ten hours a day on a bone-hard saddle and caked in stale sweat. Seriously, why couldn't I pick a more sensible ambition? Something more sedate like watching every theatre production of Shakespeare or visiting every football stadium in the UK. I had to pick the one that tested my absolute limits of endurance and happens to be far more expensive to boot. No time to look back though. Incidentally, I literally found looking back difficult as well, because I had lost a lot of flexibility in my neck after spending a decade sleeping on uncomfortable beds when I was overseas. My perspective was like my posture. I had to look forward.

I had dropped off my bike at a cycle store in Reading and she was ready and waiting in good condition at the hotel when I arrived. When I delivered her, I took the opportunity to spend even more money on last-minute supplies. Some necessary and some best described as a luxury or frivolous. I think I was organised and, if anything, I had brought too much with me. I opted to bring a large holdall that would withstand the rigours of being shipped around the country and I included a smaller, empty Ironman kit bag for any souvenirs I would pick up along the way. We were advised by Le Loop to pack the following for our bikes and general kit:

- Multitool (ideally with chain tool)
- Basic lights and basic lock (minimal use but good to bring)
- Pump, tyre levers
- Two spokes of each length (probably three lengths in total)
- Chain quick link (compatible with your chain)

- Valve extender (if you have deep rims)
- Spare cleats
- Spare rear mech hanger
- Three each of cycling jersey, shorts, socks
- Cycling shoes
- Gilet
- Good-quality waterproof/windproof jacket (ideally high-vis)
- Two pairs of cycling gloves (long and short fingers)
- For evenings: jeans, T-shirts, fleece/jumper, underwear, trainers/flip-flops
- Helmet (mandatory – you will not be allowed to cycle without one)
- Sunglasses
- Cuddly toy
- Carrier bags – for dirty washing/wet clothes
- Small packet of washing powder/soap (for rinsing clothes in the evenings)
- Tissues/toilet paper/wet wipes
- Plug adaptor
- Phone and charger (with adaptor)
- Toiletries and medical: sun cream, pain relief, chamois cream, lip salve (with sun protection), antiseptic wipes, plasters.

The organisers were superb in the information they provided beforehand and this will be a running theme, because there is no way I would have been able to organise and attempt this feat under my own steam. The support was essential and proves the old Arsène Wenger maxim from his early successful days at Arsenal: the art of succeeding with a team makes an individual stronger.

I packed most of this suggested kit and then some extra supplies on top. I brought a spare set of wheels and in the bag they were packed into I squeezed in two extra rear mech hangers, six spare tubes, a couple of spare multitools that I had collected over the years, spare tyres (reasonable to expect some wear and tear), spare rear cassette, two spare chains and other odds and ends that I keep finding in nooks and crannies of my shed.

I ignored the advice of previous Loopers and brought close to 40 energy bars, two for each day, which took up a lot of space in my bag. I brought my laptop to write a blog and to download my Garmin computer stats at the end of each day. I needed the technology because my phone was four years old and useless. That meant that I had no fear of losing or breaking the phone, which could be one less thing to worry about on the road. It also meant I bought a cheap camera at the airport because the quality of photos on the phone were sketchy at best. The laptop took up a lot of space in my holdall.

I brought the requisite three pairs of cycling shorts and six shirts (Le Loop official kit and BESA-sponsored jerseys) and I wish I had brought more. Finally, I packed way too many civilian clothes. Two pairs of jeans, three pairs of tailored shorts, one pair of casual trousers, four shirts, six T-shirts, two sweaters, two pairs of shoes, one pair of flip-flops and two pairs of trainers.

After three days on tour, standards went out the window and we all lounged around in shorts and T-shirts. Most of my clothes were dead weight and taking up too much space. I also included all manner of toiletries, including three tubs of chamois cream, which were not for sharing.

I was overcautious and covered every base, which in turn meant I had more crap to cart around than U2 on a world tour. The riding was supposed to be the difficult bit. I never found the time to write a blog and I barely updated my Facebook page. I was raring to go. Just the formalities of the first night to get out of the way.

The first three days of the 2019 Tour were based in Brussels and it provided a great send-off. Home of the legendary Eddy Merckx, arguably the greatest cyclist ever to have graced this planet, the city provided wonderful riding conditions and it was nice and easy to access. A short hop from the airport and I arrived at the hotel by the early afternoon.

The Le Loop team had been there for a couple of days and everything was in place and signposted for us. If in doubt, follow the signs. They had commandeered the car park for the mechanics, massages and even a feed stop on the second day. Seriously impressed. That admiration only increased after I checked in.

For the first three nights I would be sharing a room with a guy called Ben. He had arrived at the hotel before me, but when I walked into the room I knew there was something wrong. The curtains were closed, the air conditioning was on full blast and a slight odour of sick emanated from the bathroom. A man I had never met was laid on the double bed, his face whiter than the sheets he was curled up in. I tried to be friendly and create a good impression.

'Hi. My name's Ceri and I think I'm your room-mate for the next few days.' Or something to that effect. I ignored the fact that there was a double bed and no sign of a second bed for me. Ben looked up, stared at me blankly and muttered something along the lines of, 'We may need to see about that.' He rushed to the bathroom and was violently ill.

I would like to say that I was sympathetic towards his plight. The day before an adventure of a lifetime and he was disastrously ill. Not a slight sore throat or a niggly muscle twinge, but gut-wrenching, body-weakening, energy-sapping, soul-destroying ill.

I hope I enquired as to his well-being and offered some kind words, but the truth is the thoughts running through my head were very selfish: I hope it isn't viral; I hope I don't catch it; just my luck that I get the one room that is diseased. By this stage and after all that had gone before, I was single-minded in my quest. Sorry Ben.

I headed to the lobby and found Sarah who handled the logistics for the whole Tour. Having worked in the travel industry I can safely state that what she did for the duration was some undertaking. Over time I came to be really impressed with her and she made the whole thing so much smoother and hassle free. I don't think she ever understood my sense of humour. She impressed me right away.

I explained my and Ben's joint predicaments and she got to work. She had 100 jobs to do but she made time for me and made both Ben and me a priority. Knowing I was going to be in her hands for three weeks, this was reassuring. I had to hang around the lobby for over an hour as she juggled, tweaked and coerced the hotel into helping and this afforded me the luxury of making many new friends right away, names I would instantly forget.

By late afternoon a room was found for me. I retrieved my luggage from the original room, offered sympathy and bade farewell to Ben. I wouldn't see much more of him during the Tour because he was so much stronger than me, as he proved by making the start the following morning. Thankfully his sickness had been food poisoning and not viral. And my new room was rather nice, with a huge, luxurious queen-size bed to myself. A real stroke of fortune. Again, sorry Ben.

Conscious that I didn't want to doze off and ruin my evening's sleep I headed outside to check on Trigger. She was in great nick. I needed to tweak the gears a little bit but that aside she was gleaming and ready for another adventure with me. I just needed to know what I was doing and that would come in the briefing not long afterwards.

I wouldn't say I was intimidated at the Tour briefing, but I was intimidated. I am usually a pretty confident and positive person. I misguidedly believe in myself too much and believe that anything is possible. But I don't mind admitting that I was a little overawed by some of the riders that I shared the presentation room with that night. It seemed that every one of them was an experienced and competitive rider full of self-belief.

I saw skinny bodies attached to rippling thighs and thunderous calves. Ladies and men that glided with an athletic ease and wore T-shirts and sweaters detailing outlandish exploits. Expensive Garmin watches and high-end cycling kit adorned their frames and I felt lost in my khaki shorts and Ironman T-shirt. Wait. I've finished five

Ironman races and I bet some of them cannot swim. Then I met Richard with his thunder calves who told me in passing that he had competed for GB at all levels of triathlon.

It transpired that many others were feeling the same as I was. A cold diffidence was in fact shyness. A loud, forceful confidence was masking a fear of failure and asking too many questions was hiding a gamut of insecurities. Little did I know, but these were my people. Slight nervous tension was a good thing. It kept me focused. I was still intimidated. Then on top I had to remember everything from the briefing.

We were addressed by Rick Wates from the William Wates Memorial Trust who put us at ease and inspired us with what we were riding for. Never forget that Ceri. Sarah gave us our housekeeping rules for the next day, and the whole Tour, and we were then introduced to Emily, the professional lead rider.

Sarah talked a lot about the bubble that we would quickly find ourselves living in and she provided great advice and instruction for the full experience. Each evening there would be a briefing at dinner, where we would receive the details and timings for the next day. Emily was there to talk to us about the ride itself and give great, practical advice. I would come to adore Emily and she was, and is, one of my sporting heroes.

Emily is very warm, kind, generous, unassuming and completely without ego. She backs this up with a steely determination, professionalism and immense talent. She is the perfect lead rider for a tour. She talked through the route, the conditions and what we could expect the following day. We were given instructions on riding on Belgian roads, hopping on to cycle paths and great housekeeping at the feed stops. She also has a good nose for an excellent coffee or ice-cream stop.

The basis of Le Loop is that we cycle the route of the Tour de France exactly one week before the professionals. There are some slight differences between the Tours because this is not a race and the roads are not closed for us. We start from the same places and ride through the same finishes just without the bunting, fans and general adrenaline-fuelled fanfare, before cycling to our chosen hotel for the night. No state-of-the-art bus for us, but some extra kilometres to log in our Garmins and the odd surprise when the hotel happened to be located at the top of a steep hill. We would be spending longer in the saddle than the pros.

Obviously, we do not have the same athletic capacity as them and in many cases we have 20 years or more on them, so logic dictated that we would be slower in finishing each stage. We had to abide by the rules of the road, which would add a good 20 per cent or so to the time spent astride Trigger. We had to stick to the right-hand side of the road, there were no options to take the shortest and most efficient line. We had to stop at junctions, roundabouts and red lights. Instead of gearing up for a big sprint in the closing stretch of a ride, we might instead be unclipping our cleats and coming to a standstill as we waited for learner drivers to negotiate the correct exit on a roundabout.

We had the added benefit of four feed stops during each stage (except time-trial days) where we were fed like royalty. Royalty in a bike race that is, not a palace. This would take time to negotiate but was essential to ensure that we all made it to the finish each day in one piece. Frequently the food on the road was miles better than the hotels.

Finally, with up to 100 riders on the road some days, for obvious safety reasons we could not ride in one large peloton but had to work our way into smaller groups of ten or so. This was still efficient compared to what I had been used to, but there would be nowhere to hide like there is in a large group.

The first stage was an arduous 212km circuiting the perimeter of Brussels. The temperatures were due to be in the high 30s and we had a comfortable 1,400m of climbing to do. Nothing too strenuous. Apart from the cobblestones. I had never ridden on cobblestones, or pavé, before and I was excited at the prospect of trying something new.

Emily talked us through the technique for riding them and explained that you need to attack the cobbles and maintain a high cadence. I did not know this. If you go too slowly it prolongs the agony because they are uncomfortable. Very uncomfortable. Prolonged, bottom-smacking, bone-rattling uncomfortable. If you freewheel there is a high probability of your chain falling off and if it is wet, well then good luck. Scrap that. For an amateur plodder like me I needed all the luck that was on hand. I knew already that I hated them. Her advice was invaluable.

The excitement of the briefing carried me through the evening: a large buffet dinner where we overindulged on carbohydrates, followed by a quiet drink in the bar (fruit juice for me) full of nervous chatter about the Tour ahead. Before I hit the hay, I checked in on Ben who had managed to hold down some solids and was hoping to make the start line the following morning. That showed some guts, even if they had been displayed in the porcelain accoutrements in his hotel room. The next day a lifelong dream would start for real. I was still intimidated.

To mark the centenary of *le maillot jaune* (the yellow jersey) the Tour de France had decided to pay homage to the champion who has worn it most often, Eddy Merckx, by visiting his home city of Brussels. The first stage of the Tour itself would be 192km long, starting and finishing in the city and taking in iconic Flemish climbs up the 'wall' of Geraardsbergen and Bosberg. These were crested in the first 50km of the stage providing a total elevation gain of 800m, which meant that it would be a stage for the sprinters. The only cause for concern would be the two-kilometre *secteur* of pavé at the 118km mark, which would provide drama on the TV screens.

As always there was a bit extra for Le Loop and we eventually cycled 212km on day one and ascended over 1,400m. Still not that difficult, but the extra distance was added in because we were required to take a detour from a main road and we were required to ride to the start, and back from the finish. This made it a long and testing first day in the saddle.

Following another quick briefing to start the day, detailing the rules of the road and what we should expect along the way, we set off in groups of ten. It was an early start and breakfast was plentiful at 6am. The hotel coped excellently with 70-odd people, with riders and staff appearing en masse at the same time. I was conscious that we would be out on the road for up to ten hours and wanted to fuel as much as possible. Not easy at that time of the day but something I had to get used to.

Everywhere we stayed we would receive variations on the menus but in Brussels it was the best by far. We were spoiled. I wolfed down French toast, baked beans, fruit salad, yoghurt and cereal to the point of bursting. I needed to learn how to pace myself. Usually in a one-day event I would have a bowl of porridge, some toast and a banana. It is safe to say that I overdid it on day one.

It was positive to see that Ben had made it and I made a point of going over to see how he was doing. I am not sure if he recognised me but that was the last I would see of him for a few days, apart from the back of his jersey disappearing into the distance.

I loved the raw scent of tension in the air, the sound of nervous chatter from some and eerie silence from others. The last-minute tinkering of bikes from panicked latecomers (not me) and the inconsiderate elders stretching out muscles in a tightly packed gathering (me). I like to maintain my epic habits and I have a stretch routine I need to go through before I start any form of exercise. I have finally come to realise that I am no longer 21 and that I need to look after my body.

The air was clear, chilled for the early hour and still. Not a soul was about. The dawn chorus chirped with amusement, wondering who these Lycra-clad adventurers were, disturbing their usual peaceful outlook. Emily instructed us to ride the cycle pathways that were aplenty and again taught us how to ride the pavé. She drilled into us two maxims: follow the signs and drink plenty of water. The Le Loop team thanked us again and offered plenty of encouragement. We were off.

Interesting the sounds you hear when a peloton starts moving. It isn't a smooth glide of rubber over tarmac, but a symphony of clicks and beeps coupled with the odd expletive as a chain drops. Click clack, clickety clack, beep beep, tring, clickety clack, bollocks, clickety clack, sorry, tring and a click and then we were moving.

I have little recollection of the first 40 or so kilometres of riding the Tour de France. We skipped from one cycle path to another and barely reached speeds above 20kph. It was a bit of an anticlimax as we negotiated the city roads and gradually worked our way through commercial, to urban, to residential to finally a more rural setting.

The traffic was still quiet but picking up and tentative groups were forming as the natural order of power and excellence created an orderly queue. We all had to find our pace. I knew mine would be somewhere in the middle, with some good days thrown in, but for the first few days I was happy to hang back and save some of my matches. No point bolting the paddock before the real challenges emerge.

The roads in Belgium were flat, smooth and rolled through some wonderfully quaint villages. Everything you would expect with the added bonus of little to no wind. It was a pity that the sun had to come out and test us with a vengeance. As the day wore on it become hot. Boiling hot. Crawling in an Egyptian desert hot. Stale sweat and salt-stained kit hot. It didn't relent and we had to work harder than planned to remain hydrated for what should have been a long procession. A real test from the word go.

From Anderlecht, heading east through Ninove we rode. Roughly 40km in and we reached our first feed stop. Some more learning to do. Le Loop has a brilliant rule with feed stop one. It is usually 40km into a stage and no one is allowed to leave this feed stop until the last rider has signed in.

This meant that we maintained a unity and sense of belonging for the first quarter of the day. It meant that where possible we would ride as a group and it gave the fastest riders a chance to mingle with the slowest in the bunch. It created a camaraderie and a team spirit. It also afforded the team managing the station ample opportunity to get organised and deal with everyone over a short period. They then moved quickly to their next feed stop.

The team who managed feed stop one would also look after number three and conversely the team who managed feed stop two would manage feed stop four. It is very efficient and everyone knows what they are doing. Apart from the riders who don't know where to lean their bikes. You had 60 riders competing to find a spot to rest their bike, upright if possible. Failing that, always lay your bike with the cassette and chain facing upwards, reducing the chances of damaging it or moving your gears.

Once the bike was safely laid to rest, another set of great habits was installed: remove gloves; sign in on the board; read instructions for the next section of the journey (distance, obstacles, climbing, etc.); wash hands; apply sun cream; wash hands again; fill water bottles and then eat. The food on day one was laden with Belgian delights including local homemade waffles. I couldn't take that much on board because I was still stuffed from breakfast.

I made the mistake of not applying any sun cream. I would pay for that later. This routine would become second nature and over time we would fine-tune our transition through the feed stations, saving us up to 20 minutes at a time. Marginal gains for maximum efficiency.

Out of feed stop one, we were quickly into the approach of Geraardsbergen and the Mur de Grammont. All the significant climbs in the Tour are known as Cols and they are all categorised, but there are some short sharp shocks which are called Murs, literally translated as 'walls'. The name says it all and some of these can have quite a sting in the tail. And the body.

At roughly 60km into our ride we faced a cobbled climb of just over one kilometre with an average gradient of 9.5 per cent. Given that I was right off a bank of six months' training and my legs were fresh, I hesitate to say that this was comfortable and even enjoyable. I didn't push it hard, but I had to test the waters and gave a little burst towards the top. A little bit of peacocking to let others know that I meant business. Or was it false bravado and was I merely convincing myself that I belonged? Either way I couldn't help myself and I needed to rein it in.

That was it, one more gentle climb and that was the bulk of our riding uphill for the rest of the day. We just had to negotiate the remaining 140km in 38°C of suffocating heat and some cobblestones. Have I mentioned there would be cobblestones and that I don't like them?

A stage and a Tour like this cannot be completed without help. If Geraint Thomas needs a team of the very best cyclists in the world to shelter him from the wind, then I am entitled to ride with some interesting and talented amateurs. As the day wore on small pelotons formed and tentative friendships were made. I had the great fortune to latch on to Kenny, Kelly and Rich as we left feed stop two and we rode for a while before drifting off at different paces.

Rich was incredibly strong and was saving himself. You could sense his muscles twitching, asking him to put in a bit more. He was a very impressive rider and someone who carried me more than once. After drifting in between small groups of ones and twos I turned right, uphill, past a striking stretch of commercial canal, and headed on to a long slow drag up to a roundabout four kilometres away. I saw a lady in the distance, riding solo, and she looked very efficient, maintaining a great rhythm.

I decided to reel her in and upped my cadence a little. It wasn't that easy. I picked the pace up a bit more and she started to come back to me, but very slowly. She was strong. It took me two kilometres to finally catch up with her and find out that her name was Carmen and she was from Canada. She was to become a great friend and she would impress me with her feats of speed and endurance many times through the Tour. We caught up with Welsh Steve, whose dad had lived around the corner from my brother in Carmarthen (typical of the Welsh: we go halfway around the world and bump into a neighbour) and we hooked up again with Kenny and Rich. For the remaining 100km a gang had formed and worked together rather haphazardly all the way to the finish.

Other riders and groups joined us and drifted in and out of our peloton and we encountered three problems. We took wrong turns twice and added an extra 12km to our day. The signage throughout Le Loop was epic and guided us all the way around France with barely a mishap, so any extra kilometres was down to my misreading of the signs.

We did take a nice detour through a red-light district, which was after feed stop three and a superb pasta and rice-based lunch. Suitably fuelled we were tempted to stay a while, but with a good 80km still to cover, common sense won over frivolity. Still, it was a treat to see some scantily clad ladies sitting in shop windows.

The heat took its toll and started to sap our energy. We were all strong and fresh, but it was still a shock to the system given the temperature was twice as high as anything we had experienced in the UK (and Canada) all year. Staying hydrated was a constant concern and I forgot to put on sun cream.

The third issue had been playing on my mind, not that I had spoken about it much. For good measure we had the official two kilometres of cobblestones and an extra two kilometres thrown in on a downhill stretch just before feed stop four. That was unfair and just plain naughty.

I managed to ride both sets of pavé without falling and without damaging Trigger. I would class that as a success but my performance was at best average and my time for the day would have been affected if I had been in a race. Geraint Thomas has nothing to worry about yet.

I made the mistake of putting too much air in my tyres and this meant significantly less shock absorption with every bump I hit. There were a lot. Uneven, crooked stones scattered haphazardly everywhere, making it impossible to navigate a straightforward line through the road. The pavé was uncomfortable and difficult. It caused a great deal of stress, particularly when a car would pass in the opposite direction. Team INEOS wouldn't have to deal with that a week later. Team INEOS would also be riding the *secteur* at twice the pace I was.

The second *secteur* of cobblestones led us close to the final feed stop and by this time I was battered, bruised and in danger of overheating. I cannot express how grateful I was that they had cold fizzy drinks and access to some air-conditioned toilets. I made my way down to them and they were packed with sweaty, dust-caked riders seeking the same sanctuary. The heat had caught up with me and I had to use the facilities. After washing my hands, I filled my cap with cold water and put it on while full to the brim to cool my body down. It worked a treat. I was drenched to the bone and felt some semblance of normality.

I chose to wear a cap under my helmet for the Tour to stop my shaven head from burning and to provide a bit of sun protection. It protected me from wasp stings, which I had suffered multiple versions of in the Tour of Wessex. Once a wasp gets inside your helmet there is nothing you can do and, with no hair to protect me, I get stung repeatedly. The downside to the cap is a rather unfortunate tan line that made me look like a pool cue. From cue ball to plain old cue.

Easing our way back towards the hotel we saw a couple of ambulances carrying some British riders on stretchers. There was another charity cycling the stage, just the Grand Depart. There were more of them than us, but it is fair to say that quite a few of their team were not of the calibre of a Looper. Some of them were riding the day on mountain bikes and without cycle shoes but trainers on old-fashioned pedals. This means next to no power output in their pedal stroke, which would be exhausting at the best of times, but on a blazing day like the one we were enjoying it caused injury and exhaustion. I was relieved to be Le Loop-fit and I felt strong. Maybe I hadn't planned to fail after all.

A group of us glided into the hotel, dirty, sweaty and tired. Our bikes were dropped off: to the left, to go into storage for the next day; or to the right, if they needed attention from a mechanic. I put Trigger in for some TLC and for the gears to be aligned after the battering on the pavé. Time to shower, wash dirty kit, refuel and prepare for the following day.

One great piece of advice I had been given by a Looper in Wessex was that each day you should make sure that you could still ride for another 30km once you had finished a stage. This meant that I would not overdo things and I would be prepared for what lay ahead the next day. All part of the epic habits we needed to maintain. Thankfully the next day was relatively easy, a short time trial with time to rest in the afternoon. As I went to bed, I wasn't thinking about the next stage. I was out like a light and slept like a baby. One day down, 3,300km left to go. I dreamed of cobblestones and bumps in the road.

Distance covered: 212km
Time: 9hrs 43mins
Elevation gain: 1,463m
Calories burned: 7,570
Highest speed: 55.7kph

IF YOU ARE GOING TO ACHIEVE EXCELLENCE IN BIG THINGS, YOU DEVELOP THE HABIT IN LITTLE MATTERS. EXCELLENCE IS NOT AN EXCEPTION IT IS A PREVAILING ATTITUDE – Colin Powell

Chapter 9

1 July 2019, Brussels
Epic Habits

A TESTING first day had been successfully completed and I was very happy. Floating on air. But I knew that I had roughly 3,300km and another 20 stages to go. I needed to adapt to the rigours of the riding and quickly. I knew I needed to ensure my routines and habits were spot on if I had any chance of making it to Paris. I decided that all decisions led to Paris and that all roads led there too. It became another mantra, along with 'follow the signs' and 'if in doubt drink water and eat'.

I had time to question my mindset on Sunday afternoon following an interesting conversation with Ben but was pleased that it was mostly positive. The Sunday morning would turn out to be the most disappointing stage of the Tour.

Stage two of the 2019 edition of the Tour was a team time trial and it was designed to be smooth, flat and fast. We saw none of that. At 28km in length it started at the exquisite Royal Palace of the king and queen of Belgium, situated in the heart of the city. We had plenty of time to take in the view from the surrounding cobblestones (I really hoped I had seen the last of them) and the park that is opposite, because we had to cycle the ten kilometres into the start.

We didn't need to save our legs because this was not a competitive or difficult day. Heading off from the palace the route took in Ter Kamerenbos, a beautiful sweeping park on the south side of Brussels, before heading through the streets to the north of the city and a finish near the Atomium. Both start and finish looked fabulous and the city had served its citizens well with many opportunities for spectacular Tour-related photos. We took plenty because the riding was underwhelming. My notes on my Garmin computer for the day confirmed as much:

'Very easy and awfully slow. Team Time Trial which meant we had to ride the cycle paths of Brussels. Likely to be the most disappointing day of the Tour.'

Given that we had the rarity of not being pressed for time, plus a short route with all day to finish it in, it was time to become a tourist. For a very rare instance we were able to take in the sights, appreciate where we were and take some photographs to prove that we were, most definitely, riding the Tour. From the palace we ambled round the corner on our bikes to the Grand Place (pronounced Plas) for a cup of coffee. Most of the Loopers took this option.

The Grand Place is arguably the most memorable landmark in Brussels. It is considered as one of the most beautiful general courtyards in Europe and has been a UNESCO World Heritage site since 1998. It is the central square in Brussels and is surrounded by opulent guildhalls and two larger edifices: the city's town hall and the King's House (or Bread House building) containing the Brussels City Museum. The uneven cobbled square is framed with imposing architecture, ranging from baroque to Gothic to Louis XIV. All these eras left an imprint, giving the square an eclectic flavour and turning it into a magnet for Sunday day-trippers. Some dressed in Lycra.

I have dozens of photos from this spot, looking goofy and inane, as well as some memorable pictures from a great bicycle arch overlooking the city: a fitting homage to Eddy Merckx near the finish line and the Atomium itself. The city, the coffee and the images were remarkable. The riding was not.

On a rapid course which would have taken well under an hour on my time-trial bike riding solo, let alone with the benefit of a strong team around me, we sauntered round in double that time. We had to stop at red lights, take detours around one-way systems, hop from cycle path to pedestrian crossing and back to cycle path, wait while delivery vans reversed into spaces and while pedestrians had right of way on large chunks of the route. I swear I was overtaken by a child on a scooter at one stage.

There was nothing we could do about the road conditions except embrace the experience and take some more photos. Overall, it was very frustrating but in hindsight it was what I needed. Day one had been long and hot and had sapped energy out of me and vaporised essential salts and minerals from my system. Not applying sun cream meant that I already had an extreme tan line in bright purple and the skin on my forearms and the back of my legs was beginning to blister. I had overdone it. I hadn't taken enough care and I needed this lazy spin to recover. I needed to up my game and maintain some healthy routines to see me through to the end. All decisions led to Paris.

Back at the hotel I started my first healthy routine and I cleaned Trigger. At home I have a set routine for every ride I take. The night before, I prepare my kit, pump up the tyres and oil my chain. I make sure that the bike is ready for me to hop on and go the following morning, leaving me to worry about remembering my computer, heart rate monitor, phone, cash and food and water.

When I return from a ride, I always try to wash the bike or at least give her a quick rub-down or spray with a hose. It was time to install this routine and maintain some epic habits. This could make the difference between reaching Paris or creeping out the back door in shame to catch an early train home. Failure to look after myself and Trigger might mean a mini disaster like a clump of mud sticking in my chain, causing it to slip or fall loose. If that was to happen on a downhill or while taking a fast corner, it could mean me in a ditch and bye-bye booze-up on the river Seine celebrating my glory. I now had that image in my head to aim for. A photo in front of the Eiffel Tower, a sprint on the Champs-Élysées and a booze-up while floating under the starry sky of the most romantic city in the world. After Swansea.

That afternoon, after I had a deep tissue massage, I joined a few of the others by the hotel pool and got chatting to Ben, making up for the opportunity missed from not sharing a room. So early into a great big adventure and already this was a rare moment to unwind. Ben is ex-military and now runs his own leadership business. Being a business leader who is always eager to learn, I picked his brains and only managed to irritate him a little. A lot less than his cheese jokes would grate on us during the Tour (sorry, pun intended).

We talked about routines, mindset and focus and he gave me a bit to think about. I had had my pathway to success planned out more than a year beforehand. It had started to take shape when I had used it to run the London Marathon and the Ironmans that followed. I had dreamed big, committed myself to the challenge and I had a deadline imposed on me. I hadn't failed to plan and I certainly wasn't shy of the hard work or commitment. I felt I needed to review my living and loving of the challenge and implement some epic habits that I should maintain daily. I knew I would not be unique in this aspect so there would be plenty of support and reminders. These habits would boil down to what I did on the bike and especially what I did off it.

As for my motivation, I had an obvious desire and hunger to succeed, which is simple to maintain when things are going easy. I knew there was a chance I would need to use some of my theories when things got tough, which I expected in the mountains. At that moment, I needed to focus on the success of my personal goal. I had to complete every inch of the Tour de France. There would be no shortcuts and all decisions had to be made with that in mind. I resolved to ask myself, 'Will this help me ride into Paris?' every time a key decision needed to be made.

As I sat by the pool, I took a quick five minutes to visualise riding into Paris, sprinting up the Champs-Élysées, having my photo taken in front of the Eiffel Tower and above all celebrating hard on a boat with great friends as we floated down the river Seine. I know I have repeated myself, but it was those repetitive thoughts that would spur me on. From here on in it was time to act as if I was going to Paris. Ben didn't know it, but he gave me some clarity of thought and focus. Tunnel vision locked in, I jumped in the pool and impressed the ladies with my front crawl.

Sitting down to dinner at the end of the day I got chatting to another alumni who had completed Le Loop more than once. I asked my standard question: 'What is the one piece of advice you would give to someone riding Le Loop for the first time?' I asked this a lot and the experienced riders were always more than willing to offer advice and help an enthusiastic plodder like me. Through the course of the Tour, and previously at the Tour of Wessex, I received some excellent advice and hints and tips. On this occasion it was French Eric who inspired me:

'It is not what you do on the bike that decides if you will succeed. It is what you do off it.'

That line will never leave me and confirmed what I knew but hadn't woken up to. It is about being professional in every aspect of your daily routine and life, and it is a lesson that I now apply to everything I do. Eric talked me through the importance of looking after myself: staying hydrated, being clean, staying healthy, eating well, looking after my bike and my kit, preparing for the day ahead and a few other excellent snippets. I believe in including and inspiring others and the proof was in the pudding here. In the space of 24 hours, I had been inspired by many people and I was benefiting from teamwork in a very selfish challenge.

From that moment on, right through to the end of the Tour, I entered into some healthy routines. Not having the benefit of a soigneur or personal valet we had to do most things ourselves. The Le Loop organisers were excellent and they took care of the logistics, meals, bike support and massages (which cost a little extra) and the rest was down to us. I was not bitter about this: in fact, I would dare say that I was pleased, because it created a routine and made me stronger as an individual. Look at that. Personal growth while riding a bike. If only I had been aware of that as a 14-year-old riding my Vindec Ventura around Pembrokeshire.

Each evening at the end of every ride I endeavoured to do the same. I would clean my bike and pop it in for service if necessary. I would clean my water bottles, clean the day's kit, usually while I was cleaning myself in the shower, recharge my bike computer and phone, upload the computer results to my laptop and make brief notes on the day, drink plenty of water, put my wet kit out to dry, clean my cycle shoes if needed, prepare my spare bag for feed stops, prepare my riding kit for the next day and prepare the contents for my back pockets for the ride, including: phone, cash, energy bars and camera. It was not that complicated, but it was enough to keep me active before a massage and evening meal. The massages were an optional extra at 10 euros. I paid for ten up front and repeated it again 11 days into the Tour.

Before bed I would spend five minutes stretching and working my aching limbs. Each morning another routine took over. Wake. Drink water. Make bed. Shower (cleanliness is key). Apply chamois cream and sun cream. Put on kit except shoes, socks and helmet. Pack bag and drop off at transport van. Eat large breakfast and load as many carbs and as much protein as possible. Fill up water bottles. Visit the toilet. Stretch muscles. Collect spare bags, helmet, footwear and sunglasses. Leave room. Return to room five minutes later, to check nothing had been left behind. Depart. The bag drop at the transit van was handled each morning by Emily and Gareth, our two lead riders. They didn't just ride the whole route, they worked hard for us outside of this every day and their efforts didn't go unnoticed. I always enjoyed seeing them and I too believed in starting every day with as positive an attitude as possible, something that was hammered into me in the travel industry.

In those days I may have come off a 24-hour shift at the airport and only had two hours' sleep, but I was still expected to be professional and cheerful at every moment. People's holidays were at stake there. The Le Loop team always reminded me of that time in my life so I endeavoured to be as positive as possible.

'Morning Ceri. How are you today?'

'Any better and I would be twins.'

'Brilliant.' They would smile and humour me. It lifted my spirits and aching limbs. I hope I wasn't too annoying.

Looking back, it must have been tiresome to hear that every morning.

It was great not having to worry about my bags and my bike. Knowing that Trigger was being looked after while we were delivered by bus to the ride start, where I could pick her up, pump the tyres and go, was reassuring.

Day three was the first day that we were taken by bus to the start point and this would be repeated for 18 days of the Tour. The journey would vary from 20 minutes to a couple of hours and this would impact on our wake-up time each day. One awful day the journey was four hours and led to a horrendous ride, which turned into a memorable ride.

This was the bubble that the organisers talked about. A constant, never-ending journey of wake, eat, travel, ride, eat, massage, sleep and repeat. It was comforting and remarkable to know that it had only taken two days to fall into it, just as we entered France on day three.

Farewell Brussels. The real Tour started here and I had the shits.

Distance covered: 50km
Time: 3hrs 19mins
Elevation gain: 302m
Calories burned: 1,728
Highest speed: 38.4kph

If the first three nights had been an exercise in establishing epic habits off the bike, then the third day of riding was about doing the same on the bike. That was what I was in France for. The Tour came home and a stage finished in France for the first time on day three. Starting in Binche, a bastion of Belgian cycling, it worked its way south on a testing route to the Champagne region of Épernay. This stage was designed with the potential to blow the Tour apart.

In the first half the roads were wide open, flat and susceptible to strong crosswinds. If they were gusting during the Tour itself, it could cause great splits in the peloton. For those of us looking to survive, it would be a war of attrition and great teamwork would be needed to make it through to the rather testing second section.

The stage was a hefty 215km long and after riding for 170km we would encounter four hills. They would all be short sharp shocks and would finish with a Mur with an average gradient of 15 per cent, peaking at 20 per cent. No amount of Moët et Chandon could make that enjoyable. The idea was to soften the racers up for what was to come later in the Tour and to potentially create significant time differences in the General Classification in the first week.

By this stage I was no longer thinking about times, splits or racing. I was focusing on making it to Paris in one piece and not soiling my bib shorts that morning. The effects of the long hot Saturday ride had caught up with me and I obviously hadn't replaced enough of the electrolytes I had lost in the extreme heat. I felt okay as we travelled south for the short bus journey to Binche on the border of Belgium and France, but I had suffered a queasy moment in the hotel before we left. During the coach journey I had felt a tension in my lower gut and a small sweat developed. I put this down to nerves and drank a bottle of water.

I had encountered this many times before in my life so was not concerned. My body is sensitive and I have become adept at reading its signals. I have a strong constitution but if something is not right my body will reject it quickly and allow me to recover equally as fast. Frequently in this type of circumstance it is merely a warning to get some salts into my system. Not today.

Greg LeMond was famous in the 1986 Tour for having to 'go' whilst on the road. He had eaten Mexican food the night before and was suffering from suspected food poisoning. He ate what he thought was a bad peach whilst on the road and his body reacted to it. He screamed at a team-mate to hand him his cap (no helmets in those days). He took the hat, forced it down his shorts and used it as a toilet. After removing the cap and tossing it aside he instructed his team to bring him back to the front of the peloton. By all accounts he stank. He had to ride a further 60km to the finish, with shorts chafing and stomach turning, ignorant to the complaints of the rest of the peloton.

Those guys were (and are) on a different level. No such concern for me. We had parked next to a café which made its toilet facilities available to us. This would not happen every day, but I was mightily relieved on this occasion. The wait in line was excruciating, but I made it without accident and spent way too long in the cubicle. I was grateful that we had been advised to bring our own loo roll before we came out and I pitied the person who followed me. A good group had waited for me very patiently and we were one of the last to set off, with me praying that I would not suffer a Greg moment. We took it easy for the first 40km of the day.

I was grateful the first feed stop rule was in place because I was one of the last to glide in. A nice easy ride, plenty of water and then some solid food and I was right as rain, albeit a little tender. No chafing of my shorts. Much more fortunate than a rider I stumbled into, squatting in a bush at the edge of the feed zone. I gave him my loo roll.

We had crossed the border into France, almost without noticing, a mini disaster had been averted (I hoped) and now the real riding was about to start on the open French roads. We were lucky. The forecast crosswinds didn't materialise, although we had to battle some hefty headwinds at times and this called for us to get organised. I was lucky to be in a group with Kenny, Kelly, Rich and Carmen. We latched on to a few others including Nick and a group of ladies from Bella Velo and we tried to ride together.

Being honest with myself, there were quicker groups I could have joined. I knew that Rich was way stronger than all of us and Kenny had a huge amount of power but was a bit heavy for the hills. Carmen was a beast on the flats and is a superb time triallist but living in Toronto she was not as familiar with the hills as the rest of us. Forcing our way through the meandering roads and winding lanes we were disorganised and inefficient.

If we came across some street art, which happened to be remarkable, ones and twos would stop for a photo and the group would split up before gradually worming its way back together. The street art was something to behold and in the first few days we marvelled at old bike statues, bikes cut out of the crops in fields, polka dot jerseys grown into meadows with coloured flowers and all manner of flags, yellow jerseys and bunting on display. The country goes to town and the riders are revered, unless they happened to be Chris Froome at that time, who, on occasion, was soaked with dubious liquids. The locals are seemingly not too impressed with a serial winner. It's funny that the French are so similar to the British and that they too prefer a plucky and charismatic loser who captures their hearts over constant success.

After stage six, we would stop a lot less frequently for the road art. Not because the novelty had worn off but because we wanted to move on as efficiently as possible and make it back in time for tea and a massage.

On the television the Tour is a grand spectacle and some of the views are other-worldly. Mansions, chateaus and stone castles, which are built into cliffs or gazing upon a river, are de rigeur. Rolling hillsides resplendent with looming sunflowers that line the way are breathtaking. The reality of the Tour is that you miss so much of this because you must keep your eyes on the road and your mind on the job at hand. The romantic vision of cycling La Grande Boucle (as the Tour is also known) was still alive but reality bit hard. The reality was a bubble which blocked out much of the scenery.

After feed stop two, Rich and Kenny tried to get us organised but the hardest job was moving again after coffee and a cake. Trying to round up a group of ten riders was like trying to herd mice. Some were eager to press on, others happy to rest and refuel a bit longer. Pleasant but not efficient.

I thought along the same lines as Carmen and the two guys. Get through the feed stations as quickly as possible and focus on the job at hand. Every decision had to be made with the end goal in mind. I love Kelly and Nick, two of the most interesting people you could meet, but they loved a dawdle, an extra piece of cake, and then to go to the toilet again while the rest of us were moving. Each to their own and I had to ride my own race and they had to be true to theirs, with the aim that we would all ride into Paris together.

Around 20 minutes into this *secteur* Rich tried again. He knew what he was doing and he wanted to make us more efficient. There was no point half the group plugging away into the wind: we needed to form a train and each take a small turn at the front. He suggested riding on the front for 90 pedal turns and then drifting to the back, to gradually work your way back up to the front. Made sense to me. He gave it a go, Kenny followed and then the group resorted to anarchy again.

He rode back to me frustrated and ready to leave us all behind. He had the strength in his legs to do that easily. I suggested we give it another go and took him up to the front where we dropped in with Kenny and Kelly. Rich started again, I told Kelly what to do before following suit myself. Kenny and then Carmen dropped into the line and hey presto suddenly the entire mini peloton was an organised train. This was the first time I had ever been involved in something so brilliant and it was amazing. It felt like cycling on air.

We maintained an average speed on the flat, and into a headwind, of 28kph and Carmen exclaimed this was her sweet spot. That stuck and we would regularly visit her sweet spot through the Tour with the most puerile of jokes allayed to the greatest efficiency. The train was smooth, effective and we ate up the ground ahead of us. The joy of working as a team and involving others lifted the spirits and increased the output as the mood lightened and became highly enjoyable. I felt like a real cyclist.

Rich came up to me after a turn and asked how the hell I had managed to get us organised. I had no idea it was me, I thought it was him. Just luck, I guess. Every time I dropped to the back after a turn at the front Kenny would pat my arse and shout 'good job'. It caught on and everyone was congratulated for a decent turn on the front. He is a very funny man and he had me in stitches for much of the day. Great guy for an Irish Liverpool fan living in London.

I still had to get used to riding so close to the person in front but as the day wore on it became quite natural. The biggest issues we faced were trying to hold a steady pace at the front and not distancing ourselves from others.

When I ride I don't measure my power output, mainly because I didn't in my first couple of triathlons and I have become very adept at listening to my body and knowing what I can tolerate and for how long. Running marathons teaches you that very quickly. Not that quickly – I run marathons very slowly. I use my instincts and measure my heart rate and know what my optimum rate is for all manner of distances and objectives. It was hard to resist the temptation to pick up the pace to impress the others, but I settled down and learned how to ride in the group.

The other bump in the road was the large bumps in the road. While combining well on the flat, we all had different strengths going uphill. Every time we hit an incline the group would splinter as some failed to hold the wheel. We learned to be patient and work together but these were baby steps and new territory for me. I was loving riding with these people. It was what I envisaged the Tour to feel like.

Feed stop three is the lunch stop and is the hardest to herd the mice out of, especially when there are other groups of riders to chat to. By the time we had left, still with a good 90km left to ride, we had splintered and the great work of earlier was laid to rest. I wasn't alone but our peloton had whittled down to four by the time we approached the Champagne region and the first of four hills and a Mur. A combination of someone leaving water bottles at the feed station and having to go back to retrieve them (not me, I have epic habits) and other riders tiring towards the end of the stage and stopping for an ice cream, saw members of the gang drop back and leave us to it.

The four hills were between 900m and 1,800m in length with average gradients from 6 per cent to a cheeky 13 per cent. Nothing too difficult but enough to test the legs and warm us up for the finish. A coke at feed stop four set us up nicely for the finale and the eye-catching surrounds of vineyards draped in the early summer sun. I remember them being spectacular but not noticing that much because my head was down and my legs were pounding.

The Mur at Mutigny was only 900m and averaged 13 per cent, but it peaked at 20 per cent and brought some to a standstill at the end of a very long stage. I worked my way up it slowly. I was accustomed to hills like this at the end of a ride and with four kilometres to go this was a kicker. Great course management because it was designed to split the race apart and weaken the legs of the sprinters.

I rose out of my saddle and stamped on the pedals. Rich broke away from us with Kenny chasing him. I didn't panic. I rode my own race and I knew how to pace myself. Carmen came with me to the halfway point where she stopped to take a photo (it was gorgeous) before hopping back on and chasing after us. I overtook Kenny, who had attacked too hard at the bottom of the slope, and joined Rich who was waiting at the summit. He had some power in his legs.

Mine were starting to obey after a shaky start to the day. The climbing wasn't finished because we had another cheeky short sharp shock as we made our way back to the hotel. Rich was way ahead, Kenny strolled in with me, and Carmen was lost. She took a wrong turn and almost did the Mur a second time.

We had earned our massages that night and the right to share a hostel room with three other sweaty guys. It was a peculiar sight to see so much cycling kit hanging out of room windows to dry, but good habits needed to be maintained and I had used my three pairs of shorts once already. At dinner I took notice of the rider of the day awards and the funny/daft moment of the day prize for the first time.

Three days down and still 3,000km left to go. We were in France now and the Tour had kicked off. Some celebrated with a glass of bubbles that night. Given my predicament earlier in the day, I stuck to water.

Good job.

Distance covered: 215km
Time: 9hrs 10mins
Elevation gain: 1,911m
Calories burned: 7,864
Highest speed: 60kph

THERE IS NO NEED TO REACH FOR THE STARS. THEY ARE ALREADY WITHIN YOU. REACH DEEP INTO YOURSELF – Anon

Chapter 10

2 July 2019, Reims
Inspired

I BELIEVE it is important to have heroes in life. Especially when you are growing up. Heroes give us something to dream about. They set the standards that we should aspire to and they help us find our vision and focus in life. They help us be better versions of ourselves. It is even better if we can be a hero to those that are following us. The feeling of knowing that you have positively influenced someone else's life is beyond compare.

They say that you should never meet your heroes because they will always let you down. I must be lucky. I have met three and lived with one and they have all been nothing short of brilliant.

My first hero was my father, which is only right. There is something wrong as a boy if your father is not your hero.

I loved watching him play football. My childhood was spent following him around the county of Pembrokeshire watching him play for Kilgetty AFC. He could do no wrong in my eyes. I was happier than him when he scored a hat-trick against Neyland in a midweek match. Even better that one of the goals was from the halfway line.

I practised and copied that goal for weeks afterwards with my mates down the park. I eventually pulled it off as a 14-year-old in a county league game. The wind was strong behind me and I beat the keeper with a tricky third bounce. But I had emulated my father. That was all I ever wanted to do as a child.

My early memories of life are of living overseas where Dad worked. He was a teacher with the British forces and we were living on their bases. My first memories are of riding a tricycle in Cyprus. Mum and Dad set the standards by which I would live my life. I am one of the lucky ones because my upbringing was idyllic. This means that any cock-ups, like failing my computer science HND, are all my own doing. They instilled in me a love for travel, a sense of adventure, discipline, a strong work ethic and a very strong moral compass. I lived with my first hero and he never let me down.

As I grew older and became aware of the wider world, I looked up to many superbeings. Alan Curtis at Swansea City scoring in a 5-1 hammering of Leeds Utd in our first-ever game at the highest level still sends a shiver down my spine. I worshipped Johann Cruyff, John Toshack, Alan Curtis and Pelé. In cycling I wanted to be like Bernard Hinault and make big attacks from the middle of a mountainous stage, purely for the sheer joy of it.

I read a lot growing up, I still do, and the novels of Leslie Thomas changed my life. Whilst working in Goa I spent an evening with him and his adorable wife Diana. He was on holiday writing a travel feature for the *Mail on Sunday* and he wanted a good night out. We had dinner and drank ridiculous amounts of cheap wine into the early hours. He had me in stitches. We laughed, cried and he coached me for my writing aspirations. I was just a holiday rep. He didn't need to do that. I cherished that night and will never forget its effect on me. I was floating on air for weeks afterwards. He inspired me to write my first book, *Indian Summer*. Never forget the effect a few kind words can have on an impressionable individual.

In later years I have loved the exploits of Geraint Thomas and swashbucklers like Julian Alaphilippe. Interestingly I have been inspired by quite a few ladies. Nicole Cooke was one of the first people to bring me back to the world of cycling. Jessica Ennis-Hill winning the heptathlon at the World Athletics Championships a year after giving birth was phenomenal and Lucy Gossage is one of the most impressive people I have ever met, albeit briefly. She won't remember it.

All these athletes have certain traits in common: traits that I aspire to. They are strong, determined, focused and they are winners. They have excellent personal values as well. They are honest, nice, likeable and they stand up and fight for what is right. Too often, winners can be so driven they morph into odious human beings, losing sight of their values in their pursuit of success. Each of these individuals inspires greatness and has attributes that make me want to be a better person.

Lucy Gossage won't recall our encounter. It was at midnight at the end of Ironman Wales in 2018. I had previously raced against her in this race and finished a good three hours behind her (I am giving her 20 years' head start), but on this occasion I was supporting my friend Masao. Lucy won the women's race comfortably. She obliterated the field despite almost breaking her neck as she wiped out entering the second leg of the swim. But the reason she is so amazing is because she bounced around the course with a huge smile on her face.

She embraced the crowds, fed off their energy and was humble throughout. No hiding behind dark glasses to avoid people. At one point during the 180km bike ride I was stood with my 11-year-old niece. We had made a few signs that day that were pretty funny. The one that Taela had at that spot said 'SMILE IF YOU'VE PEE'D IN YOUR SHORTS TODAY'. Lucy, racing along at the front, saw the sign. She laughed, high-fived Taela and threw her a water bottle. My niece was in raptures and I was blown away by her generosity of spirit. Even better was to come.

After winning the race in 09:52:37 she fulfilled her duties on the podium and gave her interviews for the media and sponsors, etc. She then got changed and hung around to present the age-groupers who finished with their medals. Seven hours after she had won her race, she was stood there at midnight as my friend Masao Matsumoto crossed the line and she gave him a beaming smile and huge encouragement.

I called her over and explained to her about Masao's exploits and she was superb. She gave up her own time to chat about the spirit of Ironman when she could quite easily have been sat in bed with a glass of champagne. Acts of that magnitude should not go unnoticed. The impact she has had on the town of Tenby is massive and cannot be underestimated. All this while holding down a career as a cancer doctor. Like I said, inspiring.

I mention these individuals because they have left a positive impression on my life. They maintain the standards that I aim for. On day four of Le Loop, I met another lady of this calibre properly for the first time.

The 2019 edition of La Grande Boucle was widely regarded as one of the toughest in 50 years. The parcours was designed to break up the dominance of Team Sky/ INEOS from the outset. The Tour had everything from the cobblestones on the first day, to a summit finish in the first week, to a three-day torturous conclusion in the Alps before the procession into Paris. There would be more than 55,000m of climbing, which is the equivalent of scaling Mount Everest six times. Stage four was a comparative luxury and was regarded as a peace offering to the sprinters.

It was a lengthy 215km on a mostly flat route with only 1,400m of climbing, none of which was particularly taxing. The stage was long and more a battle of concentration. Starting from Reims it meandered through the rustic villages and bountiful countryside, heading east to Nancy. We started the day with much of the same group that we had spent the last few days with. This time we had the pleasure of Emily Chappell riding with us.

By now you will realise that Emily was the lead rider for Le Loop, an accomplished and very successful endurance cyclist of high-regard and author of two brilliant books. I took the time to chat with her and feed off her experiences as much as possible. She was so generous with her time. She was almost bashful about her exploits and incredibly interesting and engaging. She had a glow about her and I was drawn in like a moth to a flame. Not in that way. I wanted to learn as much as I could from her and seek whatever advantages I could, to get me to Paris. All decisions and actions were made with that one goal in mind.

I wanted her to like me. Childish ego boost I know, but I still worry about what some people think. I use that as a motivational tool and I would make damned sure I rode into Paris to impress Emily on top of every other motivation I had.

Having Emily with us broke up the stage. We rode harder and settled into a seamless train very quickly. I loved hearing her stories of how she won a 24-hour race and of her indomitable spirit against adversity. We swapped photos of us looking awful at the finish of challenges, completely drained from an effort. We swapped stories on the perils of writing a book (you give up your life for a passion and risk the possibility that you are one of 100,000 others whose manuscripts are rejected each year). And we discussed motivation for continuing when you had no more to give. She is incredible. Just as quickly as she had been with us, she was gone. While we stuffed our faces at the lunch stop Emily glided into the distance to hunt down and support a quicker group.

This would be the last day that we rode with all of the same people. Over the final 80km we splintered again. A couple of small uphill drags separated the group and again the issue of herding mice out of the feed stops meant we never started a section as a unit. We wasted a lot of time waiting for everyone to come together and to pick up full tempo.

Rich, Kenny, Carmen and I had been saving our legs a little because we knew there was a long way to go. I was particularly focused on stage six, which for me would be the acid test of the whole Tour. If I could survive that stage, I knew I could finish it all, so I wanted to be in the best possible shape two days down the line.

My legs were fresh but tiring. I hadn't been properly stretched but they were being worn down by the relentless challenge. Day four was new territory for me. I had never cycled more than three days in a row so I was cautious, wary of overextending myself before the true tests arose. And they would come with a vengeance. Starting with ten consecutive days of riding before a rest day.

We glided into the hotel that evening without having faced too much drama during the day. Kelly clipped a kerb and took a tumble. We were going pretty slowly, taking a corner in a town centre. He picked up a few scrapes but no major damage and his spirits weren't dampened. They never were; he was relentlessly positive. I too was quite happy because I had a very pleasant surprise.

At dinner each evening we would receive our briefing for the following day. This would be delivered by Sarah who would give us our timings, rules and housekeeping notes. She kept us on track brilliantly. If we thought getting ten cyclists out of a feed stop was like walking cats, try herding 100 cyclists to a race start. Emily would deliver the ride briefing and then we would have the fun part of the evening: the awards.

There were three prizes to give out. The first would be awarded by Emily and it was for her rider of the day. This could be for acts of chivalry, impressive riding abilities or anything that gave cyclists a good name. The second was the chapeau award. This would be decided by the current incumbent of the prize, although I am not sure how we decided on the very first recipient. The prize was a hat (chapeau) and had to be looked after until the next day when it would be handed on. The basis of this was the same as Emily's award. The third prize was a squeaky toy for the fool of the day. It was light-hearted and awarded to the person who had committed the most humorous crime against cycling. Leaving water bottles at feed stops, getting on to a bus without your kit bag, being overtaken by an old lady on an e-bike were common themes.

It turns out I had impressed Emily. I was her choice for rider of the day. It was a nothing stage after all. She was impressed with how I had managed to get our group organised and how we, as a team, did not stop laughing and maintained fantastic morale. I was very pleasantly surprised. Even better I started to believe that I could be a cyclist and that I belonged with these people. Maybe I wasn't out of my depth and maybe Paris was achievable.

It may have been a small token but coming from a new hero of mine that small award meant the world. The prize was a laminated A4 arrow with an inspiring message from Emily. It is now hanging on my living room wall in my glory corner, alongside photos of Ironman finishes and some industry prizes. That is four heroes down. I only need to meet Alan Curtis and my life will be complete.

Distance covered: 215km
Time: 10hrs 3mins
Elevation gain: 1,473m
Calories burned: 7,366
Highest speed: 54kph

The official Tour de France race guide described stage five as 'Medium Mountain, Maximum Effort' and, as it transpired, I would spend most of the day riding on my own. Stage six was still the big acid test for me and I was unconsciously saving my legs for the next day. I was still finding my feet in the Tour, becoming more accustomed to riding consecutive long days on the road and we hadn't encountered any real climbs in the first four days. Until stage five. And this was just a warm-up for what was to come.

I would guess there were seven or eight mini pelotons riding every day, with varying levels of ability. The first couple were filled with some very talented and competitive riders: people who had represented GB in either cycling or triathlon, a few who had ridden competitively since childhood or had fleeting experiences within the pro ranks and some who were born with monstrous engines. Towards the back were either newcomers to the sport or enthusiastic riders who didn't possess racing speed. These were still very talented individuals (they wouldn't be riding Le Loop if they weren't) but they lacked the competitive edge, be it through lack of speed or because of age. We had one impressive specimen with us who was a very athletic 70-year-old lady.

I had consciously been riding in a group that was roughly third from the back, and I suspect everyone who was riding with me was doing so to save their engines. We could all ride at a faster tempo and believed that we could survive a day with the faster groups, but at what cost? This was a marathon not a sprint and we had to save our legs, not just for the next day but for 17 more and the terrain was going to get steeper and longer. I knew that I could step up a level but as much as I loved riding uphill, I genuinely had no idea where my abilities lay. I was used to short steep bursts but how would I cope with long drags ten times the distances I was used to?

I wanted to test myself and see what I could do but more importantly I had to make sure I made it to Paris. I had to be more tortoise than hare, so I was saving my legs for the first test on stage six. I was put back two giant steps on stage five by spending most of the day riding on my own.

I was accustomed to long time trials, where drafting off other competitors is not allowed. But riding in a group is so much easier. If you are able to sit in a peloton, or behind another rider, it has been estimated that you will save up to 30 per cent of your effort. That is a significant saving and makes riding in a group very efficient. The other benefit for someone companionable like me is that it proves a big boost to morale. Having people around creates a camaraderie which makes the ride pass much more quickly and smoothly. Ideally, we should have been working in groups rather than toiling into the wind alone.

We entered the Vosges mountains travelling from Saint-Dié-Des-Vosges in a horseshoe-shaped route to Colmar. It was a relatively short day of 169km, including four categorised climbs in these middle mountains, none of them more difficult than a category two. This Tour was designed for climbers and the challenges were starting early. They (we) were invited to come out of the shadows when the route entered the Vosges and the medium mountains.

The course passed through Alsatian villages, each as dazzling as the next, the standout points being the Côte du Haut-Koenigsbourg, which climbs in front of the medieval chateau of the same name, and the Côte des Trois-Epis. It was a picture-postcard setting but, on the road, we were conscious of turning the pedals and surviving to tackle the monsters on stage six.

As we were waiting to take the bus to the start, I had a couple of conversations with Carmen and Rich. Carmen and I were becoming frustrated at the amount of time we were spending in the feed stations. We decided that we would improve our routine and endeavour to get in and get out much more efficiently. Rich and Kenny were frustrated at the pace that we had been riding at and they decided that they would ride with one of the quicker groups. That was more than fair. They both had strong legs and you could sense that they were both holding more back than I was. Plan set for the day. I would stay with the same ability group but Carmen and I would try and push the pace a little.

Leading us to feed stop one there was a seven-kilometre stretch with a false flat of 3 or 4 per cent. It was by no means a hill but I found myself drifting away from some of the guys that I would usually be riding with. Five days in and my legs were feeling good and they still had a little bite in them.

At the feed stop Carmen and I signed us all in, washed our hands, filled water bottles, applied sun cream (at that early hour we were heating up like lobsters in a pan), washed our hands again, went to the toilet and stuffed our faces with cakes, biscuits and fruits. We thought we would save a crucial ten minutes but, as we were ready to leave, we were forced to wait. While we were clipping into our pedals two guys decided they had to go to the toilet again. Another realised he hadn't filled his water bottles and a fourth wanted to retrieve something from his bag in the van. Carmen gave me a look. She was frustrated and I wanted to move on. So, I did.

I said that I would head off slowly and the rest could catch me up. It might provide the impetus for them to improve their habits for the rest of the Tour. If we saved 15 minutes at each feed stop, we would be back one hour earlier for a massage, food and rest each evening. The quality of our riding was not an issue, it was the bits in between.

They never caught up. I ambled for ten minutes, then 20 and no sign of company. That was a long pee someone was taking. I didn't do it consciously but I automatically found myself riding at my own tempo. I was in my own little world and in a very happy place as I crested the first little rise of the day. It was only a four-kilometre stretch heading gently uphill and it was a kind introduction to what may come from the rest of the Tour. I barely noticed it. I passed two small groups riding together plus a couple of stragglers and my legs were fresh as I pulled into the second feed stop.

I latched on to another group, hoping to share the effort for a mostly flat 50km or so. I encountered a new phenomenon, the fresh riders. Up to 50 of us were completing the Grand Loop but some days there were more than 100 people on the road. This meant that we would have other groups and individuals joining the Tour for variations of the route from three days to five days to the mountains. This day marked the beginning of the fresh groups of riders coming out and they showed me how tired my legs were compared to theirs. More importantly their minds were far more energetic than mine. I was in a bubble and was quite happy living in it. A couple of minor squabbles broke out.

As we rode along the flat and faster roads heading south between Rosheim and Kintzheim we formed a train and tried to work together. We were a mix of half a dozen new faces and the same number of tired old has-beens. Those of us who had developed useful steady rhythms dropped into our useful steady rhythms and kept up an easy pace. We had another 17 days to go in total and another five days before we had a rest day.

The ladies and gents on their first day wanted to ride hard and create an impression. They would go to the front and pick up the pace. After finishing their turn, they would drop back and shout at the rest of us for not pushing hard enough or for not pulling long enough when we were on the front. Someone (not me) tried to politely explain to them that we were tired after four tough days on the road, but they were enthused and trying to prove that they fitted in.

After 30km of proficient disharmony we let them drift away from the front. Then, 20km later we caught and passed every one of them on the Haut-Koenigsbourg, the second climb of the day, which was a little longer at six kilometres. Turns out we knew what we were doing in pacing ourselves. It also turned out that they would spend just as long as everyone else in a feed stop. After lunch I was on my own again.

I rode most of the last 60km on my own. I would catch up with people and ride with them intermittently but it was hard to fit in with other riders' rhythms. I found it easier maintaining my own pace. I was creeping up the leader board, if there was such a thing, catching up Loopers I hadn't seen on the roads since the first day.

Two more category two climbs of six kilometres in length and average gradients pushing up to 7 per cent taught me how to pace myself, how to battle my mind and how hard the rest of the Tour was going to be. Those hills don't sound that tough, but it was like taking jabs to the midriff repeatedly before you collapse in submission, rather than one horrid knockout blow.

They were hard to get a rhythm on. Just steep enough to drop to the smaller gearings, forcing me to get out of the saddle and stand on the pedals. But easy enough to allow for lengthy stretches of riding while seated. Off the back of these efforts, I made a pretty important decision.

That night I swapped my rear cassette over and fitted the 11-34 gear ratio on to Trigger. This would give me a granny gear for going up the hills and would allow me to spin the wheels that bit easier. This wasn't so much for the purpose of making it easier going up a climb, but more for preserving my legs for the next day and the day after that.

In cycling circles there is a bit of a stigma over the use of a granny gear but I have no shame. My shame gland was removed by surgeons when I was born and it was replaced with an extra awesome gland. True story.

I would be very grateful for that cassette-change the next day.

Distance covered: 173km
Time: 8hrs 24mins
Elevation gain: 2,357m
Calories burned: 6,674
Highest speed: 64kph

Chapter 11

4 July 2019, La Planche des Belles Filles Resilience

THE TOUR de France started categorising the climbs in the 1950s. The method used was by driving a car up the hill and whatever the lowest gear the car had to drop into would be the classification of the climb. The hills are classed from one to four with four being the easiest of the climbs because a car would be able to get over the mountain pass in fourth gear. This means that category one is the most difficult climb to take on because a car would not be able to ascend the mountain outside of its first gear.

This gives an idea of how difficult the climbs on the Tour de France can be and then in 1979 the even tougher HC classification was introduced. This stands for *Hors Catégorie* and translates as without category, i.e. a car in the 1950s would not have been able to make it all the way to the top of road. The latest addition to an impressive list of HC climbs is

La Planche des Belles Filles and it is already close to gaining iconic status despite only having been a part of the Tour for a decade.

The name 'Belles Filles' literally means 'Beautiful Girls', but in this case it may actually derive from the local plant life. According to Wikipedia, in the 16th century the mountain was said (in the local dialect) to be '*lieu peuplé de belles fahys*', a 'place inhabited with nice beech trees'. Later, *belles fahys* became corrupted into *Belles Filles*, though there remains a nearby village of Belfahy. The word 'planche', or 'board', comes from the nearby small town of Plancher-les-Mines.

Local folklore, in contrast, holds that the mountain took its name from something which happened during the time of the 30 Years War. According to legend, young women from Plancher-les-Mines fled into the mountains to escape Swedish mercenaries as they feared being raped and massacred. Rather than surrender, they decided to commit suicide and jumped into a lake far below. One of the soldiers then took a board and with his dagger he engraved an epitaph for the 'beautiful girls'. A wooden statue, created by a local artist, is a reminder of the legend. But again, we wouldn't notice that because we were too busy suffering up a 25 per cent incline.

Stage six was the first summit finish of the Tour. The final haul is up the steep and partly unpaved La Planche des Belles Filles, while the 157km route takes in five intermediate climbs. Peaking at 1,200m, the climb in the Vosges mountain range has established a reputation as a *puncheur*'s finish in a short time. I am waiting for them to introduce a route that establishes a reputation as a plodder's finish and rewards the slow but determined.

La Planche debuted in the Tour in 2012 and by 2019 was already being included for the fourth time, this time as the first summit finish of the race. In all three previous editions the mountain was a climb of six kilometres with an average gradient of 85 per cent. Luckily for me the 2019 edition featured an extra section of one kilometre and to spice things up this section was unpaved, except for the last 100m. Beginning with a leg-sapping ramp at 25 per cent, the final kick up is too steep for gravel. Thank you very much ASO (Tour organisers).

For good measure we had five categorised climbs to negotiate before we even dared set wheels on La Planche des Belles Filles. This was my queen stage. I knew that if I could survive this day, I could survive anything.

Race tactics went out of the window. Where the pros in the real Tour a week later would plot to chase down the breakaway and take King of the Mountains points, I had to settle for a long day on a bone-hard saddle and a battle for survival. That was all that mattered. One pedal stroke after another until I made it across the finish line. Or to paraphrase Fidel Castro, cycling is like life, it is one revolution after another. Get it?

I had had a jersey made especially for this day which would be used on a couple of other key stages. It was the same design as my BESA tops but on the reverse I had printed 'PAIN IS JUST FRENCH FOR BREAD'. This would get a lot of laughs from the French and other riders. Eric loved it. I hoped it would be my lucky climbing jersey.

There was an edge at the beginning of the day. A nervous excitement hung in the air similar to day one. We talked about our plans for what lay ahead and how we would cope with the final climb: the consensus being take it easy and then hang on for dear life. I regularly heard the words, '25 PER CENT??? You've got to be kidding me?'

I had been planning for this day since the beginning of the year but nothing I had ever ridden could prepare me for a climb this steep at the end of a long, hot and difficult ride. I was so happy. I cannot explain quite why, because I was also petrified. I was way out of my comfort zone and I knew that my whole Tour could be compromised within the following nine hours. But I had a challenge to face up to and I would find out whether I had the stones to ride the Tour, or not, pretty soon. That happiness was short-lived.

It seemed that everyone was as apprehensive as I was. Everyone had the same game-plan to save their legs for as long as possible. Somehow Jonathon – a saviour I had met at the Tour of Wessex when he gave me some spare energy bars when I was low – and I ended up on the front of a peloton of 40-plus riders. Feed stop one was roughly 35km into the stage and we rode on the front all the way there, dragging a group behind us.

Not one of them came to the front to help out. We flicked our elbows like the pros do but no one came through. We picked the pace up and they clung on. We dropped the pace and they all settled in behind. This was bizarre, but as Jonathon said to me, it would make our triumph taste even sweeter at the summit. I sprinted ahead of the group to take a video of everyone cycling past and when I re-joined two minutes later a path was made for me to resume my position with Jonathon at the front.

I burned up a few matches but I learned a lot, particularly from my new buddy. Jon is such a smooth and steady rider and he possesses great strength and a measured mind. I copied him a little and tried to learn, with little success, how to ride as efficiently as possible. Despite leading a large group into the feed zone, we were still the last to get to the cakes.

Right out of feed stop one, the climbing started. We were confronted with two climbs in quick succession starting with Le Markstein which was 11km in length with a ramp of 6 per cent. After a short dip we would rise again and peak over Le Grand Ballon at 1,300m high. I set off with Carmen, Kelly, Nick and a handful of others. Most of the group of 40 had left us behind already.

We eased into the climb. I dropped the bike into a low gear and tried to spin my way up the hill, focusing on high revolutions and low intensity. For the first five kilometres or so we had a happy group and I felt quite comfortable. Morale was high, but then again, I was in the midst of some great company. About halfway up Emily caught up with us and we started chatting. I marvelled at how easy she made the climbing look. I marvelled at how she made me a better rider.

We found an easy rhythm and we chatted freely about how we have overcome difficult periods during races. It boils down to taking one more step (or pedal stroke) and then repeating it as often as possible. I have seen runners pull out of a marathon and then walk for three miles to their hotel or car. Why not use that effort for walking to the finish? Life is simple and it takes a little effort.

Riding with Emily was seemingly effortless. We were close to the first summit of the day and my legs felt fine. I looked round to point out some inane sight to Kelly and the group were nowhere to be seen. I had wanted to ride with them for the first few hills to help each other through the day, but Emily had instead helped me find my mountain legs. She consigned me to spending the rest of the day mostly on my own again, lost in between pelotons. I was not the only one.

At the summit of Le Grand Ballon I bumped into Stuart, his wife Jackie and Eric. They were arguing over whether or not they should stop for an ice cream, so I persuaded them to take a couple of photos of me. I would see a lot more of them as the Tour wore on. On the descent I caught up with Andy who I had met on the Tour of Wessex; that level of preparation was serving me really well on a day of big tests.

We attacked the downhill. We were going so hard neither of us had time to talk, which was a Tour first. We thought we were flying until a local teenager overtook us on a corner and left us trailing in his wake. Within minutes he was a dot in the distance and we were chomping on humble pie as we made our way to the second feed stop of the day.

As the day wore on, the climbs became progressively more difficult. As the Tour ventured further into July the same pattern would apply, but first I was alone again and negotiating an 11km category one climb up the Ballon d'Alsace. Back home, as part of a training ride this would be quite the day out in its own right. As part of an epic climbers' Tour de France it was just another bump in the road.

I don't remember much about the climb. No landmarks stand out. No great twists or rises dampened the energy in my legs. I only remember keeping Trigger in her low gear and trying to spin her as efficiently as possible. I passed a few Loopers and this gave me a surge of adrenaline. I overdid it and pushed too hard, trying to make it to the top as quickly as possible. I had already forgotten that there were two more categorised climbs to battle before the denouement on gravel at 25 per cent. I saw Stuart and Jackie again and stopped to take photos with them.

At lunch I filled up as much as possible, desperate for fuel and energy. I had two large portions of pasta, rice, beans and other salad or vegetables washed down with some citrus squash drink. I was preparing for the workload ahead. I was not a patch on Welsh Steve. 'Prepare to be impressed boys,' he said as he tucked into another plate. He had a mechanical issue with his bike and had to wait for help. He had nothing else to do except eat.

Interestingly my dietary habits were starting to change. The deeper we would go into the Tour the more I craved vegetables and salad. I thought that I would be wanting more pasta and rice, which I was, but my body was craving greens like a junkie craves the next hit.

No amount of carbs would help with the low I experienced in between feed stops three and four. It was 30km of torture. Stuart and Jackie had gone on ahead of me, as had Andy, and I hadn't seen my usual riding buddies since I had left them halfway up the first hill. I was left in a void of empty lethargy.

I barely saw a soul. The route was undulating at best and there was no chance to get a proper rhythm going. I was in limbo, lost in between groups and it felt like I was cycling backwards in treacle. My legs were heavy. I was craving a siesta and the mid-afternoon sun was wearing me down. My average speed dropped by 5kph and I was delving into a dark place.

The adrenaline of the earlier climbs and the rash burst of pace was taking its toll. I felt like I didn't have it in me to pedal any further. If there had been a hammock or a sunbed anywhere on route, I would have pulled over for 40 winks. But I was in the middle of quaint, sandstone villages and empty mountain roads and had nowhere else to go except forwards.

I caught up with no one but I was left behind by a good half dozen others. It was soul-destroying. I am not sure how it happened but I somehow crawled into the final feed stop and saw the ever-cheerful face of 'Coffee Ian' who had some cheesy eighties tunes on the stereo. Darkness turned into grey. Not yet light.

I took longer than necessary at this stop. I was putting off the inevitable, fearful of the outcome and what I had left in me. I had a can of coke and some crisps. I went to the toilet. I had a chocolate bar and some caffeine. I saw Jackie very generously donate the cleats from her cycling shoes to another rider so that they could finish the stage instead of her. She was doing the first ten days, the other chap was a Grand Looper, but this still does not detract from a huge act of generosity.

Jackie is loud and you know what she is thinking, but she and her husband Stuart have the biggest hearts and the greatest moral compass you will ever encounter. Stuart left ahead of me with Deano, an American repeat alumni and awesome rider. Jackie gave me a kick up the posterior. I was suitably energised and headed off to take on the Col des Chevrères. I was about to discover if I had what it took to meet my challenge head-on.

By focusing on the final climb of the day I hadn't paid too much attention to some of the other climbs that preceded it. The Chevrères was a punch in the guts and a kick in the teeth that I didn't see coming. It was only four kilometres long but two kilometres of the ascent included stretches of 18 per cent. In layman's terms that is very steep. To make matters worse the local authorities had recently refurbished the roads with tarmac and gravel in anticipation of the Tour racing through. The day was still so hot that the tarmac was melting and the *gravillons* were sticking to our tyres. I rode some stretches leaning over my handlebars and putting my fingers on my front wheel to scrape off the tiny, sticky stones. It was unexpected and it softened us up for what was to follow. I had caught up with and dropped Deano and his group and Stuart very kindly stopped to take a photo of me nearing the summit of the climb. He would wait for Deano to ride to the base of our final challenge.

We chatted about that climb later in the day and Stuart thought I was an idiot because I said it was not that tough a climb. I had explained myself poorly. It was sheer torture. But it was the warm-up act. I was slowly rediscovering my form.

I struggled at the beginning of La Planche des Belles Filles. The late afternoon heat had sapped my diminishing reserves. A 13 per cent start to a hill that would only get steeper felt like swimming with lead boots. I have no idea where the organisers got an average of 9 per cent from: most of the ride was spent between 11 and 13 per cent. Maybe it was the 200m in the middle that were pan flat which levelled it up?

I was able to keep moving but I was quickly into my second smallest gear. I was not spinning the pedals but stamping on them. I had entered a dark headspace and my internal dialogue took over. It was time for a pep talk.

'Come on Stone. You've got this. You are epic. You can do anything. Stop being so damned weak. What is the matter with you? I need more out of you.'

'OH, COME ON LEGS. YOU ARE AWESOME. SHOW ME IT NOW. COME ON.'

Then I started to sing to myself. Some eighties earworm that Coffee Ian had stuck in my head. In German. To a song I didn't even know all the words to.

'*Neun und neunzig luft balllons*, blah blah blah blah summer sky.'

'BLOODY COME ON LEGS.'

I have had some interesting internal dialogues over the years, particularly in an Ironman swim where I am focusing on technique and chasing down some idiot who has kicked me in the face. I would be a pop psychiatrist's wet dream. Today I was hunting down Jonathon. It turns out my internal dialogue was vocalised and had been shared with half the mountain. He was chuckling away and laughing at my delirium. I would eventually get him back for this, but he broke the ride up the hill for me and as we passed kilometre five, still at 11 per cent, I found a fifth or sixth wind. It must have been the lunch. Or the coke. Or the caffeine. Or the company. Or the pep talk. I was able to pick up the pace full of the scent of glory.

With a kilometre to go we crested a final corner where a restaurant was perched, like a grandstand at a race course, full of Loopers cheering us on.

'Go on Ceri. You've got this my son.' The camaraderie was deafening and I was given a much-needed lift. I loved the team with Le Loop; we were riding for so much more than ourselves. I hit the 20 per cent slope, passed through a gate and hit the gravel. It was the hardest course I had ridden in my life.

Cycling uphill on gravel is impossible. At a gradient that precipitous I had to rise out of the saddle to put down the power I needed to move forward. Each time I did so, my rear wheel slid all over the place and I would come close to a standstill. I had to stay seated, but then I had little to no power.

People were watching me. I had to guts it out. I tried to pick the best line and follow in the tracks of those that had gone before me. It didn't help much because loose stones meant close to zero traction.

Dig in. Push hard. Come on legs you've got this. My muscles were burning. I was in agony. I was euphoric, because this could be one of the greatest physical achievements of my life. This was all five of my Ironman races rolled into one. This was the agony of failing the computer studies HND, my first real challenge in life, coming back to haunt me. I was in a battle for survival, an epic duel against myself worse than stepping into a ring with Mike Tyson. If I failed now, it would be all over for me.

I screamed inside. It came down to a question of how much did I want this? I asked my legs for one more push. They gave it.

I asked them for a couple more. They delivered again. I hit solid tarmac and only 100m of riding to achieve eternal glory: 100m of a 25 per cent wall after a long, steep and hard day on the road. It was shit or bust time.

I went all in. There was no other choice. If I didn't, I would not be able to say that I had cycled the Tour de France. I rose out of the saddle, lungs burning, heart rate up to a frightening 190 beats per minute (my maximum is supposed to be 170). I stamped on the pedals and I weaved.

There were two guys ahead of me and they were zigzagging in an uneven pattern using up all of the road. I set my sights on them. I didn't let up. I couldn't let up. If I took a breather I would fail. If I paused, I would tumble. There was no choice but to dig in and push on. No inner voice this time, just sheer blind determination and the screams from a handful of Loopers waiting at the top: '*Come on Ceri. You've got this.*'

It was the last push I needed and I stormed over the crest of the hill to summit La Planche des Belles Filles.

I was exhausted. I was soaking wet with sweat from the exertion. My body ached. My legs were trembling as I put my bike down to take in the view. I struggled to catch my breath. I was close to tears. I was ecstatic. I had to help the next few riders make it over that hill.

I very happily cheered on the next half a dozen Loopers and gave them the help that had been willingly given to me. We developed friendships and a team spirit on that hill: an elite club that would only be bettered by the professionals a week later, who flew up the thing.

I didn't want to leave the top of La Planche. I lingered and took dozens of photos. Adrenaline was coursing through me and I chatted excitedly with the others who joined us at the top. I had set my sights on this day and I had made it a big target. I knew that by finishing this stage I could take whatever the Tour would throw at me and I could make it all the way to Paris. All I had to do was hold myself together.

Jonathon was right as well. Our triumph did taste that little bit sweeter after the early effort we had put in. Plus, I had gained a new lucky climbing jersey. The question was how much had it taken out of me? Physically, mentally and emotionally. The best day of my life would lead to some of the most difficult days of riding I would experience. I had used up everything I had and I was spent.

Distance covered: 158km
Time: 9hrs 10mins
Elevation gain: 3,923m
Calories burned: 7,153
Highest speed: 67kph

IF YOU WANT THE POT OF GOLD
AT THE END OF THE RAINBOW,
YOU'VE GOT TO EMBRACE THE
RAIN – Mahatma Gandhi

Chapter 12

5 July 2019, Belfort
Hard Work and Teamwork

AFTER THE exalted highs of La Planche des Belles Filles my body was shattered but my mind was still coming down from the thrill of cresting that 25 per cent beast. With the relative success of thriving on my queen stage, emotions got the better of me and I wanted to extend myself to see how good a rider I could become.

I was engulfed with the thrill of the Tour and my heart was ruling my head for a brief period in time. I would come back down to earth with a rather sharp bump as I discovered my true place in our pecking order. I had a vague notion that I could maintain a swifter race pace for a couple of stages, so I set off in pursuit of proving this to myself and those that I had trundled in behind during the early days of our tour. I should have listened to my legs.

I caught up with a group ahead. I hoped that maybe, just maybe I would arrive back at the hotel a bit earlier that night. I had seen Rich and Kenny move up a gear and ride with faster groups and they were benefiting from the experience. I wanted some of that for myself: to ride with a stronger pack and to see if I could cope.

I didn't pick the lead peloton. They were way out of my league and I didn't want to kill myself when my goal was to reach Paris in one piece. I selected the second-fastest group (at least I think that was who they were) and tried to join in. They were well known for riding at a strong and consistent tempo. They were highly regarded for being well organised, despite being new to each other a week ago. They were borderline professional in their approach. I wanted a piece of this.

I had told Carmen, Kelly and a few others of my plans before the stage started. They encouraged me to give it a go. Maybe I should have asked my chosen group before I latched on to them first.

We headed out from feed stop one and I gradually sidled my way to the back of the train. As I had come to believe, and so they proved, they were indeed a very well-drilled outfit. There were ten of them. A nice even number. I made 11.

I loved the discipline of the group. Everyone did exactly two minutes on the front at a given power ratio. That could cause a problem because I did not ride with a power meter, I had always used my heart rate monitor and listened to my body. I was good at it as well.

As the first riders pulled off the front I moved up through the group. I caught a few funny stares and a couple of welcoming smiles. I held the pace pretty well and didn't look out of place in the peloton. The test would be whether I could sustain it for the next 40km or, even better, for the rest of the day.

The lead rider pulled off the front and took a second look after seeing me in the line. Bit odd. I took my turn on the front and put every ounce of my concentration into holding the speed and tempo. I did my two minutes and was pretty pleased with myself. I had held my own and I knew I could hold it for the rest of the day. I drifted to the back and took my place in the line, ready to go through it all again. No one shouted 'good job' like Kenny did.

'Hi Ceri. This is a bit awkward but what are you doing?' One of the leaders of the group had dropped back to ride alongside me.

'Sorry. Didn't I hold the right pace? Was I too slow?' I was a little embarrassed. I wanted to do the right thing. I wanted to belong.

'No. It's not that. It's just, did you ask if you could ride with us today? We like to be organised from the beginning of the day. It allows us to keep a good tempo. We don't remember you asking.' I was starting to feel a little uncomfortable.

'I am not sure I understand. Can't I ride with you? I thought we were all in this together?'

'It's not that. It's just that we don't want to disrupt our rhythm. We like you and everything. You're quite funny. But. You know. We can't risk being held up. Sorry.'

Those may not be the exact words that were intimated, but they were what I understood. The direction may well have been far more encouraging than I remember, but I also recall the feeling of being crestfallen so soon after the previous day's high.

I was dumbfounded. Throughout the infancy of our Tour I had gone out of my way to bring struggling riders into the pelotons I was involved with. I had nursed some weaker cyclists back into our groups by letting them hold my wheel. I wanted to contribute. I wanted to be better. I wanted to soak up the whole team experience and I wanted to belong.

I wasn't wanted. That hurt. It made me angry and sad in equal measure. I wouldn't forget that moment or that mood. I chose to bury my rage and store those feelings for a later date. I let myself sulk for a while. I would recall that anger when I needed it most. There would surely be more testing times down the road when I would need all the inspiration I could lay my hands on. I was pissed off.

I drifted back, riding on my own and struggling to hold on to other pelotons until we reached feed stop two. I was a firm believer in teamwork and helping other riders. The time would come when I would really need the help and I wanted credit in the bank. I care about other people and believe that we all work better as a group.

I envisioned seeking my revenge somewhere down the line; being realistic the odds indicated that I would not be riding at that rarefied pace again.

I want everyone to belong and work together but I could also bear a grudge. I had heard that this had happened to Rich and Kenny and I didn't want to believe it. I couldn't get the look of disdain from one strong rider out of my head. Someone I had hoped would be more inspiring than harmful to my morale. I was upset. I sulked. I vowed not to forget this moment.

After La Planche des Belles Filles I would need the support of a team. I would come to rely on good friends. We all would. We were into the second week of the Tour and had four days of riding before we would get a rest. Heading south from Belfort, we covered a lot of kilometres. We had experienced the steepest mountain on the Tour and immediately afterwards we encountered the longest stage of the whole event. My legs were shot to bits and my body was struggling to adapt to the rigours of multi-day riding. I wasn't the only one.

La Planche was the first stage where we saw some casualties. Almost 50 of us started out as Grand Loopers with the sole intention of cycling every kilometre of the Tour de France route of 2019. Stage six was the first where some of that number did not complete the full stage. A couple did not make it past the last feed stop. A few others finished late enough that they didn't have time to make it to the top of La Planche des Belles Filles. They made it as far as the restaurant, and our coaches that were parked on the corner. They were not able to climb the final kilometre up the gravel ascent and the final 100m of torture.

This Tour would have to be earned and we would need all the help we could get. Legal help that is. I was determined to make it to Paris with no shortcuts and without the help of any illegal substances. The odd iron tablet or vitamin C pill yes, but EPO injections or salbutamol or tramadol? No. Stage seven saw a couple of others fall short.

If we had been riding the Tour as a professional race, those who didn't complete a stage would be off the Tour.

Given that we were riding a grand tour for charity, we all carried on with the adventure. Mind you, if this had been a race, I would have been six hours behind the leaders already with no hope of winning.

I know my place in the peloton. If I was a pro rider I would have no chance of winning the GC and I do not possess the speed or potency to be a sprinter, so the possibility of stage wins would be very limited. I lack the power to be of service on long flat stages and I am a complete and utter scaredy-cat on descents, which hinders my chances for an overall win. I don't have the stones to attack hard on a downhill stretch and it takes a while to build confidence in my handling skills, a battle I am constantly engaged with. However, I am relatively light and my power-to-weight ratio is conducive to trudging uphill at a steady pace. I would be a domestique in the mountains and that would be the extent of my ambition.

Maybe I would cling to a pipedream of a breakaway on a hilly stage, but at this stage of our tour, survival was the name of the game. I was glad everyone stayed together. For selfish reasons. I was in need of the support and the extra morale.

Stage six took a lot out of me. I had targeted the stage from the beginning of the year and I had placed too much emphasis on finishing it. Not just finishing it but with a little style. I had pushed too hard and burned a lot of matches that day. I had a huge adrenaline surge and after the surge I was faced with a come-down.

Cycling stages of the Tour de France is like a drug. I do not partake and never have, but the thrill I had from climbing La Planche must be what cocaine users feel on a Saturday night. The rush and the euphoria were on another level, it was hard to control my emotions. The gradual come-down was like a great depression, but I had to keep riding. The Tour organisers were very generous and they gave us a lot of kilometres to cover on stage seven. The longest day of the Tour in fact. Thanks once again, ASO.

With the first mountainous section of the Tour out of the way, we moved straight on to a stage for the sprinters. We could have been forgiven for thinking that it would have been flat, fast and straightforward. Instead, the 230km from Belfort to Chalon-sur-Saône provided nothing short of mental torture.

I had cycled this distance once in my life and that was two weeks before the Tour started. I was so relieved that I had put the preparation in. In theory it was a downhill stage but we still had an elevation gain of 2,200m and three categorised climbs that we barely noticed. In an Ironman that is regarded as difficult, on the Tour it is regarded as a descent.

The day was hot (*quelle surprise*), and after I had been rebuffed by my first choice of riding partners it became fragmented. It saw a couple more casualties. I drifted into feed stop two on my own, not long after Rich and Kenny's group, who had passed me on the road, and followed shortly by a small group containing Carmen, Kelly and Nick. A few others had drifted like I had, struggling to find a rhythm and energy after the exertions of the previous day.

The highlight of the day was a small man-made pool adjacent to our food truck. After sandwiches and drinks, we took the opportunity to sit in the water and cool down. Never had a soothing dip been more gratefully received. On what should have been a fast ride into town, the groups I attached myself to never really got going. Some fresher riders pushing too hard, some very tired riders failing to take their turns on the front. It was a disjointed day and never looked like falling into place until after lunch.

Our main meal was taken late in the day. Too late. We were losing time and moods were becoming frayed. Having eaten, some of us were eager to get going where others ambled through the process of shifting into gear to start turning the wheels again. Andy was the one who stepped up. Emily had urged us to get a move on and Andy took the lead. He cajoled a group of a dozen fragmented souls into order and set a tempo. There was still bickering and mixed tempos. There were still a few team-mates who tried to shirk their responsibilities. I tried to keep my head down and just do my job. I wanted to survive and make it through to the end of the day. One revolution after the other. All roads lead to Paris. I was an invisible cog in the wheel most of the day.

I pulled when it was my turn and I supported when friends became frazzled. We were breaking new ground with this distance and the effort was having a detrimental effect. The puerile jokes disappeared for the last couple of hours and they were replaced with a grim and intense silence. This was the first day of the Tour that I had ridden with both Andy and Eric and they were equally strong.

Eric was so durable he simply rode away from us without realising the strength he had in him. It was an impressive feat of riding. It was effortless. Later in the evening someone tried to make an issue out of it but I was impressed and wanted to ride with him some more. He had no need to apologise, but he did anyway. It showed the class of the man.

Stage seven was an interminable day. It felt like we were cycling in a sweltering abyss. It was made notable by another couple of Grand Loopers catching a lift back to the hotel from the final feed stop. Seven hard days of riding, rising temperatures and the toughest parcours in decades were taking a toll. I was glad to survive to ride another day.

Distance covered: 234km
Time: 10hrs 45mins
Elevation gain: 2,123m
Calories burned: 8,601
Highest speed: 67kph

The official Tour magazine described stage eight as a maelstrom of medium mountains. It was a brute of a day and that was not taking into account the torrent of hailstones the size of golf balls.

Par for the course, this year's event offered no respite. It felt like the organisers had gone looking for every possible climb in the 198km between Mâcon and Saint-Étienne. Some were longish climbs of seven kilometres while others were shorter at three kilometres but harnessing some double-digit gradients. There was something there to test the strongest of legs and splinter the most well-drilled groups.

The forecast had predicted some rain but we had no idea how much. We were advised to take our waterproof jackets with us, just in case. It all kicked off right out of the gate of feed stop one as we hit the bottom of the Col de la Croix

Montmain, a six-kilometre climb with an average rise of 7 per cent. In theory a gentle warm-up before the sterner tests that lay in wait.

I had recovered some semblance of strength in my legs but I couldn't get my heart rate up. I usually ride at a heart rate of between 130–140 beats per minute at a comfortable pace. If I am racing, I will push this above 150 beats and, on a climb, I expect to hit somewhere between 160–170 beats depending on the severity of the test. Ever since La Planche my heart rate was sitting at a comfortable 100–110 beats per minute and was struggling to get above 140 on the climbs. I didn't know if this was because I had hit a level of peak fitness and the efforts were becoming very easy or because my body was exhausted and it was no longer allowing me to exert myself. I suspect it was the latter. For the rest of the Tour, my heart rate consistently remained at these low levels. Either way, I was enjoying the first climb of the day. Until the storms happened.

They came out of nowhere. One minute we were riding in warm, humid sunshine and the next we were cycling upstream in a fast-flowing torrent of water. There was a loud crack of thunder. Flashes of lightning could be seen in the distance and they were edging closer to us. A couple of riders turned round and headed back for the general safety of the feed trucks, hoping the storm would pass. They were the wise ones. Then the heavens opened.

It wasn't just a simple downpour or a summer shower that we would be used to in the UK. It was heavy, torrential rain like water being poured from a bucket. The spray and the mist were similar to the damp vapour that wafts from

Niagara Falls. It was mind-blowing and treacherous. The rainwater gathered apace and formed little rivers that flowed down the hillside.

We were caught riding against the tide and forcing ourselves to move at a snail's pace. I hadn't bargained for this when I signed up for Le Loop. Neither had I bargained for the hailstones. It is no exaggeration to say that they were the size of golf balls and they were painful. Like a golf ball being hit from the tee into your thigh painful. If you search through the photos on the Rideleloop Facebook page you will see pictures of the stones taking up the whole of a grown man's hand. They were big, fast and painful to be on the receiving end of. By the end of the day there were more than a few welts on thighs, worse than an epic paintball battle with no armour.

Some of the Loopers with common sense took shelter under trees and waited for the storm to pass. Most of us, who knew this would be a long and tough day, chose to carry on. I was soaked through. My posterior was chafing against the saddle. I hadn't time to put my rain coat on. It meant I was drenched and had red blotches where the hailstones hit their target. They were bouncing two feet off the road and right into our path. The choices were either to take shelter or plough on as best we could. I chose the latter.

I gutsed it out and confronted the pain head-on. The adrenaline was back and I was going to make it to Paris come rain, hail or shine. Incredibly I had some company. Carmen, Doctor Fi and Andy all rode with me and we paced each other up the hill. I must have had some strength in me because I was lucky enough to be able to ride alongside some absolute titans. They were immense. Carmen had a wish to be known as a badass cyclist. On this day she proved it in spades. Not only did she glide up a mountain, head-first into a maelstrom of friendly ice-borne fire, but her disposition was relentlessly positive and she carried the unusually quiet Andy and me with her. Just as suddenly as the storm arrived, it disappeared.

The descent was horrendous. Rivers of dirty rainwater drifted across the road and we negotiated a tricky descent as slowly as we had travelled up it. My hands never left the brakes and my eyes never left the road. I have never felt so alive and so frightened at the same time. That set the tone for the whole day.

The route was lumpy at best and downright cruel at worst. There was not a single stretch of flat land: the road either led up steep inclines or arced down tricky descents. It made it difficult to ride in pelotons and gather any momentum. We were stretched and tortured in equal measure and the weather switched quicker than a schizophrenic psychopath. One minute we would glide along in balmy sunshine with a misty haze wafting across the road, steam rising out of the fog of endurance, and the next we were blown off course and drenched like a frog in a waterfall.

By lunch I had latched on to a mixed-ability group of some very determined riders. Legs were aching, backs were sore and welts were starting to bulge their deep red pain. We had a brief respite and decent tempo on a long false flat downhill stretch that took us to the base of the Côte de la Croix de Part. Deano had led the group brilliantly, keeping us in order and looking after the well-being of us all. He was heaven-sent for an hour of riding until we hit the climb. We splintered again for the final time.

I took it quite easy. I let others take the lead and surge ahead. It was only 5km, with a steady incline, but it peaked with bumps as steep as 15 per cent and it would prove to be a challenge. It didn't take long to find my climbing legs and my rhythm.

I was starting to become accustomed to the hills and dare I say it beginning to enjoy them. I wouldn't say I was thriving but I was surviving better than some others. I started picking off some of the group and by halfway I had left them all behind, only Andy was keeping pace with me. We looked back and we had put 500m into the group.

By the top of the hill Andy magnanimously chose to wait for some of the others to help them along. I kept going. He was one of the most unselfish riders of the Tour and always looking out for others. I enjoyed riding with him, even if he did talk more nonsense than me. I was consigned to another torturous stretch on my own, paying the price for my vain exploits.

It was hot on the hill and I had drunk a lot of water. I was running low and I still had a good 30km to the next feed stop. The road took us through country farmlands that weaved and undulated and tested my resolve. I rationed my intake but with the heat and the humidity I was very thirsty.

I thought about waiting for the others but I hadn't seen a soul for ages and there was no sign of anyone in the distance, both ahead or behind. I persisted up the constant, niggling climbs and ran out of water just as the next storm and machine-gun attack of hail descended upon us. I used my initiative and took the top off one of my water bottles and let the rain fill it up to halfway. No sooner had I done this than out of the haze I saw a group of riders huddled under the awning of a Le Loop-emblazoned feed stop. Time for some shelter.

After more than 160km of treacherous terrain, I was now cold again and there was a danger of it getting dark quite quickly. I didn't have a light with me and I didn't want my legs to seize up through the cold. Most of the gang taking shelter were cold and disheartened. Except for Welsh Steve. Everyone should ride with him just once in their life. He is powerful, fast and relentlessly good-humoured.

'Hiya Ceri. What's occurin'? Hot dogs for tea, is it boyo?' I paraphrase some of our colloquialisms. 'Are you fit? These miserable sods aren't used to the cold. Fancy a gentle ride?'

Oh, hell yes, I did. Steve set off at pace and I fought with all my might to cling on to his coat-tails. He was a legend and saved my day. At one point, he asked where we were. I told him we were in the Loire Valley and he said something along the lines of, 'Oh crap. Better speed up then. I'm banned from here.'

He told me the tale of a camping holiday he had had with his wife and some friends the year before and how they had drunk too much and upset a local police officer. As a result, they were moved on and asked never to return. Steve made a final hour pass in minutes and we dropped quite a few riders on the route, before making it back in time for 'tea'. No hot dogs though.

This stage had everything: great climbs, tricky descents, sunshine, rain, thunder, lightning, hailstones and great people. It was pretty much every stage of the Tour rolled into one. I was surviving through a lot of hard work and some superb team work. I knew that I had been able to help some of the others on the challenge so far, but I wasn't going to be able to do this on my own. I was so grateful for the help of some team-mates, but I thought I had found my legs. The next day I hit a wall.

Distance covered: 195km
Time: 10hrs 51mins
Elevation gain: 3,853m
Calories burned: 8,533
Highest speed: 60kph

A TEAM IS NOT A GROUP WHO WORK TOGETHER. A TEAM IS A GROUP WHO TRUST EACH OTHER
– Simon Sinek

Chapter 13

7 July 2019, Saint-Flour
Dig Deep and Rest

WHEN I say wall, I mean Mur. A steep, nasty, smack in the gonads type of Mur. The kind of Mur that provides a knockout punch in the first round and then they insist you carry on fighting for another ten rounds for the sheer hell of it.

Nothing great is ever easy. And never was I in so much need of a friend and team-mate than when Kenny caught up with me. I may have been able to do this thing on my own but sharing the load with great friends would make the burden so much easier. We weren't helped by the fact that a cut-off time was imposed on us for the end of the stage. If we didn't make feed stop four within a given time-frame we wouldn't be allowed to ride the final 40km to the finish of the stage because we had a lengthy transfer from there to our hotel for the night.

Day nine of a difficult Tour and a tough day lay ahead. My legs were starting to feel it and they were craving a rest day. To compound matters we had the added pressure of having to increase our speed to make it inside the cut-off.

I had a conversation with Rich over dinner the night before. The Tour was starting to take its toll on us and it was showing. Like half the peloton, we had badly chapped lips from the relentless wind and sun. Our bodies were aching and although not letting us down they were suffering. Over a bowl of pasta and chicken we swapped sob stories.

Neither of us had ever ridden for more than three consecutive days. We were into pastures unknown and at the same time taking on the toughest sporting challenge in the world. The route for 2019 was arguably the toughest Tour route in 50 years. If you don't believe me, that came from Eddy Merckx, the greatest cyclist who has ever lived. This route was designed to break the spirits of the best professional cyclists in the world and here we were, a bunch of enthusiastic amateurs proving that the pros are the toughest sportsmen on the planet.

We were both finding it hard to warm our legs up to the challenge each day and it would regularly take two to three hours before we found some semblance of form. We both felt like we could cycle all day long but equally we both felt as if we had lost all power and speed in our legs. We felt like we had become genuine plodders.

The great thing with Rich is that he is as tough as nails. He lifted my spirits by talking about how we would reach Paris and how we would celebrate. There was no talk of failure. There was no talk of quitting and there was no talk of taking a rest. Unlike a couple more of the Grand Loopers who had already taken that option. The Tour was taking its toll and collecting its prisoners one by one, but it would not take us.

Day nine of riding saw me meet the only person from the whole experience that I did not warm to. I don't wish to focus on another person's negative energy, I would rather maintain a positive outlook, but sometimes obstacles are put in your path to test your resolve. This individual I will call Buddy. He had all the gear but no idea. Although that applied to most of us.

He rode a beautiful bike with matching kit and he lectured me on riding technique and success strategies, but he never delivered himself. I found him quite negative to be around so I politely chose to stay close to riders with a similar mindset to mine. Positive, honest and with a puerile sense of humour. I believe that behaviour breeds behaviour and I preferred to mingle with like-minded fools. All glib facades masking interiors forged with steel.

On day nine Buddy opted to miss the stage and travel by bus to the hotel. To be fair to him, he had completed the Tour a couple of years previously and he was a faster rider than me. There was a lot I could learn from him, but quitting was not something on my agenda. Digging deep and supporting my team was more my cup of tea. Buddy was the polar opposite of Rich.

Given that it took a couple of hours for our legs to properly warm up, it was only fitting that it was a stage for the *puncheurs* and that the knocks started coming in round one, straight out of feed stop one. We were heading deeper south through the middle mountains from the industrial, and sopping wet, city of Saint-Étienne down to Brioude, the birthplace of Romain Bardet. The route barely featured a flat metre and travelled from one hill to the next. If we survived the cut-off, we would crest the Côte de Saint-Just, with its consistent steep slope over four awkward kilometres, before a tricky descent, flying down to the line in Brioude. But first that wall.

I had managed to sit in the middle of a large peloton leading up to feed stop one and there was no oomph in my legs. I was uncomfortable. Because it had been so wet the day before, I had suffered a little chafing around my groin area and I had the first tentative signs of a saddle sore. Nothing big but enough to irritate. Even worse was the fact that my bike shoes had not dried out properly so I left them in my holdall and wore my spare pair.

I know a workman shouldn't blame his tools but there was a big difference between the two pairs of shoes. My spares had a plastic sole which had a little flex in them, whereas my main shoes had a carbon sole which meant that they were stiffer and lighter. This doesn't sound like much but if we go back to Team INEOS's aggregation of marginal gains, the difference in power transfer from the carbon on to the pedals could be felt. I would need the power transfer that was missing.

After filling up with cakes, bananas and water we headed out of the feed station and attacked the Mur d'Aurec-sur-Loire. I had positioned myself with people like Andy, Eric, Carmen, Kelly and Nick, all good riders but in theory I should be better going uphill than them. Within 200m they had all left me behind.

I had nothing in my legs and I had nothing inside. No energy, no fire, no power and no oomph. I was empty. There was still three kilometres of a Mur to climb and 140km of a *puncheur*'s stage left to negotiate. I was treading water in treacle. Riders who had spent the previous week way behind me were starting to drift past. For the first time in my life, I contemplated walking up a hill.

No one needs that kind of negativity in their life and I quickly shook off that thought. I focused purely on one revolution at a time (good old Fidel Castro) and set myself small targets. A tree was 100m ahead, well let's make it there and re-evaluate my position. I reached the tree and could still turn the pedals. Next up a stone-walled house 200m away. Done. Then a couple of ladies who were walking by the side of the road with picnic baskets. Done, and a little bit easier. I was breaking it down and picking off the targets one at a time.

After two kilometres, my legs were no better but I saw Eric ahead of me. I reeled him in very slowly and we were able to support each other for the last 800m or so, Eric fantasising about ice creams and me craving a kebab. I don't even like kebabs, but I must have been short of some salts and fats and the image of a steaming pile of donner on a stick never left my focus. We had hit a wall on a Mur and survived. One revolution at a time and we had crested the rise to find a long stretch of open and windy roads at the top of a mountain. Eric dropped me.

I still couldn't get my legs going. There was nothing inside and my morale was cracking. I should have been ten kilometres further up the road but I was struggling on my own, lost in a dark abyss of self-pity. I had no oomph. Then along came a singing Irishman.

I had not been so relieved to see Kenny throughout the whole Tour. Like many others he was relentlessly good-humoured, always laughing and joking and quick with a tall tale to pick up our spirits. He had struggled on the Mur but had found his second wind. He was feeling strong and he took me under his wing.

I don't think I have ever laughed so hard as I did over the next 20km, when we not only picked up the pace but lifted our spirits. We dropped one or two slower riders but also picked up and helped out a couple more. We kept paying it forward and a second wind was gratefully welcomed. By feed stop two we had joined up with a strong group, faces I would see a bit more of as we approached the real mountains following a rest day.

After lunch I suffered my first puncture of the Tour on a slight incline and was left to my own devices to repair it. It was fiddly and took a bit longer than usual to fix, but ten minutes later I was on my way, riding solo again. It took 30 minutes to catch up with a strong band of brothers to finish a testing ride into Brioude.

Deano took control of the group and organised us into an efficient train. He was awesome. Jonathon and Stuart led the way and set a healthy rhythm that ensured we would comfortably beat the cut-off and we were freed from the shackles of that tension. They were awesome. I hid in the shadows, rediscovering some form and doing what I could to survive. If necessary, all the way to Paris. We freewheeled into Brioude.

Our hotel that night was in the dramatic, ancient walled town of Saint-Flour. It was facing what looked like a castle sitting high into a cliff face and the resulting sunset provided the most epic of weather-beaten photos. I was sharing with Nigel and one other. Nigel had been with us for the last 50km of the day. He was quiet, steady and very impressive.

We were both worn out and ready for the usual routine of wash, clean, eat, massage, prepare and rest. There was one double bed and two single camp beds between three. As we entered the room, we saw Buddy.

'Hi guys. Hope you've had a good ride. I've had a good rest day today and am feeling fresh. Also hope you don't mind but I've nabbed the double bed.'

I looked at Nigel and suspired.

Selfish wanker, I thought. To myself. Just

There are many times in my life when I have had no filter. I have a tendency to verbalise what I am thinking and some home truths that cut right to the heart of the matter accidentally slip out. I kept my mouth shut in this precise moment. I wouldn't have been ashamed if it had slipped out. I was simply too tired to carry my holdall to my part of the room, let alone argue over sleep.

I didn't even want the double bed; Nigel was far more deserving than me.

There had to be one individual on the Tour who I wouldn't get on with. I would steer clear of Buddy wherever possible. I knew that before I dare criticise someone, I should walk a mile in his shoes. That way I would be a great distance away from him and I would have an expensive pair of shoes that matched my bike. One more day to survive before the first rest day.

Distance covered: 177km
Time: 8hrs 44mins
Elevation gain: 2,847m
Calories burned: 6,796
Highest speed: 61kph

The last four days leading into the rest day in the town of Albi were the days that I appreciated the benefits of teamwork the most. For the first time in my life, I was on the verge of riding consistently for ten consecutive days and I had no idea how my body would react to it. For the most part it was good.

I was waking up fresh each day and refuelling well. I had established and maintained some epic habits and I was loving the bubble that we were living in. I was capable of riding for ten hours or more every day. What my body was depriving me of was consistent power and strength. There were periods when I had nothing. I could not predict when I would suffer these dark moments but they would creep up on me. The only solution I had was to work harder and keep on turning the pedals.

Being immodest I know that I contributed to the groups that I rode with and I know that I was good for morale. I constantly kept spirits high and I remember laughing a lot with the teams around me. Occasionally I needed it back in return. The day before, Kenny had been heaven-sent at exactly the right moment, and on day ten I was indebted to Carmen. She is an incredible human being.

I think my mind had drifted to the relative ease of the rest day and I wasn't prepared mentally to cycle 217km south to the very charming town of Albi. This was classed as a flat parcours, designed for the sprinters in the Tour de France, when it would be seen as a deciding stage in the battle for the green jersey. We would be descending 3,500m, but as is customary with these routes on the Tour, that meant we also had to climb over 3,000m. No such thing as a flat stage. Emotionally I wasn't ready for the incessant rises and the four categorised climbs. I wanted to freewheel into Albi and have my first drink in six weeks. Thank heavens for Carmen and our new-found friend Kirk.

My notes on my Garmin computer for that day pretty much summed it up:

'Really long and lumpy stage and very hot again. Rode all day with Carmen and joined by Kirk for the last two *secteurs*. Great company but the climbing for a flat stage when your legs are spent was heart-breaking. Time to rest now. Carmen conquered her demons from yesterday and was awe-inspiring. My legs are tired and have no power right now. In theory they should get stronger but for now I just keep turning the pedals. One incredible 10k downhill.'

Carmen and I are different riders. I am pretty light and am generally very good going uphill. When I get a rhythm going, I fall into my happy place and I am easy to hang on to and ride with. I fidget on the bike a lot. I am never comfortable but I am very consistent with my pacing and I know how to judge an effort pretty well.

Carmen is outstanding on the flat and she would make an epic time-triallist. Like me, she has completed an Ironman and it shows in her brilliance. She can slip into a rhythm, set a high tempo and sustain it for very long periods. Her disadvantage is that she does not have confidence in the hills, which is hardly surprising given they have none in Toronto.

I like to think I am relentlessly positive and my expectations are often unrealistic. I believe I can do anything if I put my mind to it; I need to set my mind into gear more often. Carmen is too hard on herself. She seeks perfection and she beats herself up if she is not performing to the levels that she is capable of. She needs to ease up on herself a little and realise that she is epic. She proved it on stage ten. She carried me.

At one point, as we hit the bottom of the third categorised hill of the day, my internal dialogue was vocalised. I needed to get a handle on it.

'Not another bloody hill. How many hills do we have to face on a flat day? Seriously? What is wrong with these route designers? Come on legs. You've got this. You are awesome. You are strong. Nothing will defeat us. Come on legs. Time to show the road who is boss. Get a grip Stone. You're better than this. Paris here we come. Oh, for crying out loud. Where did this hill come from?'

Carmen glided past me up the rise, laughing at my nonsense. At least she was happy. I was drifting into a dark place. Then Jackie went flying past us with three guys clinging on to her coat-tails for dear life. That perked me up.

Jackie was on her final day and she wasn't going to leave any effort out on the road. She was steaming and she was a sight to behold. We tried to latch on to her little group but it was too much. After a couple of kilometres, we let them drift away and we maintained our healthy pace that would get us to Albi and eventually to Paris. All roads lead to Paris.

By the time we reached feed stop three for lunch Jackie had left and the guys who had been riding with her had given up. They were happily tucking into ice creams from the shop that was next door. One of them was Kirk and we picked him up for the remainder of the day. He had been on the Tour for three days and he would be leaving after stage ten. I had roomed with him his first night and we had got on really well. It was nice to be able to ride with him on his last day and maybe share a glass of champagne before he departed.

Leading up to the lunch stop Carmen impressed me immensely with one little burst of power. We were in our own little zone when we were joined by three guys who were pretty fresh in the legs. They too were only doing the three days. They sat on our wheels for a while without taking a turn on the front. We carried them with no gratitude from them or effort in return. We thought nothing of it until they dropped us. They rode past us as a unit and didn't offer a solitary word of thanks or support. I suggested that we make the effort to catch up and ride with them, but Carmen rightly said no. They weren't worthy of her efforts.

A little further down the road we did catch them. They latched on again as we headed out of some industrial town that blended from one into another. The road pulled uphill steeply for a couple of kilometres.

'Hang on,' Carmen shouted. I did as I was told.

We left the three of them for dust. They tried desperately to cling to our wheels and suck the air out of them, but Carmen was way too strong. She blew them out of the water and left them panting for air. They had burned their matches trying to hold on to us, but she was having none of it. She made me dig deep and I had a lot of fun in the process. It broke up the day.

'Serves them right,' she said, as we turned off at the top of the little climb. 'I'll help anyone but don't take advantage of my good nature.' Top lady.

Albi is a town on the Tarn river in southern France, north-east of Toulouse. Dominating the skyline is the 13th-century, red-brick Sainte-Cécile Cathedral, a Gothic landmark with large interior frescoes such as the dramatic *Last Judgment*. The centuries-old Palais de la Berbie houses the Musée Toulouse-Lautrec, honouring the Albi-born painter. The roads seemed wide and inviting as we turned a corner and crossed the bridge over the river that led us gently into our hotel in the heart of the town. A pleasant spot to spend a day and recover a little.

I enjoyed my first drink in over six weeks and celebrated the end of a very difficult ten days of riding. Only 11 more tougher ones to go and we would be in Paris. Next up, the mountains.

Distance covered: 217km
Time: 11hrs 3mins
Elevation gain: 2,938m
Calories burned: 8,239
Highest speed: 61kph

AN EMPTY LANTERN PROVIDES
NO LIGHT. SELF-CARE ALLOWS
YOU TO SHINE BRIGHTER – Anon

Chapter 14

9 July 2019, Albi
Hard at Work Resting

ONE OF the great advantages of riding the Tour de France is that the route introduces you to towns, villages, communities and cities that I would never have considered visiting. The great disadvantage of riding the Tour is that you don't get the opportunity to either see or experience them properly.

The first rest day after ten days on the road, consistently riding for up to ten hours at a time, was in the southern town of Albi. It was amazing for two big reasons: the first being that the town was beautiful and charming and the second that we got to sleep in the same bed for two consecutive nights. Already a rare luxury. The day of rest hadn't come soon enough.

In theory all we wanted to do was spend the day in bed; eating, drinking, letting our bodies recover and maybe watching some of the real Tour on TV to see how the pros coped with the course we had ridden the week before. As it turned out we didn't want to do that last one. It made me feel inadequate. But this is the Tour and there is always something to be done.

I planned on sleeping in until late in the morning but by 7.30am the riders' WhatsApp group was busy disturbing the peace with constant alerts. I was awake already but didn't want to be disturbed. The alerts were worthwhile for a group of 50-odd middle-aged plodders looking to clean their Lycra. Someone had found a launderette and it was empty. They had also found a bike store, a pharmacist and a barber shop within walking distance. That was my day planned already. But first I met another lady who would have a major impact on my challenge.

After a leisurely breakfast, I stumbled around in a haze a little bit lost, not knowing what to do with myself without the routine of Sarah telling me where to go and with no arrows to point me in the right direction. I was immersed in the bubble and I loved the feeling of warmth from the security blanket of Le Loop organisation. First order of the day was to tinker with Trigger and give her some love and affection and thank her for looking after me so well.

At 10.30am I was booked in for some more therapy. I thought I had been looking after my body. I was stretching each morning before we started as well as each evening before bed, and I had received regular massages; I was trying to preserve my legs and I was listening to my body but I was still in some pain. After the magnificence of La Planche des Belles Filles something hadn't been right with my legs. I was devoid of power and energy and it took me a good three hours to properly get going each day. I was concerned that my body was breaking down beyond mere fatigue.

The massages I had had up to this stage were excellent and had allowed me to repair and go again each day but the rest-day pummelling took it to another level. A quarter of an hour on the table and Katy from the Le Loop team had pounded me like an Eastern European shot putter. She didn't pull any punches and she cut right to the core of the matter. I had a lot of stiffness and sore muscles around my hamstrings, glutes and quads that required attention. She dug her elbows into my glutes, wiggled my legs around and I winced and squealed like a little baby losing its favourite blanket.

She dug deep into my muscles and teased me for my over-sensitive reaction, which in turn took my mind off some of the agony. I didn't enjoy those 15 minutes in the slightest but as I got off the torture table, I swear I felt like I was walking on air. I was ready to go for a mid-morning run such was the spring in my step. It could have been the fact that this was the first massage that I had had which wasn't following eight hours on a saddle or the fact that I was relaxed after a good night's sleep, but either way some of the damage I had put my body through was repaired. Rest day was having its effect.

The remainder of the day was taken up with essential chores and a bizarre three-language conversation. I went with Carmen to do our laundry and we found the bike store at the same time. She bought some new kit and I stocked up on protein bars (I was craving help for my muscles), new gloves and spare inner tubes. It seemed that the owner of the bike store was quite pleased to see a large group of cyclists ride into town. All his Christmases had come at once and he would have the real thing to follow up with in a week's time. I bet Geraint Thomas wasn't washing his smalls and buying protein bars; he would have had a professional to do that for him.

I dined with the Canadians at lunchtime and we filled our faces with carbohydrates and more muscle-repairing protein. I charmingly (ahem) taught them all how to speak English correctly instead of going 'aroond aboot the hooses, hey,' and then headed into town with American Kelly for a gentle stroll. We explored the quaint and easy charm of the place and grabbed a coffee while we watched the finale of stage four.

Kelly is ridiculously charming and he is a magnet to all around him. He has such a calming aura and by the time we left the café we had made half a dozen new friends who were intrigued by the American and Taff who were cycling the Tour. I taught Kelly how to speak English correctly and then showed him where the bike store was before stocking up on lip salve, sterilising washing liquid for my kit and bottom cream for my, well, area that should never see the light of day, at the pharmacy. I finished the afternoon with a little treat by dropping into the barbers for a head shave.

The barber was Moroccan and spoke no English and only a form of pigeon French. I spoke pigeon French but his mate spoke fluent Spanish, so we conversed in a form of Spanish/French and I think I impressed them with tall tales of exploits traversing the delightful French roads and with my perfectly shaped cranium. He didn't cut me once and he gave me something for the weekend.

I was so looking forward to the rest day but in the end it had been full of gentle little chores and by the time I had finished the day was over and it was time to refuel yet again. My mind had been taken off the riding for a while and my body was ready for the second half of the Tour. I was ready for the real mountains.

Kilometres: 0
Massages: 1
Haircuts: 1
Siestas: 1

SMOOTH SEAS DO NOT MAKE
SKILFUL SAILORS

Chapter 15

11 July 2019, The Pyrenees
Hard Work

A NICE side effect from riding for eight hours or so every day for three weeks is that you lose a bit of weight and become a bit leaner. However, I hadn't noticed any difference leading up to the rest day and, if anything, I felt a bit bloated. It was explained to me that in the first week of the constant exercise we undertake, the body adjusts to the stress it is put under. It stores up fat and fuel to allow it to cope with the effort it expects to be under the following day. Muscles were slowly starting to grow in my legs and core but there was no definition because a layer of fat was being stored to help that growth. On the rest day the body seemed to relax and it allowed the excess weight to fall off a little. I was a tiny bit slimmer and this would be to my advantage in the mountains.

I am not exactly heavily built as it is. I was always the skinniest kid in school and I have never had a big frame. As I frequently lament, I possess no natural power or speed, but

I have strength and endurance. Essentially, I am weak and I can be weak for really long periods of time.

I am probably an average build nowadays, with a healthy predilection for beer showing around my midriff. I am not fat, neither am I muscular nor well-toned, I just seem to be rather average. In France I would be heading towards skinny again and I was delighted. No great science to the theory of the weight loss, just constant intense exercise.

I was consuming close to 8,000 calories a day and I was losing a few pounds in the process. The food I was eating was very rich in carbohydrates and protein and for good measure I would chomp on an extra protein bar each day to combat the muscle fatigue. This all combined to help with my power-to-weight ratio and I hoped I was fairly well prepared for long days climbing steep mountains. This is what I was in France for. It was strange, but with 11 stages under our belts and having travelled more than half of the Tour already, it was on stage 12 that I had the feeling that the Tour and the great challenges were starting for real. We simply had to reach the Pyrenees.

Getting to the Pyrenees was no straightforward feat. They had been a looming presence for the previous few days, both in our minds and visually in the distance, with their magnificent peaks rising like gladiators above the mist. They were challenging and tormenting us in equal measure and their beauty was intoxicating.

Every waking thought and every pedal stroke took us a step closer to romance and battle. I had been dreaming of moments like this my entire life and following a brief 120km they would be upon me.

That approach seemed to last forever. The thought of the mountains fragmented some sturdy groups as riders were defeated by the mere presence of the mercurial mountains creeping ever nearer. Some chose to ease up and save their legs for the two monsters at the end of the day. Others picked up the pace, taking advantage of the flat, smooth tarmac which was like a pristine charcoal-grey carpet. It was easy to glide along, if only we could all work together. As usual the quicker groups surged ahead and the remainder of us inconsistent plodders tried to find a way to work together. It was not easy. Unlike the day before.

Stage 11 had passed in a blur on a relatively short and flat 167km sojourn. I had the great fortune to ride with Carmen and Eric in nigh-on perfect unity and our efforts rendered the day efficient and without drama. That would change on stage 12.

It felt like there was no game plan or leadership from any of the great people I had ridden with for 11 days. In the early part of the day, I too drifted in between groups and found a steady pace hard to come by. Eventually the day clicked with two old reliable friends. I had known these people for such a short period of time but already I had come to call them trusty friends. I was lucky to have ridden with so many great people and come to learn who I could rely upon in times of need. I instantly knew who was the funny one (me), who was the quickest (not me) and who I could count on (occasionally me). I could trust every person in our Tour bar one very odd one.

Out of feed stop one I settled into a comfortable rhythm and easily found a heady pace with Carmen and Eric once again. We didn't need to talk, or rather they preferred me to be quiet, and we gelled. In no time at all we were eating up the tarmac ahead of us and gliding past some slower groups. We still had 90km to travel when we had set off and they seemed interminable. The Pyrenees were calling to us but they were still at arm's length.

Before long we caught up with a larger group who should have been doing well but were sadly disorganised. They included a few friends like Nick, Stuart and Kelly but they were struggling with Buddy and they lacked leadership. We latched on to the back and our pace noticeably slowed.

Two things then happened which splintered the group. Firstly, a wasp flew into my shirt and stung me three or four times on my right-hand ribcage. That smarted. No seriously, it really stung. But adrenaline is a great masking agent. I slowed to a standstill, unzipped my shirt and freed the tiny little foe. Stuart and Nick stayed with me as the rest surged ahead. Not a problem. Stuart is a stand-up guy. We shared a similar opinion of Buddy. He nursed me back to the group and we aimed to get firing again.

At this point, still with 40km before we reached the first mountain, Buddy rode off the front, taking with him a couple of others. He had moaned that us weaker riders were holding him up and that he was too good to be labouring with us. Interesting. He had taken one full rest day (plus that double bed) and had fallen short on at least one other day and caught the van back for the last 40km. Not a man of substance in my low regard.

It left us with a core group of seven or eight who delivered us all to a much-needed feed stop in the shadow of the Col de Peyresourde. My legs were in good shape, my body was holding up quite well and I was having to calm my adrenaline levels down. I was raring to get stuck into the mountains and test myself.

Could I survive and would I enjoy them? All of my questions about the Tour and about myself were about to be answered over the course of the next ten days and I wasn't sure I was going to like the answers. The road doesn't lie.

The Col de Peyresourde had been the first Pyrenean mountain ever to be included in the Tour de France, back in 1910. I can't bear to imagine what it would have been like for the titans who were racing back then, wearing woollen jumpers and carrying spare tyres, inner tubes and toolkits. They weren't allowed any assistance in those days. Their bikes were a very heavy steel with none of the modern-day lightweight carbon fibre aerodynamics. They were not designed for a mountain pass, let alone one with a gravel track rather than the smooth tarmac that helped us glide up. The Peyresourde is neither the toughest nor the steepest of the Pyrenean challenges that lay ahead but it softened us up for what was to come.

Heading west out of Bagnères-de-Luchon, a spa town whose existence is due to springs of super-heated water emanating from deep within the Pyrenees, there was a solid 8 per cent to kick things off. This led to a prolonged gentle slope to give the legs a chance to recover and gain false hope. Halfway up, the slope peaked at its most difficult 10 per cent and was followed by a series of steep switchbacks, resembling a flight of stairs that lead to a grassy gnoll maxing out at 1,600m. I found it to be quite hard but that was all my own doing.

I had struggled to keep my enthusiasm and adrenaline in check and I attacked the bottom of the climb way too hard. Knowing on paper that I was a stronger climber than most of our group, I pulled alongside Eric and Carmen as we approached the climb to have a chat and bid my farewell.

'Hey guys, we need to talk,' I said sheepishly in a faux break-up apology.

'Yeah? What's up?' Carmen, not tolerating my crap.

'Well, you know, this is all me. It's not you. It's me and I take full responsibility for this, but I think we should go our separate ways. You know, I've loved our time together and we can't say we haven't given it our best shot, but all good things come to an end. Deep down I will always share a piece of my heart with you but we just cannot go on as we are. As I said, it is all me and not you. But the mountains have my heart and I have to be true to myself. So, goodbye. Are we good though? We can stay friends, right?' Not quite Hugh Grant in *Four Weddings and a Funeral* but I thought I had crammed in enough break-up clichés.

'Quoi?' That was Eric.

'Dumb Welshman thinks he's funny,' said Carmen. 'Humour him and say goodbye.'

'Au revoir, Taffy.'

And then the Peyresourde slapped me right in the face as my body called a time-out almost at the start of the climb. I had attacked it too hard and hadn't learned a thing from my months of training.

We were in the peak of the midday sun and exposed on the side of a mountain in a temperature in the mid-30s. After my initial burst I hit a wall and needed to slow down and recover quickly. I was gulping down water and was close to running out so early into a 15km ascent. Carmen, Nick and Eric started to gain on me and I cursed my naivety in showing off so early into a challenge; then along came a tiny miracle.

I love the French. I love their attitude to cycling. They give so much respect to cyclists and we are actively encouraged on the roads. The quality of the roads are ten times what they are in the UK. The quality of the driving is ten times what it is in the UK. Back home when I am struggling up a hill and cars gather behind, I can guarantee that at least one kindly soul will shout some obscenity asking me to remove myself from the road. It is not uncommon for the odd car to veer dangerously close to my bike to give me a little scare. In France they wait patiently and shout encouragement as we concentrate on one pedal stroke after another.

'Bonne chance mon ami. Oh, and your shirt is very funny.'

They think of us on the roads as well. Dotted along every hill we traversed there were natural water stops cut into the mountain face, or wells on the edge of a pass, and four kilometres in I saw a couple of guys from a faster group filling their water bottles. I was ecstatic and received a fresh burst of energy.

I dunked my head into the mini pond and cooled my core temperature. I filled up my bottles and then waved to the approaching gang that they could fill up here as well. This time, I steadied myself and paced myself into the hill. More tortoise and less hare. If the plan isn't working then I need to change the plan. Never change the goal. A lower gear, slightly faster cadence and find a comfortable pace that would maximise my abilities.

In no time at all I found a rhythm. The hill was consistent and I felt like an intrepid racer from 1910 experiencing this fresh torture for the first time and overcoming it. I had the granny gear on the rear of my bike and I dropped it into one of the lower cogs. I spun my way up the hill, negotiating the tight turns and started to pick off guys who had been riding in much faster groups than me.

I was starting to find my feet. Sweat was pouring off my brow and I was in ecstasy. It wasn't the toughest of hills but it was ground-breaking for me and I took so much encouragement from it. By the time I reached the top I had overtaken 15 riders and been caught by none. Maybe I had found my forte and maybe I was not just someone who would cling on at the back of a peloton. I stopped for a coke with Andy at the top, took a lot of photos to prove that I had scaled that first peak and then set off for the valley that led to La Hourquette d'Ancizan.

The Hourquette is a ten-kilometre climb averaging 8 per cent and it was a stiff challenge at the end of a long day. It led to the fastest and most surreal run into the finish of a stage.

It was still hot as we tackled the bottom of the climb and I knew it would be a challenge to complete my second-ever mountain pass in the Pyrenees. I was breaking very new territory. This time common sense prevailed and I paced myself a little more sensibly at the start.

Again, I found a constant rhythm spinning my wheels in a low gear. No punching out of climbs for me, I am a one-litre diesel and there is no two-litre turbo in my engine. I kicked up the hill and picked off a few more riders, then I had two solitary moments of encouragement.

Firstly, the views were spectacular. 'Will. You. Take. A. Fucking. Look. At. That.' I exclaimed as I rode alongside another cyclist. It turns out he was east European and couldn't understand a word of what I said. No matter, we smiled and pointed at the vista around us. Glorious green-crested peaks peering over the mist with sun-baked hillsides slowly adapting to the influx of caravans who were marking their spots for the week to come. It was heavenly. As was the moment I saw Buddy sat under a tree, face ashen, white as a sheet, ready to give up. I did the decent thing.

'Are you alright mate? Do you need any water or help?' I asked. I didn't like him but I had standards and couldn't leave a fellow Looper in trouble. I was using frustration with him as an energy and a great form of motivation, but I was still a team player. If I was to succeed in this challenge, I had to do it the right way.

'No mate, I'm fine. Just overheated and need to cool down for a bit.'

He had overcooked the two hills and paid the price. The road never lies. I didn't gloat as I went past.

I crested the hill, enjoyed crisps and a drink at the summit and then sped off for a bizarre descent. I had left behind a few guys who I had been trailing for the past ten days plus a few newcomers with fresh legs. I was floating on air, accepting that I may just belong with this crowd. Well, some of them; the guys at the very front were on another level. But I was finding my legs and picking up my pace. Until I nearly ran into a donkey.

It was surreal. There were a few donkeys casually strolling on the road. I was racing along at 60km per hour when I had to brake sharply and navigate my way through the four-legged chums. They were charming and wished me luck. Not like the eerie dolls and dummies in the Fete des Mariolles village. That was like a night of the living dead with the village resplendent with dummies dressed up as corpses. Zombies ready to pounce on unsuspecting cyclo-tourists. I picked up my pace and rode through there a little quicker and towards an evening meal at a restaurant in Bagnères-de-Bigorre.

When I reached the finish, the first coach had already left for our hotel with the very fast riders but I was one of the first people to arrive for the next coach. I sat and had a soft drink with Rich and a very interesting guy called Wim. I hadn't met Wim before because he was always ahead of me, so this was a good chance to learn from a superior cyclist. Instead, we talked about the effects the Tour was taking on our bodies. More specifically the fact that neither of us had had an erection since we arrived in Belgium.

The body is very good at looking after itself and, if necessary, it will shut down some senses or functions to concentrate on what is needed. There are many stories of Olympic rowers or marathon runners crossing the finish line with no sense of smell, taste, hearing and/or feel. They will have pushed themselves to the absolute limit and beyond, and the body allows them to do this by shutting down the senses that are not needed.

It turned out that my body had decided that to allow me to cycle the route of the Tour de France I no longer needed a desire or sensation involving the General. It was a peculiar realisation of how the body works. I still had my taste buds and I wolfed down 2,000 calories worth of pasta, rice, chicken and broccoli. I would need that and more for the Tourmalet, which was around the corner. The wasp stings were killing me.

Buddy finished over two hours behind.

Distance covered: 211km
Time: 9hrs 33mins
Elevation gain: 3,028m
Calories burned: 8,042
Highest speed: 68kph

GREAT THINGS NEVER CAME
FROM COMFORT ZONES – Anon

Chapter 16

13 July 2019, Col du Tourmalet
Overcoming Mountains

COL DU Tourmalet baby. The mountain is epic and is a rite of passage for anyone attempting to ride the Tour de France. Its status is right up there with Mont Ventoux, Alpe d'Huez and the Galibier. In this edition we would be cycling up the Tourmalet and the Galibier in what was labelled the Tour of the high peaks. The Tour has climbed the Tourmalet 83 times and it has a rich legacy of broken forks, epic battles and cries of 'Murderer!' On 13 July 2019 it was time for me to earn my stripes, cycling up the western passage.

In theory this was a shorter stage at 120km, heading south from Tarbes. We would be softened up by first tackling the Col du Soulor before finishing atop the giant of the Pyrenees at a mouth-watering 2,200m above sea level. At no stage would we be riding on the flat. At every point in the stage we would be tested and we would gain the full experience of the Tourmalet's monstrous heritage.

The first time the Tourmalet was ascended in the Tour was way back in 1910. At this stage the mountains were still relatively new to the racers and the quality of the roads was a little worse for wear compared to our smooth, pristine tarmac. They covered a few more kilometres than us as well. In 1910 the stage ran from Luchon to Bayonne and was a not insignificant 326km. As well as the Tourmalet, the riders climbed the Peyresourde, Aspin and Col d'Aubisque. That doesn't bear thinking about. It was uncharted territory.

During the course of my training, I had researched this hurdle incessantly. I found the legend best summarised by an article in the *Cycling Weekly*, 'Cycling's Iconic Places' series:

'Tour founder Henri Desgrange had not even seen the high Pyrenees until the day before the stage, but what he saw then gave cause for concern. Early in the morning of that historic stage Desgrange drove to the top of the Col de Peyresourde and waited. The roads were treacherous, nothing more than mule tracks in places and the scale of the place was overbearing. Desgrange was worried that he had taken his race a step too far. He waited.

'Out of the gloom a lone figure gradually trudged into view. He was pushing a bike, stumbling as he went but determination writ large all over his face. He was covered in mud and at first Desgrange was unable to recognise him. He spoke to the rider, trying to find out where the rest of the peloton was, but so exhausted was the racer he couldn't speak, or possibly refused to speak. He was spent.

'Next along was Octave Lapize, a man whose name is synonymous with the mountain. He would go on to win the 1910 Tour and would later lose his life serving as a pilot in World War One. He spoke to Desgrange. "Murderer," was all he would say. Others followed but Lapize was the first man to reach the summit of the Tourmalet before going on to take the stage. Only 40 riders made it to the finish and the last of them was over seven hours behind Lapize. Desgrange felt vindicated with his choice of route and the Tourmalet has become permanently etched into Tour folklore.'

We would have a mountain to climb if we were going to ride the Tour in 2019. Literally.

The Tourmalet was everything I had signed up for and more. I was like a pig in the proverbial and I felt like I was trudging in the mire when I went up it, but first we had the matter of a time trial on stage 13 and the Soulor at the beginning of stage 14.

I had mixed emotions about the time trials. This was supposedly a fast stage at a mere 27km around the attractive town of Pau. In the Tour itself it would be an opportunity for the professionals to flex their muscles and decide the order of the General Classification riders heading into the mountains. Ideally, I would have loved to have brought my Ceepo Katana TT bike, donned a skin suit (I don't own one) and raced around the route, taking unnecessary risks to beat my PB. In reality the route meant we would have to negotiate a couple of crossroads, some tight turns on busy town roads and roughly one-third of it on cycle paths. There was no real possibility for hammering the course so common sense prevailed and we tootled around at a leisurely pace saving our legs for the hills that would follow. My Garmin notes for the day said as much:

'A gentle little tootle around Pau with a 400m ascent. Very attractive town but in effect a rest day.'

What was significant was that I had shared a room with Stuart for the first time the night before. As we went deeper into the Tour I would come to see more of Stuart. Like many riders, he was too strong for me on the flat but we were fairly consistent with each other in the hills. I became good friends with him.

During the first ten days his wife Jackie had been riding and he had spent a lot of his time cycling alongside her. After she left, he was free to ride his own Tour and he had to adapt to sharing with other Loopers. There are a few things about Stuart that are instantly recognisable. He is a stand-up human being. You know where you stand with him and he has a tremendous sense of right and wrong and a strong moral compass. Stuart is a very loyal friend and a tremendous ally.

What really stood out for me was that he was incredibly organised and we shared a similar level of anal retentiveness. We both maintained epic habits, but Stuart (or his wife Jackie) had come to the Tour prepared. As a result of sharing a room with him we now had antiseptic washing liquid for our kit, sterilising tablets for our water bottles and a multi adaptor to recharge all of our phones, computers and other unnecessary electrical equipment.

There would be no fighting over the sockets or whose turn it was in the bathroom. He was a perfect room-mate and when he asked would I mind sharing with him for the rest of the Tour it was easy to say yes. Stuart doesn't like change and I like epic habits. There was one minor problem. I couldn't understand a word he said.

Stuart has a very strong Scottish brogue and you have to listen very carefully to everything he says. It was like being caught in the middle of an Irvine Welsh novel. I fully expected Begbie to wake me in my sleep each night. At the beginning of our journey, I was happy to have a different room-mate each night. It gave me a chance to meet new people and to learn from each of them. But Stuart brought a sense of order and calm which I benefited from. I would come to rely on him a couple of times in the coming days. A new sense of order and a gentle stage 13 was great preparation for what was to follow.

Distance covered: 29km
Time: 1hr 32mins
Elevation gain: 344m
Calories burned: 1,115
Highest speed: 46kph

Before we could attack the Col du Soulor at the beginning of the titanic stage 14, we had to make it to feed stop one, which was a battle in itself. The road was hardly flat as we cycled the early stretch of a truncated stage and we were thrown a major spanner in the works.

The team who put the signs and arrows out for us on the route did a fantastic job. They would rise at the crack of dawn and drive the whole route ensuring we knew where we were heading. They covered every turn, junction, crossroads, roundabout and obstacle that we would face for 21 days.

They were faultless and second to none and they would have made the experience effortless, if we didn't have to cycle all of it.

At the end of each day, they would then retrace their steps and collect the signs and act as a broom wagon for the last placed riders. They were awesome. What wasn't awesome were the unpredictable factors that came into play. On stage 11 an impish prankster had moved a sign and on stage 13 it was an oblivious van driver.

Heading through the heart of the town of Bénéjacq, slightly north of the Pyrenees, we had to take a left turn off the main road leading through it. This was a sleepy market town cradling the church which was the epicentre of all activity. Just past the church was a bustling, cobblestoned market square and in front of that was our turning. The signs telling us where to go were placed on a lamp post on the corner of the square. We couldn't miss them. Until a market trader parked his van directly in front of the lamp post.

I was lucky that I was riding with Handsome Nick. As well as a set of rippling muscular thighs that powered his bike like pistons on a steam train, he happened to have a pretty decent set of eagle eyes. He spotted the signs from a long way out and he made sure our little group didn't miss the turning. Unfortunately, those riding some way ahead of us had missed it and some poor souls added up to 20km on to their day. It held us all up at feed stop one, which was a chance for me to rest my legs and refuel for the day ahead.

After the missed turn we still had 15km or so to the feed stop and we caught up with one of the leading quick groups. I had forgotten about the time I wasn't allowed to ride with a faster group, until this moment. Inadvertently I had latched on to them again. We were only heading to the first feed stop so surely there wouldn't be a problem this time? I was relieved that there wasn't. Given that I had regularly spent time carrying people from the front of the pack when we headed up to the first break of the day, I was happy to be a wheel sucker and sit at the back of the group. The pace was quite strong but bearable and I drifted into the first tented rest area of the day. It transpired that more than one or two riders had missed that turning. We would have a little time on our hands.

The rider who had gently let me down in the first week was polite. I was told that it was nice that I was able to ride with them and good on me for keeping up. I felt a little patronised and am sure it wasn't deliberate. It was expected that I wouldn't be heading out with their train. Through the whole of the Tour, I met hundreds of very strong and generous riders and I learned from all of them. Just 1 per cent not seeing eye to eye with me was more than tolerable. All roads led to Paris and I was here to ride my own race.

The feed stop itself was stupendous. The sun gently warmed our limbs and we were in the shadow of the Col du Soulor. A large and impossible evergreen beast that was in turns imposing, threatening and yet so heart-achingly beautiful. I was seduced and frightened all at the same time. Its arcing green peak fought through a gentle mist leaving a glow on the verdant hillside. We would attack that straight out of the rest area. Elitist little groups be damned, the road never lies.

The Soulor is 13km in length and a consistent 7 per cent ramp almost all the way. Making our way out of the feed stop, we dropped down into a cooling valley with the scent of rainwater wafting through our nostrils before heading up the consistent, meandering roadway. The profusion of trees surrounding us created damp shadows and played havoc with the satellite signals on our computers. That was of little concern; my goal was to reach the top with enough energy to attack the Tourmalet later in the day.

Given that the col was so early in the stage and because we had the benefit of an extended rest, both from the food break and the easier day beforehand, my legs felt fresh. I dropped into an easy gear and tried to spin my way up the hill. I had learned my lessons from two days before and I knew how to get the best out of my legs. Preserving my energy and not getting carried away would be big concerns throughout the Tour.

I tend to sit on the front of my saddle when I pedal up hill and I try to keep my back straight. When I tire my back hunches and I lose some of my technique as my core muscles weaken. I tend to ride hills half seated and half out of the saddle, rising as the road steepens in an effort to maintain rhythm and keep my muscles fresh. It rarely works and I learn to embrace the suffering. The Soulor was an exercise in pleasure.

From the bottom of the climb there were plenty of riders ahead of me, most of them big and strong. I aimed to pick them off one at a time and use this to break up the monotony along the way. It made the climb go quicker as I passed a new rider on average every 500m. My internal dialogue remained internal for once. I chose to focus on small details and not on berating my lack of strength.

By fixating on the minutiae of a rider's make-up I could focus on that foible and make it my primary goal to reach the guy with a white shirt, or rippling calf muscles, or annoying Trek bike, or quaint aluminium frame bike. I tapped into a little bit of annoyance, I wouldn't go so far as to call it rage, just enough to give me a tunnel vision. All I could see was an offending piece of kit and that would give me a clear path to my next goal. I broke a big climb down into small chunks and I fixated on the tiny goal ahead of me. I was a little schizophrenic with my internal dialogue but it took my mind off the pain in my legs and the lack of wind in my sails.

I've got you white shirt. You're mine: 50 more yards and you will be dust. I'm coming for you white shirt. Come on Ceri, keep the rhythm and you'll sail past him. He's in sight. He's in touching distance. Almost there. Got him. Up yours white shirt. I managed to keep it all to myself and the hill passed a little quicker than I had planned.

'Alright mate, how are you? Good job. You're looking good. See you on the other side buddy.' The focus on the negative instantly gone. White shirt was my best friend again. Now for the Trek bike. *I'm coming for you Trek bike.*

In all I overtook 24 Loopers and none went past me. There were plenty who were still a dot, far away in the distance but I was finding my place in the mountains and it was further up in the pecking order than it had been on the flatter stages. I was able to break the hill down into 500m stretches and did not need to look any further than that. It was nice and consistent and so was my cadence. That was a decent start to the day.

With four kilometres to go there was a brief but nasty 20 per cent ramp which delivered us on to 3.5km of 9 per cent riding. The finale is why the Soulor needs to be recognised as a mountain in its own right and not only the hors d'ouevres to a more treacherous beast. It was a punishing fight through beautifully rugged terrain, green moss lands similar to the Brecon Beacons at the summit, standing proud under the gaze of the rocky peaks ahead.

What I didn't appreciate were the ceaseless false-flat roads that lead to Luz-Saint-Sauveur, the base town before we attacked the Tourmalet. They were never-ending and I was lost on them on my own once again, caught in a void between forced speed and sluggish self-doubt. Maybe an elite little group would have been helpful right then?

I guess it was a mixture of a large peloton so fragmented by the first hill and some riders feeling fresh where others were already wasted from their efforts, because rarely did I get any shelter on the open roads that led to the small skiing town. That approach was far more difficult than the Soulor and the buffeting wind took its toll. I did latch on to a couple of small groups but one or the other of us would be dropped. No consistency could be found and my legs were suffering as we stopped for lunch.

Lunch was ideally situated in a car park at the base of the Col du Tourmalet. It wasn't attractive but it was in a bustling little tourist town, more famous for its winter sports, which afforded us a few very welcome amenities. There was a proper set of toilets, rather than the usual bush, and a very tempting souvenir shop with some stylish-looking Tourmalet cycle tops. I had my eye on one of those but there was no way that I would tempt fate by purchasing one before I had reached the top.

I overfed at the lunch stop. I was apprehensive about what lay ahead and I wanted as much energy as possible. I ate too much. I had a fizzy drink and my body disagreed. Never had I been so relieved that we had some public amenities nearby. It turns out that I wasn't the only one. Nerves had got the better of a few of us.

I could put it off no longer, I had to attack the longest climb of my life and ascend the Col du Tourmalet. Time to follow in the footsteps of Lapize and every other intrepid winner who has scaled that mountain.

The Tourmalet is roughly 20km long with an average gradient of just above 7 per cent. We were approaching from the west side and the air was about to get thin. Not only was the distance new territory for me but so too was the altitude. I have cycled steep hills but never this high. I was intimidated, yet after the relative joy on the Soulor, quietly confident.

Approaching the town of Luz-Saint-Sauveur was daunting. The beast was looming above. A giant of a challenge, its rich heritage tormenting. The summit was barely visible through the thin cloud wafting over a sunny green peak. No right-thinking individual would attempt to scale this monster, yet without doing so I would fail. Scaling this mountain was a necessary road to Paris. It was a hill and I had to get over it.

At first the route wasn't that sexy. It felt more like a false flat as I trudged out on my own, through the town and gradually up the side of the mountain. For the first five kilometres I couldn't see the summit or the meandering paths and neither did I see another cyclist on the road.

I was caught in a desert of barren climbing, with only my demons for company. I needed someone to talk to, or at least someone in front to focus on. Anything to take my mind off the slow torture. I am collegiate. I am a team player and I am a talker. Company frequently brings out the best in me. At that rate I felt I would never make it.

I contemplated easing up and possibly stopping to wait for someone behind. I looked back down the hill and saw nothing. If I was going to surmount this goal, I would have to defeat it on my own. Being Welsh, we have the patron saint of David and this David was facing his very own Goliath. Substitute a slingshot for two wheels and I was fortunate that my giant was going nowhere. A bit like my legs.

About seven kilometres in I passed through the town of Barèges and saw my first cyclists. That had been a long time to ride on my own. They were sat in a café having coffee and ice cream. I was beckoned in but I have my rules and my epic habits to maintain. I have never ever walked or stopped on a hill and I wasn't going to start that habit on the Tourmalet.

For me the view changed and it was no less intimidating: 13 more kilometres of climbing, gradually working their way like a snake up a barren green hillside. Ironman Wales was a walk in the park compared to this. It hurt my neck looking up but now I had some riders in front I could focus on. There was a group of three. I didn't know them, they had joined up with us a couple of days ago, but they knew what they were doing and they had fresh legs. *Catch them Ceri. You can let them carry you some of the way.*

I had a new focus and my eyes locked on the rider in the rear, a black-and-red BMC racing kit, I think. That would do for me. They compete with Geraint and this meant I was now representing Geraint Thomas. I couldn't let G down. I was his mountain domestique. *I'm coming for you BMC. You are mine. Let's do this.*

The Tourmalet was no longer a 13km trudge uphill in treacle: now it was a steady battle to bridge the gap of 500m to the trio in front. That I could do. I stopped looking at the misty green hillside and was oblivious to the majestic beauty of my uphill foe. I saw only the black-and-red kit. I was on them in no time. Time to ease up and let them carry me a little.

I had found a new rhythm and a slightly higher cadence and I dare not waste it. I kept on going and sidled past them. One of the three gave chase but in a matter of 300m he was off my tail. I was in my happy place and I was climbing again. I loved it. Loved it. Loved it. I was in a bizarre sporting nirvana.

I would never be the best rider in any team but in that moment I was the very best version of myself and I liked what I was seeing. I believed that not only was I a match for the Tourmalet, but that I could make it all the way to Paris. Self-belief is a superpower but this was no time to get ahead of myself.

Another five kilometres passed and not once did I regret not stopping for an ice cream. I didn't have the time nor the energy to do so. It was hot but I had enough water and the forecast said it was going to cool down a little. I passed six or seven more riders and only one passed me. He took me really easily. It was a little soul-destroying but I tried to strike up a conversation anyway. Turns out he was a local club cyclist out for a training ride. That made me feel better. He knew this hill. He was familiar with it and more importantly he hadn't gone through what I had in the previous two weeks.

In my pidgin French I explained that we were cycling 'tous le Tour de France, un semaine avant La Grande Boucle'. He called me crazy and that made me feel good about myself. He carried me for a kilometre before dropping me with the ease of a Harley Davidson racing a cyclist. (There were a few of those machines on the mountain as well.) But that was okay because it had used up another kilometre and now I could see Colin.

Colin and I had swapped places on the hills a few times. He was another rider who was stronger than me on the flat but someone I could keep pace with going uphill. We were now into 9 per cent territory and it was only going to get steeper. I had a clear focus. I bridged over to Colin and struck up a conversation that was short.

He had headphones on with music to drown out the suffering. Given his choice of tunes I think that was torture enough. He was going through a rough patch. I offered to work with him but he told me to ride my own journey. Top man. I left him but he never went away. Where I had used others as a carrot in the past, now I had become the hare and he was the greyhound chasing after me. I developed a lead of about 60 to 80m but it never went further than that. We overtook five or six others but he was a bad itch I couldn't get rid of; he wouldn't leave me alone.

All the while the slope kept hitting us hard, the more dramatic the scenery the more violent the incline, back and forth as we ground our way up the savagely primaeval landscape. The misty green was becoming a more barren grey and the air was getting thinner with every pedal stroke. This affects some people greatly. I was lucky in that I found the thin air to be quite refreshing. That smell just before a huge rain storm hits was how it felt. Cold, fresh and thinning.

I have a theory here and I think I benefited from it. I suffer with my sinuses and had operations as a youngster to help sort them out. They made no difference. I had my adenoids cleared as a seven-year-old and I was called back in a few days later to repeat the operation. I had record levels of mucus as a child. I will always be susceptible to colds, flu and a build-up of mucus. It isn't pleasant, but it ensures I maintain good habits. I avoid foods that hinder me, such as citrus fruits and dairy products. Oh, I miss cheese, but it is not healthy when I am in a bank of training.

But as the air gradually became thinner, so too did the catarrh in my sinuses. I felt the small amount of mucus dissipate and my sinuses felt clear and free. Contrary to how others were feeling I was opening up my airways and I could take oxygen on board. I felt like I belonged up there at altitude.

Every switchback I glanced back and still Colin was there. The gap never grew and he avoided eye contact. He was toying with me. I would dig in and put in a burst when I was out of sight but, true to form, at the next switchback, there he was again. I just couldn't cut the cord. He was very impressive. I could have done with his company to make the climb easier but I think he preferred to listen to Abba rather than chat with me.

Switchback after switchback he was there goading me with his rhythm, frequently gaining on me. Again, I contemplated easing up. Again, I refused to waste a good rhythm and put that thought to the back of my mind; I may never get it back. Then we hit the final kick in the teeth.

Delivering a killer blow, the final kilometre took us to kickers averaging above 11 per cent. After 19km of difficult ascending we now had to rise out of our saddles and dig ever deeper for the finale. Colin still wouldn't leave me and I could see him planning a cheeky attack. I should really have focused on what was ahead, but I had to get rid of the itch.

He rose out of his saddle and gradually picked up his pace. No chance sunshine. I did the same and pushed hard, stamping on the pedals, no longer turning them but grinding out a lumbering pace. I was in the last 500m, four, three, two.

'Come on Ceri,' I heard in the distance. It was Handsome Nick. Holy crap, I was close to riding with the big boys. I still hadn't caught up with the team-mate who wouldn't let me ride with a lead group, but cresting the summit to see the laughing face of a good friend like Nick was plenty of success for me.

'Well done mate. I've been watching you. That was impressive.' Heady praise indeed, but Nick is a positive soul.

'Hang on,' I said. I turned and gave Colin a hug. He had ridden up La Planche with me and he had now tormented me on the Tourmalet. He laughed when I asked him if it was deliberate. He said that he had seen me looking over my shoulder at every switchback and decided to keep me within about 50m. Turns out he had done us both a big favour. Our focus had been on each other and together we had scaled one big old primitive mountain.

The view looking back was awe-inspiring: grey lines weaving their way up the side of a long and steep mountain, misty green with challenges faced and dreams shattered. If I hadn't been so exhausted it would have taken my breath away.

We queued up to take obligatory photos with the statue of Octave Lapize and felt an odd kinship with the intrepid pioneer. He may well have been right. Murderers indeed. But we had lived to tell the tale. Col du Tourmalet baby.

The gift shop was rubbish. So was the hotel we stayed in on top of the mountain.

Distance covered: 124km
Time: 6hrs 55mins
Elevation gain: 3,688m
Calories burned: 5,872
Highest speed: 68kph

LET THE FIRE INSIDE YOU BURN
BRIGHTER THAN THE STORM
OUTSIDE – Joshua Graham

Chapter 17

14 July 2019, Foix Prat d'Albis
Rage

I WASN'T that angry. I was simply tapping into a form of rage as a means of motivation. My dream was on the line and there was no way I was going to fail. I used whatever tools were at my disposal and, in that moment, rage helped me ride a little quicker.

The hotel at the top of the Tourmalet was like something out of *The Shining*. It had a lot to answer for. Le Loop had decided to give us the treat of staying on top of the iconic mountain, which was a brilliant idea in principle. The hotel itself left a lot to be desired and it also meant a very early start the following day for a long day of back-to-back riding in the Pyrenees. Tour de France, baby.

The hotel was perched on the side of the hilltop, not far from the summit. The great benefit was that we didn't have far to travel after we had climbed the Tourmalet. After such a monumental effort, that was a great relief. Two or three kilometres downhill and Nick and I were at the head of the queue for a massage.

I had time to give Trigger a clean and then let the physio pound on me and hammer the lactic acid out of my aching limbs. That pain was very welcome. While I was waiting for the physio I got chatting with Butch. He is from Hawaii and an awesome rider and epic human being. He had ridden at a high level in the nineties and he made what we were doing look effortless. I loved watching him ride because it gave me something to aspire to.

Butch had joined up with us for the mountain stages from day 12 onwards. He told me the story of his first day with us and how he had put the wrong cassette on his bike. It meant he rode up two Pyrenean mountains with an 11-25 gear ratio. For non-cyclists that is like trying to ride a moped up the hill with just your legs for power. It was a schoolboy error and he had made it look like a breeze. There were some characters on this Tour and I wanted to soak up as much of it as possible. I promised myself that I would no longer moan about my struggles uphill on a very light carbon fibre bike. I couldn't make the same promise about the hotel.

Actually, I quite liked it. It had character. Being an ex-holiday rep, I have seen all manner of holiday accommodation and have worked in much worse than this one. To be fair to the resort, they do not usually cater for large groups in the summer months. This was a winter ski-resort and we were intruding on their rest and they did the best they could.

The rooms creaked and I opted for the camp bed and let Stuart take the big double bed. It looked magnanimous but we had to rise at 5am so I didn't want to get too comfortable and resent getting out of a comfy space. We were sharing with three other guys in an adjoining room and I pity the maid who cleaned up after we left.

Before we had checked in, videos were being circulated on the WhatsApp group of the tap water flowing a deep shade of brown. It was frightening but was just a bit of scaremongering. After a couple of minutes, the pipes ran through and the water was fine for showering and drinking. I desperately hoped it was fine. My bidons were filled with the tap water for the following day's ride.

We left the hotel shortly after 6.30am for the transfer to the start of the stage, tired and grateful that Jack Nicholson hadn't burst into the room screaming 'Here's Johnny'. I exaggerate but there were a few who didn't sleep well. Given that we would stay in something in the region of 20 different hotels, there had to be one that was the stuff of nightmares. It gave us stories to tell as part of the adventure and it wasn't the reason for a difficult stage 15. That was the late start.

The transfer should have taken two hours and we should have been cycling by 9am at the latest. But we were held up, the journey took longer than predicted and we didn't start the stage until roughly 11am. It was a long and hilly stage from Limoux to Foix Prat d'Albis, covering 185km (plus an extra descent added on at the end) and climbing four hills with a total of 4,700m of ascent. Three of those hills were category ones. This was not a day for the faint-hearted; this would prove to be a true war of attrition for even the best amongst us.

I had a plan for the day and that instantly went out the window. I wanted to take it easy and ride with Carmen,

Kelly, Canadian Ian and a few others. We wanted to help and support some of those that were slower than us. This was an ideal stage to give a little back. But with the late start, nerves were frayed and the road was uneven.

I settled into a group with some usual friends being the Canadians, Stuart and Eric; a great group of people that I was comfortable riding with. Some others would take a shortcut and miss the stretch to the first feed stop to give themselves a head start. That was not on the agenda for the gang I was riding with. We were all determined to ride the full route to Paris, come what may.

Carmen was in a difficult headspace at the start of the stage. She likes everything to be organised and in its place. She puts a lot of pressure on herself to be the best she can be and she needed to work it out. She was beating herself up before we had started. Stuart, Eric, Ian and I put our heads down and rode. Her disposition worked in our favour because Carmen settled into time-trial mode and we struggled to hold her wheel for long periods. She didn't want company or the inane banter, she wanted to find the right frame of mind to be the best version of herself and she did that by riding into her happy place. Impressive stuff.

After surmounting the first hill of the day at seven kilometres, we formed our group and Emily joined in. My legs rather pleasingly felt quite fresh after the previous day's efforts and the long coach ride. No real power in them but a little energy to pep my spirits; again I think Katy was the real hero there after the pummelling she had given me on the Tourmalet. We established a decent tempo that would see us through to the end of a long day.

As we rode, we seemed to pick up more riders. We were riding strong and there were a few cyclists new to Le Loop who were drifting. I invited them on to ride with us. Stuart then became a little cross when they refused to take their turn on the front. We had a strong bunch which had grown to 15 or so, but it was the same five who were doing all the work: Carmen, Eric, Stuart, Ian and myself. It was frustrating but I let it go. I had to because once again I would be stranded.

Running along a fast section of flattish road, roughly 15km from the second feed stop I picked up a puncture. I shouted 'stopping' and let everyone past. It didn't take long to fix. Emily offered to stay behind and help but realistically there was nothing she could do. As I ran my finger along the inside of the tyre, I felt two nails. Just as well that I had checked because I would have had multiple punctures for the rest of the day. I was sorted in five minutes and caught up with the group as they were approaching the feed station, feeling half-decent.

Straight out of the feed stop we hit the bottom of the first categorised climb, the Port de Lers at just over 11km. We were now taking these in our stride. Carmen was uncomfortable at the beginning of the climb and asked to be left alone. Ian and I ignored her. We rode alongside her as she repeatedly told us to leave her be. We didn't say a word and let her find her own rhythm, until we passed a group of two who were up ahead.

'One and two,' I counted, checking them off for my benefit. So it continued: Ian and I counting off the riders we were consistently picking off. By the time we had crested the top and rolled into the lunch stop we had overtaken 14 riders.

Carmen on a bad day was still dropping people on the hills and she and Canadian Ian were ridiculously good company. Despite their funny accents. At lunch everything changed.

A couple of Facebook reports later that night said that 'rags were being lost' at this point. That was a bit of an exaggeration but the mood changed and Stuart and I were a little peeved. Emily had been told to let us know that there would be a cut-off time at the bottom of the final climb, the Foix Prat d'Albis, for health and safety reasons. We had to be there at a given time to make sure that we were not riding up the hill in the dark. It made sense. It made us upset.

The reason we were four hours behind schedule was because we were late setting off. I was a little upset in that I was trying to enter into the spirit of Le Loop and was going out of my way to help other cyclists in our tour. I wanted to contribute to the whole spirit of the event and I felt that I was being penalised for it. It wasn't particularly fair. I could quite easily have gone off on my own at the start of the day or with a faster group and I would have been close to that final climb by that point. I felt for Emily because our reaction wasn't pleasant.

Both Stuart and I were piqued. We have a similar sense of right and wrong and we felt hard done by. I explained to Emily that I was going up that final hill come what may. They could send a taxi to bring me back down in the dark, but I was going to finish the stage. I hoped that I had explained the point politely. My whole year of training, preparation, fundraising and dreaming was in jeopardy and I was upset. The look on Emily's face said that I had probably overstepped the mark. She is so warm, generous, kind and without ego. She is a sporting and humane hero of mine and I felt awful. I finished my lunch of rice and beans very quickly. I had a small shot of coffee and asked Stuart what he was doing.

'I'm with you,' I think he said. I still couldn't understand him. I sought out Carmen and Ian and they told me to go. They didn't want to hold anyone back and they supported their friends. Brilliant people. I picked up Trigger and sped off down a hairy descent with Stuart hot on my heels.

I wasn't angry. I was frustrated. Stuart shouted to me to calm down. That wasn't necessary, but I knew the next hill was a brutal challenge before we attacked the final summit finish and I needed an energy to tap into. I exaggerated the anger in me. I fuelled that fire and I fed on it. I was seething but at the same time I was deadly focused.

Generally, I am a great big scaredy-cat on descents. They are not natural or comfortable for me and like the swim in Ironman they are something to both improve and to survive. My concentration was heightened, almost laser-like, and my senses were on red alert. I took risks that I wouldn't usually dare dream of. I was no Deano, and Stuart comfortably held my wheel, but we flew, taking a few others on the way until we hit a wall.

The Mur de Péguère to be precise. A nine-kilometre climb with a gradient of 8 per cent, but a torturous three-kilometre stretch where that wall averaged out above 18 per cent. These climbs were a brilliant combination to shake up the General Classification in the main race and the Mur shook us to our core. At the bottom of the hill Stuart was shouting at me.

'Ceri, take it easy. Don't blow yourself up yet. There is a long way to go.' I ignored him. I was on a mission and I wasn't going to lose this burst of adrenaline. I was holding on to this feeling for as long as possible. Even under pressure, Stuart was thinking of others.

It was a cooler day than usual. Slightly overcast as we headed into the late afternoon. The Mur de Péguère was a single track, narrow road with uneven tarmac in places. It was long, straight and steep. We saw a couple of riders walking by the side of the road. Not me. Never. This was like the Hean Castle hill, leading out of Wisemans Bridge on the Ironman Wales route. I had grown up on that hill. The Mur was ten times longer.

Trees lined both sides of the hill. We couldn't see the beautiful terrain around us; we could only feel the gentle breeze and the cool air blowing into our faces. The immediate road ahead was all that mattered.

It took forever. I had dropped into my bottom gear and was out of the saddle for much of the steepest part, stamping on the pedals again. It was like climbing stairs on an escalator running in the opposite direction, knowing that I was moving forward but feeling like I was going backwards. I very slowly caught up with Scottish Brian. He was weaving across the road. There were still two kilometres remaining on this ramp. As I approached, he asked me what I was doing. I told him I was struggling.

'No. Are you sitting or coming through?' I told him I was coming through and he told me to get a move on and make it quick. Fair enough. There wasn't much room on the road. I surged. Another burst of effort and I felt the rage spur me

Do what it takes to cross the line – courtesy Desmond Stone

Le Grand Depart

Le Grand Depart 2

Road art

Refuelling

La Planche des Belles Filles

Tourmalet

Octave Lapize and me

Survived a crash

Battle scars and tan lines

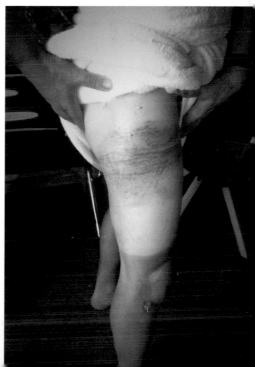

Pain

Col de L'Iseran – Like cycling in treacle
– courtesy foxphotos.fr

Col de L'Iseran – Eventually at the summit

Col de L'Iseran – my Jour Sans – courtesy foxphotos.fr

Reward

Le Loop – I would have achieved nothing without their superb organisation

Thin air

Oh yeah

A birthday I will never forget

Last stop Paris

A team effort

Success

on. I was wasting matches. In no time Brian was behind me and I maintained that burst of energy. I caught Jonathon towards the top. He was funny. He was delirious. He had caught my internal dialogue on La Planche des Belles Filles and his was equally as daft near the top of the Mur.

'Pixies. They're dancing. Look on the side of the road. Can you see them? Pixies dancing. Why won't they help us. Oh, they are beautiful.'

'Keep going Jon, you've got this. Almost there.'

'Wait. Who's that? Oh Ceri, didn't see you there. I wasn't talking, was I?' I chuckled and the energy from that gave me a lift. We all had to deal with this dark spot in the best way we could. Be it anger, laughter, fantasy or sheer determination. I crested the top and knew I would make it but I still attacked the descent. No point in wasting the rage.

The descent was longer than what we had surmounted but not quite as steep. There was a chance to refuel at the final feed stop near the bottom. Coke and crisps for me and I was off. There was no hanging around with a deadline looming. As I approached the town of Foix the road levelled out and Stuart caught up with me. Absolute legend. He had ridden through some pain and was there to join me on the beginning of the final climb of the day.

As we hit the bottom slopes anger faded and a cheerier delirium enveloped us. We rode together for a little while, setting a healthy tempo on the 12km hill, tackling a consistent rise of 7 per cent. That was a doddle after what we had covered in the past few days.

The temperature dropped and the wind picked up. This climb was not sheltered like the Mur, this was in the open and we were subject to the elements. The light was fading. Stuart set a decent pace for the first few kilometres and then pulled to one side for a comfort break. I pushed on.

On this hill there was plenty of encouragement and my mood lifted. The lead riders were gliding back down the slope on the same road that we were travelling up. Without fail every one of them shouted some form of morale-boosting toast. I loved Le Loop and these people were on another level. I felt like I was part of an exclusive club and there was no way I was going to let them down.

I was now riding for a team and I picked up a further incentive to succeed. One final focus for the remainder of the stage. The sun was starting to fall and I wanted to reach the summit to catch the sunset. Just the hill and those winds to navigate.

This was a strange climb. Plenty of switchbacks as it writhed its way up the southerly edge of the hillside. Splendid open verdant terrain on a smooth and unyielding road, casting panoramic views across the Pyrenees. It was stunning and by some peculiar twist of fate I was arriving at the best time of day for a glowing ember vista.

The wind was either right in our faces or immediately on our backs. It helped me glide up some sections and forced herculean battles on others, but the time passed swiftly. I reached the top of my mountain bang on time. The sun set as I crossed the finish line and the signpost marking the summit of Foix Prat d'Albis. What a stupendous ride. One of the best of my life. Two in two days. I was now in celebratory mood. Rage had subsided and led to a calm satisfaction. All I had to do was navigate my way back down to the bottom.

The descent was horrendous and treacherous. I had a light that was next to useless. I joined a group of five and we shared what lights we had. We crawled down the tight road, turning back on ourselves as we meandered lost in the dark night. For a short while we were lucky. A car pulled up behind us and guided us with his beam. It was incredibly generous and not something British cyclists are accustomed to. It turned a very long descent into just a difficult one.

On the way down we passed Eric, Andy and Ian who were still making their way to the top. They were borderline heroic and their resolve was a sight to behold. We shouted encouragement. They really impressed me with their determination to make it all the way to Paris. They shouted congratulations in return.

We assigned each other numbers and counted ourselves off on each corner. Stuart had caught up with us and he took the lead. It was cold and our fingers were getting numb. I hadn't allowed for this in my training. It is just as well that I am from Wales. The conditions were like a summer ride in Pembrokeshire.

It was late when we arrived back into Foix. We were cold, hungry and thirsty. We were fed, watered and warmed up. We dropped our bikes off and caught the bus to the next hotel. Thanks to Kenny I had a room all to myself. Kenny was sharing with Rhys throughout the Tour but for some reason he had booked and paid for a room to himself on this evening. After checking in I went to my room. I was down to share with Rhys. I banged on the door and shouted, 'Hello big boy,' to be greeted with a sleepy-eyed Welshman in pyjamas.

'What's going on?' he asked. I told him we were sharing and he replied that Kenny was already there. Sure enough, Kenny was already in his single bed half asleep. That was quick. I went back to reception to see what had happened, to be told that Kenny had made a mistake. I was given his pre-booked room. Result. I had a room to myself and we had a rest day in Nîmes the following day.

Two epic days under my belt and they were two of the most eventful days of riding in my life. Foix Prat d'Albis will live long in the memory. It could have been one of the worst days of riding ever, but it turned into one of the most memorable. I had learned how to use different energies to fulfil my goals and I had produced one of my favourite rides ever. I felt great and I loved the Pyrenees.

Before I went to my room, I found Emily and apologised for my outburst earlier in the day. I had been wrong. My intentions were good but my tone was wrong. She had been nothing but a guiding light for me and I had repaid her with rudeness. I was genuinely sorry.

But I had smashed the stage. I wasn't angry. I had found a way to harness another energy. From rage to delirium to exhaustion. I felt like nothing could stop me now, apart from a really unfortunate or catastrophic accident.

I slept like a contented baby in my own private room. Thank you, Kenny.

Distance covered: 200km
Time: 10hrs 25mins
Elevation gain: 4,700m
Calories burned: 8,600
Highest speed: 71kph

Chapter 18

16 July 2019, Nîmes
Resilicnce

ACCIDENTS HAPPEN in slow motion. As a general rule you don't suddenly wake up on your back wondering what the hell just happened. Time seems to stand still. You see the crash happening and you see a way of preventing it. It just doesn't happen quickly enough. It is like a bad dream where you are chased by a monster. It gradually gets closer and closer to you and, no matter how hard you run, you cannot get away. And then you find yourself falling. This happened 40km outside of Nîmes.

My hands were on the top of my handlebars, close enough to grab the brakes. I remember the shout of 'stopping' and the bike in front doing exactly that as it turned in front of me. I saw where the point of impact was going to be. I saw there was no chance of avoiding it. I screamed something along the lines of 'watch out!' and I hit the brakes.

I still see the light-grey concrete from a driveway edging closer towards me. It took forever for me to hit the deck but when I did, it was with a big thump. It hurt. I was momentarily lost. Lying on my back I heard the shouts and the screeching of brakes. Fear flashed through my mind. Pain was the last thing I thought of. Maybe that was the adrenaline kicking in or maybe it was a sign of where my priorities lay.

Was the crash the fault of the guy in front? No. Emphatically so. He had a puncture and he needed to stop. Did he stop too soon and without warning? He gave a warning shout before he braked. He did all that he could. Do I blame him? Absolutely not. I was behind him and he did nothing wrong. So, this begs the question, were we cycling too fast? Categorically no. Was I too close? Possibly. I was 6 to 12 inches away from his wheel. Our wheels were not overlapping, Emily made sure that never happened; we had epic habits in that regard. After 16 days of riding together we should be able to ride in close proximity to each other. Could it have been avoided? Possibly. Was I at fault? I ask myself this all the time. My natural instinct is to prove that I am not, before I take absolute responsibility. I don't think I was. Was it simply one of those racing incidents that can happen? I think so, yes. Was I hurt? I was the worse for wear and bore the brunt of the fall.

I hit my head very hard and my helmet saved the day. Whatever you do, always wear a helmet, kids. Without mine I would have ended up in hospital. That is a cold truth that hurts. I had banged both of my hips and they would become very badly bruised. I had ripped my shorts to bits on the right-hand side. One pair less to clean I suppose and a dubious souvenir of a great adventure. I had badly cut my right knee, my right elbow and somehow both shoulders. My sunglasses were smashed to bits. My Garmin computer survived but took a few minutes to find. I would need to buy a new helmet that night at a local store, once we had arrived back at the hotel.

Fatima had called the Le Loop organisers and they were outstanding. They were better than that. They were with us within ten minutes to help get me back on the road.

The issue with a crash is not the physical pain but the emotional and mental torture. I was in a Le Loop bubble and I did all I could to remain in it. I was initially angry, mostly at myself for crashing. I was embarrassed and ashamed. I was worried about what all of the other riders thought of me. I desperately wanted to be accepted with these great athletes and to be recognised as a Le Loop cyclist. I so wanted to belong to this elite group of human beings. Embarrassment and shame. I couldn't shake them off.

Then came fear. The thought of not making it to Paris flashed before my eyes. The hours spent training. The cost of the whole adventure, the effort put into raising all of the sponsorship, my whole life for a year had been focused on this one lifelong dream. It wasn't just an adventure. It was everything. If I couldn't finish the stage that would be my Tour over. I wouldn't be able to live with myself. I had to do whatever it took to make sure I cycled back into Nîmes.

I gingerly rose to my feet. I could feel all of my limbs and I could move my arms and legs. That was a relief. No pain in my back, that would come six months later. I walked around and swore a little bit. I could move and I wanted to get back on to my bike. Then I thought of the guy in front of me.

'Are you alright mate?' I asked. He was sheepish but okay and his bike worked. Time to look at mine.

I picked up Trigger and apologised to her. The handlebars were askew, the brakes needed to be straightened and the pedals were intact. A cursory glance said the frame was in one piece. Unlike my shorts that were in bits in a small pool of blood on the concrete. I spun the wheels around. The front was fine. The back wheel didn't budge. It was jammed into the rear derailleur, the bar holding it was bent. The mechanic would need to sort that out.

Carmen and Fatima dragged me across the road to get some shade and some water in me. They ordered me to sit. I preferred to stand and to keep moving. I feared that if I didn't my body would seize. Stay mobile and keep thinking. Le Loop were with us in no time. We sent the others on their way but four key friends stayed with me. I will forever be in their debt.

The Le Loop team went to work like the very well-oiled machine that they are. Yogi, all-round food and mechanical expert, picked my bike up and instantly fixed the bracket and a few other problems. I liked Yogi. He had high standards and could be curt, but he had a great sense of humour and he did things right. He was always great with me and, in that moment, he kept my dream alive.

He straightened the brakes, the front wheel and the rear derailleur. He told me it would need to be replaced that evening but the bike would get me back to the finish line. Only, Yogi wouldn't let me ride off just yet. Quite rightly he wanted to make sure I hadn't suffered a concussion and that I was fit enough to ride. If I wasn't then in my mind I would walk with the bike. I had a goal to realise but it would be easier if I was fit enough to cycle. Cue the physio.

'Okay Ceri, how many fingers am I holding up?'

'Two.' Followed by four, three and then a tricky eight.

'What is your middle name?'

Eric, quick as a flash, said: 'Tell him he's Geraint Thomas and put him back on his bike.' Exactly what we needed.

'Desmond,' followed by a few chuckles. 'But that's my dad's name,' then sheepish silence.

'What day of the week is it?'

'I haven't got a clue. I know it is stage 16 and we have been riding for 16 days with two rest days. But day and date no idea.'

'Where is the finish line today?'

'Nîmes,' and that was the end of the interrogation. She checked that I had no blurred vision, no headache, no drowsiness and she gave me a gentle shove to check my balance. I was given the all-clear but ordered to visit the doctor that night.

I lied. I had a splitting headache. I figured that some exercise would help clear it up.

I rode with Eric, Stuart, Andy and Carmen back to the finish. Eric and Stuart in front setting a steady pace. Andy next, making sure I was okay and Carmen behind taking great care of me. I apologised constantly. They never let me take the lead and their pacing was bang on; quick enough to get us back in time for me to sort bike, kit and doctor out, but at the same time steady enough to ensure I wasn't under any pressure. Remarkably we covered the ground without incident and finished ahead of a few groups who had ignored Carmen after her puncture at the very beginning of the stage. Eric never did get the ice cream he had been searching for.

There are two types of cyclists. Those who have had an accident and those who are about to have one. Every one of the Loopers had suffered some form of crash over the years, many much more dramatic than mine. They put me at ease. The team of Loopers lifted my spirits and really helped me through the next couple of days. Incredible bunch.

That evening at dinner I was given the Chapeau award for cycling excellence. I was very sheepish and didn't feel it was deserved. I was recognised as a team player because I had gone to help Carmen with her puncture. I felt the four who stayed with me when I was in peril were far more deserving. I was very grateful to be honoured. I felt that possibly I did belong with these epic people.

Over the course of the past couple of days all extreme facets of my very frail human traits had been exposed by the Tour. The road truly does not lie. I had lost my cheery, calm demeanour on the way to Prat d'Albis. I had shown my gallant side by helping out a friend in need and then a careless side by crashing. I took full responsibility for my actions and faults and I guess that was appreciated. Most pleasing for me, I had stared adversity square in the face and I had persevered. My powers of resilience were intact and my dream was still alive.

I truly believe that if you want to meet the one person who can make your life better you need to look in the mirror. I had done that and liked what I saw staring back at me with a massive shiner on my right eye. The same couldn't be said for Trigger.

After dinner I worked into the night with the mechanics. These folks were as awesome as the rest of the Le Loop operation. Every night they worked into the early hours repairing bikes, tweaking gears, fixing brakes, swapping cassettes, etc. They were always generous and good-humoured and I learned a lot from them.

We needed to ensure that the rear derailleur was okay and that the rear mech hanger was straight. As we gave Trigger a cursory once-over it was obvious that the rear seat stay and rear chain stay on the left-hand side were cracked to the point of snapping. It was a miracle that I had been able to ride the bike back to Nîmes in one piece. Maybe my luck was in, perversely. There was no way Trigger could be repaired so we explored my options.

As per the terms of my entry, I was able to use a loan bike for two days and then I would have to hire a bike for the remainder of the Tour, just the last three days. They removed my saddle, pedals and computer holder and placed them on to a spare bike that would fit me. I had only one option at this late hour and it was a Trek branded bike that I could not get to grips with. The next day would be one of my worst on tour.

Distance covered: 189km
Time: 8hrs 7mins
Elevation gain: 1,574m
Calories burned: 6,474
Highest speed: 56kph

I didn't think I could ever have been so grateful for the fact that I was sharing a room with Stuart. The guy was organised, considerate and went out of his way to make sure that I was alright. I had spent the whole evening and morning putting on a false bravado. I was in a lot of discomfort but I didn't want to lose face. I wanted to be accepted so I pretended that I was alright and that everything was a big joke. That is my default mode for coping. Make crass and inappropriate jokes to deflect from my true feelings and weakness. I would keep it up until the end of the Tour and for weeks afterwards.

'I'm okay. It's just a scratch. Just embarrassed.' It would be my go-to answer. Either that or I would sing Chumbawumba's song 'I get knocked down, but I get up again. You are never gonna keep me down.' That would make light of the pain I was in and keep spirits up.

I had five more days to get through, three of which were some of the toughest the Tour had ever witnessed. I needed to stay positive. I wanted to keep a winning mindset and I didn't want to let anyone down. Not my family. Not my new-found friends and I especially didn't want to look weak or foolish in front of the rest of the Loopers. If I could keep my ego satisfied, I could push through and make it to the end.

I blocked out the pain and pretended that everything was okay. I would confront the reality of my situation after the Tour. Maybe. Or maybe I would lock my crash into the grey area of my brain which forgets past failures.

A headache in the first 40km of a long ride didn't help my cause. I am not just talking about the crappy bike.

My Garmin notes for the day were pretty succinct:

'Long old day in the saddle on a loan bike. It was a Trek but I couldn't get to grips with it, at no stage did it fit well and the whole day felt like I was cycling in treacle. Was hot and uncomfortable but had great company with Carmen, Stuart and Eric. Guess I was suffering from an adrenaline come-down from the day before. Long day.'

I picked up the loan bike after we had been transferred to the start by bus. The start was down a narrow street with a zebra crossing and Handsome Nick insisted we mimic the old Beatles album cover. It was cheesy but I appreciated his constant efforts at keeping spirits high. If ever there was a day for me to falter it was this day.

I was feeling a little low, probably due to the adrenaline come-down from the day before. Not dissimilar to the stage after La Planche, where we had a long, hot and tedious ride with no zip in our legs. I had a bike I didn't like and my head was throbbing. I'd chosen not to visit the doctor the night before, not out of bravado but cowardice. I was frightened of what Dr Fi might say to me. She could potentially take me out of the Tour, so I maintained a positive charade and hid like a coward.

I did ring my parents to let them know about the accident and to forewarn them that I would be putting some uncomfortable pictures on Facebook. It worked. The sympathy vote generated a further £750 for the William Wates Memorial Trust. The accident was almost worth it and I wondered if I should maybe crash properly in the coming days? Possibly at high speed on a descent? *Stop it Ceri. That might become a self-fulfilling prophecy. Think positive. Stay positive. Be positive.*

I put the dubious images of a downhill fiasco to one side and moved on with the day. It started with me waking up in blood-soaked sheets. The cuts and bruises were worse than I thought and the sheets had to be peeled off me that morning. I had been wrong, I should have visited the doctor the night before. She rightly told me off that morning and kept an eye on me for a while. We decided not to bandage the wounds but put some Savlon cream on them and let the fresh air heal them naturally. I refused any form of pain killers, not even an ibuprofen, because I was determined to cycle the whole Tour clean. Vitamin C was the extent of drug-taking for me. It could be done. Once I started pedalling, I barely noticed the wounds.

Getting going was the issue. I don't particularly like Trek bikes. They look sexy but they built their brand off the back of Lance Armstrong's success and that doesn't sit well with me. I tested a Trek bike when I was looking at buying a new one before the Tour and it wasn't for me, both in physical comfort and peace of mind. I had a mental block regarding the bike before we headed out.

It also took time to get the damned thing to fit and become comfortable to ride. I adjusted the seat position close to a dozen times but at no stage were the ergonomics suitable for my body size and riding position. By the time I had found a seat position that I could tolerate, every one of the hundred-odd riders had already left for the day. I was last on the road and playing catch-up.

Because of the excellent first feed stop rule I didn't have to panic about racing to bridge the gap to the peloton. I tucked in and set my own pace and a couple of ever-reliable friends drifted back to keep me company. It was the headache that was causing problems. I was aware of a tense throbbing above my right eye. The perfect shiner. It was dull and constant and was causing some irritation. I couldn't shake it off before we reached the feed stop. I was a little concerned and wondered if I should talk to the doctor about it. But that would have meant risking her pulling me from the stage. I decided to have some food and drink first and then take stock. That worked.

Actually, taking my new helmet off did the trick. As we dismounted, I removed the shiny new lime green protection and almost instantly my head started to clear. It was like sunshine breaking through on a rainy day. I think the strange fit of a new helmet was taking a little bit of getting used to and in my over-cautious desire to be safe I had secured it way too tight. Schoolboy error. More to the point a huge sense of relief. I sought out my buddy who I had collided with. He was okay and in good spirits, so we broke out into song.

'I get knocked down …' It wasn't a pleasant sound, but that would prove to be a highlight of the day.

Stage 17 was a long and arduous 206km from Pont du Gard to Gap with two small climbs of note. It was hot (quelle surprise) with some strong side and headwinds in the first half of the day. It would be a fast day for the pros but a day of survival and a long slog for most of us Loopers. We already had one eye on the following three make-or-break days in the Alps. This stage was designed to bridge the gap all the way to those infamous tests.

As we headed out of feed stop one, I stopped by the side of the road for a comfort break and found myself on my own again. The next 40km were the worst of the stage for me. I was battling into a headwind on a strange, ill-fitting bike, and I had no support nor anyone to shelter with. I put my head down, sang some happy songs and eked out a rhythm. Before long I saw two guys I could latch on to. They were only a few hundred metres from me but it took forever to reach them. I was being buffeted by the wind and it was blowing me across the road at times. I should have held my pee in earlier on and gutsed it out for a little bit. I wouldn't have been dropped then.

Eventually I caught them and suggested we ride as a group. They looked spent and politely agreed. It didn't take long before I was on the front, heading into the wind on my own again. They weren't too happy about working with me and it seemed like I was doing all the pulling on the front. I wanted to work with them but they wouldn't hold a steady tempo. To their credit they told me to ride at my own pace and they would see me at the next feed stop.

The highlight of the stage was riding with Eric, Stuart and Carmen and witnessing Eric's delight when he finally got his ice cream with roughly 30km left. There must have been something in the sweet little treat, because on the final hill he dropped us like hot potatoes. Eric was a man possessed and a sight to behold. As the Tour was getting longer, so he was getting stronger. This stage had one final nasty little surprise, which did provide ammunition for my handing over of the Chapeau that evening. It was a phenomenon commonly known as a Mur d'Hôtel.

Following each stage, we would have to cycle to our next hotel and on a couple of these excursions we received a cheeky little ramp as a treat. Our hotel for this evening was a basic two-star situated in the most idyllic of settings on the outskirts of Gap. We dined al fresco underneath a wooded shade and had massages in the gentle garden grounds, a soothing breeze tingling our aching muscles. They ached after that final kick in the teeth.

Cycling a steep hill is not really an issue at the level of strength and fitness we had reached, the difficulty was the surprise at the end of a long day. Only one kilometre but reaching a wall of 18 per cent was more than cheeky. On a bike I didn't like, that was painful. I was delighted to have the use of a different loan bike for the following day and that one was a keeper.

At the bottom of the hill, Thunder-Calves Richard set off, attacking it with a verve seen by sprinters chasing down a finish line. By halfway he was floundering. He was overtaken by one of the Australians with us, who sauntered past one-handed and took a selfie with Rich. We couldn't let that one pass and the Chapeau went Down Under to Martin. The new loan bike came to Ceri.

This time we made sure it fitted perfectly the night before. We added my saddle, pedals and computer holder again and I took it for a little test ride. It was love at first sight. I had been given a Pinarello Dogma F10, with disc brakes. This is a top-of-the-range bike designed specifically in the wind tunnels for Team Sky. I chose to keep this machine for the rest of the Tour, happy to pay whatever the rental would be for the final few days.

This bike would spoil me for all other bikes; we were a match made in heaven. It would be like dating Kylie

Minogue and then trying to talk to any other lady down the pub. Ruined in a beautiful way. I was in love with an inanimate piece of carbon fibre and my morale sky-rocketed with this one small change in equipment. Until I saw the doctor and she told me off again.

Next up, three massive days in the Alps for this workman. I could no longer blame my tools if anything went wrong.

Distance covered: 206km
Time: 9hrs 15mins
Elevation gain: 2,361m
Calories burned: 7,390
Highest speed: 58kph

FALLING DOWN IS AN ACCIDENT,
STAYING DOWN IS A CHOICE –
Anon

YOU'LL NEVER KNOW HOW GREAT
YOU ARE UNTIL A MOMENT CALLS
FOR GREATNESS – Anon

Chapter 19

18 July 2019, The Alps
Dig Deep and Work Harder

I PREFERRED the Pyrenees to the Alps. It wasn't even close. If I had the cash to buy a holiday home in France it would be in the Pyrenees. We did discuss this in idle moments during the Tour and the vote was pretty evenly split. But it was the Pyrenees for me for a number of reasons.

Firstly, I found them to be a little bit more attractive and that little bit quieter. It was as if the world was aware that they are a hidden gem but hasn't quite bothered to go there yet. Cycling the roads in the Pyrenees was that bit easier. There was a little less traffic and what traffic there was, was mostly French and they were very respectful towards cyclists.

In the Alps there were so many tourists. The roads were busy, particularly going up the hills, where we had to fight for space with a cavalcade of motorcycle groups who were time-trialling the same routes that we were. Plus, the roads in the Pyrenees were far superior. The tarmac was mostly new and fresh, quite possibly for the Tour or simply because of better management from the local authorities. Either way they were smoother and easier to ride. Don't get me wrong, the Alps had mouth-watering vistas to die for. I could quite easily make them my second home. Indeed, I felt at home riding on both sets of mountains. The Pyrenees edged it but the Alps were more memorable.

We had three monster stages in a row, with no respite, beginning with the queen stage of the Tour. Starting in Embrun we cycled 209km, ascending four mountain passes, three of which were above 2,000m in altitude and in total we would travel upwards for 5,400m. The air would become decidedly thin in this stage. There was a category one mountain followed by two 'Hors Catégorie' mountains, finishing with a hairy descent into the ski resort of Valloire. This was a stage that was designed to sort out the men from the boys, or the women from the girls, or the tough from the quitters.

We were offered a short-cut at the beginning, but not for me and those determined to cycle every inch of the route. Still without drugs. It was going to be a long day for us amateurs. The coach transfer from Gap to Embrun meant an early start but, oh man, was it worth it.

The first 25km were cycled around the Lac de Serre-Ponçon. It was spectacular, bordering on other-worldly; so beautiful we barely noticed that we ascended the first col of the day in the first 15km. As the sun rose and the day began to warm up, a slight mist glowed upon the lake, stationary like a mill pond. Crystalline blue waters were intoxicating and took our minds off what was to come, until Eric told me the story of how the reservoir was made.

The lake was created to control water flow after disastrous floods caused severe damage and loss of life in the mid 1800s. First proposed in 1895, construction started in 1955 and was completed by 1961. During its development, approximately 3 million cubic metres of material was moved. The dam was constructed and the valley slowly became a lake, in the process flooding all of the local villages. This flooding is the subject of the movie *Girl and the River* (1958), starring Guy Beart.

According to the official website of the Muséoscope, the 'museum of the largest dam in Europe made of compacted soil', Lac de Serre-Ponçon includes a hydroelectric power plant with a 380 mega-watt generator. In addition to the power plant on the lake itself, the dam provides the reservoir and overall water management to facilitate an additional 15 hydroelectric plants along the Durance and Verdon rivers in south-eastern France.

Isolated within the lake is a small chapel, Chapelle Saint-Michel, which had been built on top of a hill in the 12th century. The chapel was originally condemned during the construction of the dam and lake, but survived, its hill becoming an island in its own right. It is accessible on foot during winter and early spring.

I loved riding with Eric, his passion for France made an epic voyage even more interesting. I had forgotten almost all of this by the time we reached the summit of the Col de Vars.

The Vars was just over a nine-kilometre climb with your regular Alpine gradients. In week one this would have been tough; it was tough, but we were stronger and more prepared for it. Our plan was to spin up the climb and save our legs for the rest of the day but the mood was becoming a little fractious.

The approach to the climb itself was a long false flat of over 45km. I was riding with my usual friends and this terrain was perfect for the powerful riders like Stuart, Eric, Carmen, Kenny and Rich. We had been joined by a handful of other cyclists, many of whom were new to Le Loop, for the Alpine stages, and this caused a little discord. We had settled into our usual rhythm of two minutes at the front but before long we realised that it was the same five who were doing all the pulling.

I think I have mentioned that Stuart has the most tremendous sense of right and wrong and a very generous disposition. But he is not the man to cross or take advantage of and he was in no mood to tolerate this behaviour. Two of them in particular were winding us up. Stuart referred to them as the 'Trek Brothers' (I did mention that particular brand doesn't sit well with me). For love nor money, they would not take a turn on the front. Apparently, they were saving their legs for the mountains.

'What the hell do you think we have been doing for the past 16 stages?' Stuart asked, but it fell on deaf ears.

The route leading to the col was lined with idyllic little picnic and camping spots, fern trees lining the roads and soft green verges bordering fields adjacent to small rivers and lakes. Ideal for a group comfort break and to let the 'Trek Brothers' ride into the wind on their own. Two minutes later we started up again and formed a very soothing tempo that ensured everyone took their turn. Effortless, unspoken, teamwork at its best. We felt like Team INEOS without the money. Moods settled down as we approached the bottom of the climb, and eventually caught up with the brothers once again.

For all their bluster we dropped them within the first kilometre. They were saving themselves for a climb and still couldn't hold our wheels. I was ahead of our gang at this stage and hunting trophies in the form of stronger Loopers and those that had taken the shortcut on offer.

I flew up the climb, by plodding, middle-aged, amateur standards, and in hindsight I should have held something back. I was learning my lessons but they had to be repeated more than once. I would pay for that effort, both on the Izoard that followed and in the days to come. I cannot resist a cheeky hill. There is something about a long incline that triggers a fast twitch impulse in my brain. I have to attack it and either go hard or go home.

The Izoard I found to be really tough going at the beginning. Once again this was because I had found myself in a no-man's land with no one to ride with and another 20km or so of false flat to contend with. This time I was playing catch-up because I needed another tube change at feed stop two, which was halfway down the other side of the Vars. The upside to that was having a few targets to chase down as we climbed the Izoard. First, I had to get there.

The false flat didn't appear to be that tough at first glance, it gave the illusion of riding downhill and I couldn't understand why I was struggling in a slow gear. The course was playing hefty tricks with my mind and we still hadn't reached lunch yet. The only positive was that the view continued to be sensational. A small river or large stream (not sure which) ran alongside the road, resplendent with tourists bathing and catching the sun on its little rocky outcrops. Small tufts of whitewash punctuated the flow in the same way my ride was struggling. It was this stream (or river) that showed we were most definitely going uphill and saved my sanity. Until I hit the Col d'Izoard.

The Izoard was 14km with an average climb of 7.5 per cent. As we quickly discovered, the hills in the Alps have a more flexible view of the word average than the Pyrenees. In the Pyrenees if a mountain is seven per cent it will fluctuate between 5 and 9 per cent, but doesn't yield too many unwelcome surprises. In the Alps, on an average 7 per cent climb some flat sections may be encountered; this in turn means that there may be some 15 per cent sections which come right out of the blue. The Izoard was baking hot and open to the elements, which in this case was a scorching sun. It was testing our mettle with a constant incline pushing the limits so early into the stage. I was running out of water and beginning to worry.

Legs tired from the Col de Vars and sapped of energy from the heat, the ascent became a difficult trudge. I was out of the saddle early on and struggled to take in the scenery. I heard crickets by the roadside, tormenting my feeble efforts with their chorus. I focused on one rider at a time and tried to pick them off, only I couldn't. There were bigger and heavier athletes than me but they were gradually leaving me behind. I was at the beginning of a long climb and I was in a dark place.

I stopped chasing down riders. I dropped to my lowest gear, ever grateful that I had bought the 11-34 cassette, and slumped into a rhythm. I have experienced this before and there is only one solution: keep turning the pedals. Slowly at first, just find a routine and maintain it. One revolution at a time, so it is in life as it is on a bike and how leadership was for Fidel Castro. It was long, slow and painful and it hurt to see lesser climbers drifting away from me. In every desert there is an oasis though.

Roughly halfway up the hill was a small tourist village and in the middle of the village was a well. I was almost out of water and on the verge of begging from other riders, but all hail the French and their consideration for intrepid adventurers on two wheels. I very nearly didn't see the tiny village; my head was down, my body was rolling and I was fixated on the tarmac. Deano saw me and called out. He pretty much saved this stage for me.

It transpired that there were eight or nine Loopers in the same predicament but I couldn't see them in the way that I couldn't see the wood for the trees. I was indebted to Deano and I would repay him by dropping him the first chance I got.

I gulped down ice-cool spring water and filled both of my bidons. Eric was there with a can of coke and he gave me a sip. It instantly provided the tiny sugar rush I needed to get going. I didn't hang around.

The road got steeper, the Izoard reached gradients in excess of 10 per cent for most of the final seven kilometres. But I didn't care, I had found my rhythm. It was remarkable what some fluid and a sugar kick can do for you at an opportune moment. I picked off a dozen riders, some in as dark a place as I had been only 20 minutes earlier. I embraced the thinner air.

It was cold at the top and it took way too long to take the celebratory photo to prove that I had been there. The area was crowded with European tourists who lingered round the signposts at the summit and they would not budge. None offered to take my photo until Deano caught up with me again and politely kicked some posterior.

I wolfed down two helpings of lunch and had plenty more of a sugar-based drink because we still had the big climb of the day to come. I did mention this was the queen stage and it was designed as such for a good reason.

I couldn't keep up with Deano on the downhill, very few can. You need stones the size of watermelons to ride at the speeds he does and I think I may have mentioned that I am a bit of a scaredy-cat. I was improving and becoming braver and faster but some, like Deano and Eric, left me trailing in their wake, eating dust. Nevertheless, the descent was rapid and without incident and brought us to the resort town of Briançon where I witnessed an incredible feat of strength.

It wasn't an easy town to ride through because the roads were narrow and filled with inattentive tourists, ambling through the streets. We had to slow and be extra cautious. It was a very attractive resort. Wooden-framed buildings with red tile roofs were enchanting and quaint. It was like something out of Heidi or Hansel and Gretel, and the beer terraces overlooking the road were so enticing that a couple of our team jumped off their saddles and settled in for the afternoon. I believe some cricket was on the big screen but I couldn't let myself be distracted.

Coming out of Briançon we approached a roundabout where we had to turn immediately right and head up a sharp incline. The road was jam-packed with lost hire cars and we came to an abrupt halt. When it cleared, a couple of Loopers took the right turn, where I decided to go all the way around the roundabout. They thought I was foolish but it gave me precious seconds to clip into my pedals.

The road we were on went up at 8 per cent for about a kilometre. Welsh Steve hadn't been able to clip in but he pushed it all the way up the hill, pretty much with one leg. I have rarely witnessed a feat of cycling that powerful yet he was blasé about it.

'Hot dogs for tea boys,' he shouted back at me.

From Briançon there was yet another false flat of about 15km before the climbing started in earnest. Steve organised a group of seven of us and we all pulled on the front for a couple of minutes. He had everyone's respect and shirking wasn't allowed. No 'Trek Brothers' here; they were a long way back.

We were into an open headwind which was growing stronger by the hour and the going was tough. Once we hit the climb it would get tougher. I was getting a second wind. It was the extra portion of lunch that did it, so yet again Yogi and his lunch stop had saved my bacon.

I was finding that on my turn I was starting to pull away from the others. These were bigger and stronger riders than me but we were all in different stages of pain and recovery. Some were scrapping to find a third and a fourth wind. I eased up to work with them and fought to hold on when I was in their midst.

As we approached the climb I drifted away. It wasn't deliberate. I was lost in a happy place turning the wheels and daydreaming about the Col du Galibier. Just the mere 23km with another Alpine average gradient of 6 per cent which progressively steepened the more the air thinned out. I zoomed in on a group ahead and focused on catching them for our group. I thought I was pulling everyone along but when I looked back they were nowhere to be seen. I ploughed ahead.

The Galibier is sensational and long. Its landscape is fairly barren and grey with pockets of snow near the top. The steeper it rose out of the haze the shallower the air became and the colder the ride. The wind was up and straight into our faces. Respite would come halfway up with our final feed stop of the day. I was on my own again. I was in heaven and almost as high as the heavens. I bloody loved it.

Nirvana for me is finding that strength and rhythm in unison. I was on my second wind and that usually is a stronger, more durable energy burst, having recovered from a debilitating low. The early slopes were averaging 6 per cent and with the open moonscape we could see most of the roads leading to the summit. I saw the people I wanted to pick off and chased them down. I moved up through the gears, not knowing where the strength came from but grateful nonetheless and I quickly made it to feed stop four for a coke, chocolate and crisps. It was time to don my rain jacket because the cold air was making me shiver. A nearby donkey approved and Coffee Ian sent me on my way with another obscure eighties earworm stuck in my head. I was now riding with some of the big boys, I was finding my level in the mountains and, bizarrely, the more difficult the terrain, the more I excelled.

'You must be out, of your brilliant mind. Da da dum.' Cheers Ian.

The road rose more steeply. I could see my friends kilometres below, a dozen or so switchbacks behind. I called out to Carmen and Stuart but heard no response bar a tuneless Welsh echo. It was late afternoon and as the air became gloomier my mood was lifted. I saw Australian Martin and Thunder Calves Richard ahead but could not reel them in. I had a strong tempo and turned the wheels quite smoothly but they were on another level. I dreamed of emulating their feats.

I kept them in view and used them to drag me along and help overtake a few more people, including three riders ahead of me who had skipped the first stretch at the beginning of the day. That gave me the final lift I needed to break free of the summit and marvel at the views from 2,642m high. I felt like a god and punched the air in delight. I was in celebratory mood but still had two tough days to follow and a hair-raising descent to negotiate. That brought me back down to earth.

What goes up must come down and when I passed Deano pushing up a hill I would always see him on the other side. I went down the final rapid 20km as tentatively fast as I could. My hands were cold and in danger of freezing and the light was in danger of fading. It was at that point that I lost sight in one eye.

After smashing my prescription cycling glasses to smithereens in the accident on stage 16, I was forced to substitute them with an ordinary pair of prescription sunglasses, aviator style. The descent was so rapid and the wind so abrasive that one of the lenses popped out. I was left with a streaming right eye and vision in the left. It was good enough to get me back to yet another idyllic ski village of Valloire and the denouement of the queen stage.

I wolfed down my dinner and sought out Sarah to help me with a favour for the coming Sunday; she was as brilliant as ever. I then tinkered with the new bike a little before sleeping like a baby at high altitude on the floor. We had four squeezed into the room but I didn't care because I had completed the most epic day of cycling in my life. For the first time during the whole Tour my dreams were starting to incorporate a party in Paris.

This Tour just kept on giving. It was surpassing all of my expectations and I was improving as the days passed. I had stuck mostly to my limits during the day and had overcome a rough patch. I was very strong on the Galibier and I felt privileged to be riding Le Loop.

The 'Trek Brothers' crawled in after dark. So much for saving their legs.

I would learn the meaning of the word 'suffer' the next day.

Distance covered: 209km
Time: 11hrs 25mins
Elevation gain: 5,400m
Calories burned: 9,221
Highest speed: 60kph

*I DIDN'T COME THIS FAR TO
ONLY COME THIS FAR* – Tom Brady

Chapter 20

19 July 2019, Tignes
Included

IN THEORY this was a shorter stage but that didn't make it easy. It was designed for the true climbers to attack pretty much from the word go. We were at the tail end of three weeks of riding and I was in bits. July 19 would prove to be a very interesting day and also the day when my body almost gave up.

In France they call this a '*jour sans*' and every cyclist will have experienced this phenomenon at some stage in their lives. It literally means a 'day without' and is an apt description of that feeling where you have absolutely nothing to give. No energy, no power, no speed and no form, no matter how hard you try to coax your legs, body and mind into gear. It is debilitating and soul-destroying but also a perverse rite of passage in the adventure of surviving an epic climber's tour.

Mine seemingly came out of nowhere but had obviously been building over the course of the preceding three weeks.

Maybe it was the ultra-challenging stage the day before? Maybe it was a delayed reaction to my accident three days earlier, once the adrenaline had dramatically worn off? Perhaps it was a result of pushing my body to the limit for 18 days so far, or maybe it was the culmination of all of this. Either way, I suffered on the road to Tignes.

My memory of the stage is solely the Col de L'Iseran but there was so much more to it than that. We started from our base in Valloire, reluctant to leave the warm sanctity of a tourist resort, which beckoned us to put our feet up, linger a while and enjoy a cool glass of beer. That thought was so tempting given how I felt that morning. But we had to first make it to the start of another day of plodding backwards uphill. I love the hills but this was becoming a bit much.

Stuart noted that his hands felt like claws when he woke up. Possibly a form of carpal tunnel syndrome but, as he pointed out, at least they were brake-shaped claws. It meant he was adapting to the rigours of speeding down rapid descents.

The stage ran from Saint-Jean-de-Maurienne over four mountain climbs and culminated in a climb to our hotel in another resort of Tignes. These resorts were a distraction from the monotony of the Tour, but they were also an unwelcome temptation. I resisted and made a mental note to come back here one day without a bike and sit in one of the hotel bars with a beer. I would watch everyone else scale these peaks, be it on two wheels or skis, while I gloated.

I had downloaded some official Tour notes before I headed to France and they summed up the stage pretty well:

'The riders depart for Tignes on a short yet demanding route. The road goes up once the flag is dropped, not dramatically but stoically. On rolling and constantly sloping terrain the riders reach Montee d'Aussois after almost 40km and following a short drop it continues like before.

'The route moves through Lanslebourg-Mont-Cenis and tackles the Col de L'Iseran, a mountain pass of 32.9km. Sure, the sheer distance is a killer (this race is for the pros remember), but even more so are the last three kilometres with double digit ramps. Following the descent to Val d'Isere it levels out for a few kilometres. An ensuing drop leads to the foot of the final ascent, a tough eight kilometres at over seven per cent.'

This was destined to be a long day and my body was broken.

That morning it felt like it had all caught up with me. I was aching from the efforts of the day before. There was no energy or zip in my legs, only stiffness and lethargy. My mind was a little fuggy – maybe that was the early hour – and my whole body ached. I still bore the scars from a bad crash and I had bloodstained sheets and a throbbing black eye to show for it.

Over the past few days my adrenaline levels had surged up and down like the peaks we were scaling and it was hard to regulate my mood and my fitness. To compound matters, I had no sunglasses, prescription or otherwise, and the cuts around my knee were deepening rather than improving. I couldn't pick a short flat time trial for my 'day without', could I?

Over breakfast I gave myself a talking-to.

I fuelled and then over-fuelled. I needed every bit of sustenance I could force down. I focused on what my end goal was. I told myself I had not come this far to only come this far and I reminded myself that we only had three days of riding left. I had completed 18 stages, so surely I could make my way through three more. I was in a dark place but the camaraderie of the Le Loop riders helped pull me through. I would come to learn the benefit of teamwork, resilience and inclusion before the day was out.

It felt like the whole stage was uphill. Didn't the guide notes say just that? I had a mental block I needed to get out of. I reminded myself that I loved cycling uphill and being realistic there were others who would be feeling much worse than me. I guess they were because I didn't see a lot of my usual buddies for the next two days. Remarkably some were behind me.

I recall very little from the first two hills. I remember it being warm, with not a cloud in the sky but a soothing breeze helped to cool us down. The roads were decent on the lower slopes and the views and archaic tipsy villages very pleasing on the eye, but that didn't detract from the constant pain as we kept on traversing uphill. Very stoic indeed.

It was as we were plodding up the Col de la Madeleine that I was caught by Thunder Calves Richard. He stayed alongside me and listened to my moans for a few minutes, which lifted my mood. He improved it further by donating a pair of sunglasses. He had spares in a choice of colours. They weren't prescription but my short-sightedness was not that bad and they eased the glare from the sun. A small gesture that made a huge difference. I chose the white ones.

Richard is a gentleman. He is tall, strong and forever cheerful and he rides like an express train: all smooth rhythm and bustling power. A great wheel to suck from. Like me he races triathlons and we ended up talking about our adventures over the multi-disciplines. Unlike me he is competitive in triathlons and has competed for GB on more than one occasion. It was a genuine honour to ride with him for a short while and I was determined to learn from him as much as I could. Even at our lowest lows there is still room for development. My greatest weakness is an opportunity for growth and that development took my mind off the ascents.

Ordinarily the Col de la Madeleine would be a focal point of a stage and it has been used as a summit finish in previous tours. In 2019 it was a mere hors d'oeuvre for what was to come. We reached its summit at a meagre 1,700m. No thin air just yet and we dined in the shade of pine trees on the side of the road. Richard had stayed with me for the three or four final kilometres and I was grateful. We weren't even halfway into the stage but it was lunchtime already and all we had done was ride upwards. As it would transpire, the first 90km were pretty much all uphill.

On the approach to the base of the Col de L'Iseran we had a brief downhill and a false flat out in the open for a few kilometres. I was happy that I had some company and headed out clinging on to the coat-tails of a big engine. My first issue was that I couldn't descend as quickly as him and my second was that I was wiped out and had nothing inside. I told Richard to move on and ride at his own pace. He humoured me and said something about feeling the effects from the previous day, so if it was alright with me, he would stick around. I knew he was only being kind but I appreciated it no end. I was happy to plod along, feeling a little guilty that I was holding up a top rider.

At 76km the climbing started in earnest. Seriously, what had we been doing for the rest of the morning? It's a hell of a way to earn a living, Geraint Thomas.

The Col de L'Iseran is utterly breathtaking. One of our gang stated that it felt more Himalayan than Alpine, such were the giddy thin-aired heights we were reaching. This was the roof of the Tour alright. We approached it from the south with temperatures at a breezy 34°C leading away from the pleasant village of Bonneval-sur-Arc, which is protected from the looming monster above by a gentle valley. The average gradient is close to 8 per cent but it is steep from the off with the first ramp at close to 9 per cent. Knowing that there were a couple of flattish stretches, these ramps would become ever steeper. Richard led us up, patiently sticking to my pace. I expected a little adrenaline surge but none came.

I was aware of the dull grey tarmac meandering its way up the craggy green mountainside to a pointed summit. Warm sunshine and blue skies at the bottom with our goal of a snow-capped peak reaching into the heavens. I saw a lot of darkness. I locked myself into a bubble. I dropped down to the second-lowest gear, hoping to have something in reserve for the steeper ramps and I focused on one revolution after another. So it is on the road, so it is in life and so it was that Emily came to join us. For her this was effortless. Richard kept spirits high and she joined in. I wanted to quit.

The thought crossed my mind. I wasn't in pain but I was lifeless. I was devoid of energy or adrenaline and the pace uphill was sluggish at best. Richard and Emily were brilliant. They chatted continuously about inane crap and races they had competed in. Anything but the challenge we were facing and the ultimate *jour sans* that was overwhelming me.

I tried to make a few cheap jokes to lift my spirits but I was better off focusing on the next pedal revolution. I banished thoughts of quitting from my mind very quickly. I focused on photos in front of the Eiffel Tower and I concentrated on the next couple of pedal strokes and breaking the mountain down into tiny, manageable chunks. My negativity was a fleeting moment and I had a sense that maybe the worst was over. I was wrong.

As was always the case on this Tour, just as I felt like I had nothing left to give, the Tour gave back. God bless the roads, they never lie. In the same way I cannot resist a cliché when I am devoid of creativity.

We caught up with a group of three relatively fresh riders. We reeled them in and chatted briefly before very kindly dropping them. I thought I was in a bad way but there were others who were worse off. I make no apologies for the fact that their suffering gave me a lift. I was clinging on to anything that would get me through this. That was another 800m chunk ticked off a seemingly endless list.

We were only four kilometres in and then another gift. A flat section. It wasn't long but it was enough. Enough to catch my breath, to drink some water and to gaze at the monumental peak above us. As I had the day before, I focused on the views we would see from the top; they would make the whole ordeal worthwhile.

I have seen footage of the Tour de France where mountain domestiques ride hard on the front for most of the stage and then all of a sudden, they come to a standstill. They suffer the hunger knock or completely blow up and they have nothing left to give. They struggle to crawl up the hill and are borderline static while the peloton moves on without them, barely registering their pain.

That would best describe how I had been feeling but the calm lifted me. I wasn't suffering a hunger knock, I was just tired and weak. That I could deal with. A positive mood helps. I worked on that and focused on the next switchback or the next group ahead as every kilometre passed. I envisaged the reward of stupendous panoramas from the summit.

The terrain didn't get any easier but I had a little bit more in me to be able to contribute. I was able to join in the conversations again. Richard and Emily were making this look easy and I was embarrassed that I needed the help. I wanted desperately to be a helpful team-mate and to be worthy of their company.

What lay ahead was just plain nasty. A further six kilometres of 10 per cent climbing into cooler, thinner air. What fresh hell was this? Miraculously my dark mood was lifting from black to light grey. Hardly a sunny disposition but the higher we went the brighter my outlook. The power of positive thinking was having some effect. It was just brutal on the legs. The col was exposed, there was no shelter and the temperature was dropping but once again we caught and dropped a couple of other smaller groups. More suffering for others to ease my own melancholic torment. It couldn't get much worse, until it did.

The final three kilometres didn't let up and we reached the maximum ramp in the double digits. Not that steep a punch, but at the end of 90km of constant climbing, with thin air and after 19 days of effort, I was on the ropes. If it had been a boxing match the bout would have been stopped out of mercy. I kept apologising to Richard and Emily and they tried to reassure me that it was tough going for them as well. Judging by how they kept checking on me I knew this wasn't the case.

Vast cavalcades of snow and ice adorned the hillside, some forming mini tunnels above us. It was surreal, like something out of a James Bond movie: the hidden lair of a supervillain locked inside these pristine white outcrops. Little rivers of melted snow drifted across the road and we focused on one pedal stroke at a time.

That was one of the most difficult climbs of my life but I was indeed right. The views were worth every inch of the suffering. We felt like gods looking down upon mountains, clouds and snow-capped peaks below us. I had been forced to dig deep and I had relied on the moral support and backbone of two heroic individuals. I had long preached the value of teamwork and on this day I had reaped the benefit of it.

Emily had the energy to take a perfect moving selfie of the three of us and then jumped off her bike and took celebratory photos of us overlooking the undulating vistas below. Time for food and to witness Yogi being shouted at by an angry café owner.

The guys who man the feed stops had a difficult job to do. Finding locations at regular 40km breaks isn't easy, but they did an outstanding job in securing idyllic havens in which we were able to wolf down our daily treats. Apparently on top of a cold, windswept mountain is the wrong spot. Yogi had parked the van and pitched our food tent on some empty scrubland not far from a remote café. Before long the owner showed her displeasure by coming out and with a lack of grace asked him to move on, just as Richard and I were ready to move on. The irony was that she had some solid business from over 100 Loopers buying coffees, cokes and sweet treats but she didn't want us near her café. This summed up the Alps for me: a superlative mass of peculiarities and contradictions.

The quality of the roads in the Alps was not that great. I don't know if it was the weather that caused them to break up and pothole or maybe it was down to a lack of care. They were the worst roads we trundled along in France. The rest of the country had been pristine, bordering on anal retentive and the tarmac had been a rolling treat. It easily added two or three kph to our average speeds. The Alps could be a little treacherous, particularly when we had to compete with tourists in rental cars or motorbikes racing us down the mountainsides. Long stretches were spent hidden in pitch-black tunnels hoping your front wheel didn't disappear from underneath you. On top of this there was the local gendarmerie who seemed to be on permanent patrol, ordering us to ride in single file and not two abreast. The rules of the road in the UK and in France state that two abreast is preferred but the local police were having none of it. None of this excused the fact that I couldn't hold Richard's wheel on the descent.

I remember little about the drop in elevation apart from the fact that it was hard to catch a cold breath and that it passed very quickly. By the end my hands were like Stuart's braking claws and Richard was waiting for me yet again at the bottom. The man was a Trojan. He was ready for us to ride to the summit of our final eight-kilometre climb, with yet another healthy punishing ramp, to our hotel in Tignes. A breeze compared to what we had just been through, but not in the state I was languishing in.

Just ten minutes into the ride Richard had problems with his electronic shifters and it meant that he couldn't change gear. This was a problem on a climb. He pulled to one side to manually put the bike into a low gear so that he could spin his way up the hill. I didn't want to stop. I knew that if I did, I may not get going again, plus I just don't believe in stopping on a hill. I did the right thing and slowed down and offered to help. Richard told me there was nothing I could do and that he would be right behind me. That was pretty magnanimous. I accepted and rode on. I felt guilty leaving him behind after all that he had done for me that day. I owed him a debt of gratitude but my legs didn't seem to have it in them to relent so late in the stage. I needed to ensure I rode with him again to repay the favour.

In the final five kilometres of the day I found a second wind. Goodness knows where it came from, given all that I had been through, but I glided up the second half of the hill, passed a handful of other Loopers and had something to spare when I finished.

I hung around in the hotel car park for a while. I waited for Richard to come in 20 minutes behind me. I apologised for leaving him and I thanked him profusely for riding with me all day. He had saved my day. I am confident I would have completed the stage under my own steam but he made it so much easier and highly enjoyable. I had benefited from the camaraderie and teamwork of a true sportsman. I owed him a beer when we reached Paris at the very least.

I had my massage and cleaned my bike and hung around to savour the atmosphere. We were high up in the Alps and I had survived the greatest cycling ordeal of my life. I was on cloud nine, both literally and figuratively. I decided to give a little back and helped a few of the riders who trailed behind us by cleaning their bikes. As a reward we were treated to the best hotel we would stay in during the Tour. With the most fantastic buffet.

I had mixed emotions that night. I felt like I had ridden through a perfect storm and I was feeling fresher again. We were so close to Paris and I could almost reach out and touch it.

On the other hand, I was in the middle of the greatest time of my life and I didn't want it to end. I loved life in the Le Loop bubble and I knew that life wouldn't get much better than this. That night at dinner, Carmen remarked that we had all been living in each other's pockets for three weeks and in a couple of days it would all be taken away from us. We may never see some of these people ever again. That knocked me for six.

After barely surviving my 'day without', I vowed to savour every last moment of the remaining two days. As much as you can savour the longest mountain climb ever to grace the Tour de France.

Distance covered: 129km
Time: 7hrs 56mins
Elevation gain: 3,789m
Calories burned: 6,011
Altitude: 2,770m

*WHEN EVERYTHING FEELS LIKE
AN UPHILL STRUGGLE, PICTURE
THE VIEW FROM THE TOP* – Anon

Chapter 21

20 July 2019, Val Thorens
Succeed

'WHAT IS it that you say you are doing?'

'I'm riding Le Loop.'

'Oh, cool. And what is Le Loop exactly?'

'It is a fantastic charity ride where we cycle the route of the Tour de France one week before the pros race on it.'

'Oh wow. And what stage will you be doing?'

'All of them.'

'Right, but what stage will you be doing specifically?'

'All 21 of them. Specifically.'

'Right. So, is it like L'Étape du Tour? They do one of the stages a week before the pros, right?'

'Yes, they do. But we are riding Le Loop which is the whole of the Tour de France. All 21 stages.'

'Okay I think I understand but I don't get which stage of the Tour you are riding in. Is it the queen stage or a mixture of a couple?'

'WE WILL RIDE THE WHOLE OF THE TOUR DE BLOODY FRANCE. Ah, what the hell, yes, it is L'Étape and we will ride stage 20.'

'Wow, that's impressive. And what other events have you done?'

'Well, I've competed in a few Ironman triathlons.'

'Oh. My. Word. That is incredible. You've done an Ironman? How does someone even go about doing that? That must be the toughest thing you have ever done?'

'Actually no. Cycling the Tour de France will be the toughest thing I have ever done.'

'What, like L'Étape?'

'Oh for … Yes, L'Étape.'

Seriously, I must have had that conversation 100 times. No one I spoke to could conceive that we were cycling the whole of the Tour de France. What I found frustrating was that even when they did finally comprehend what we were taking on, they were not that impressed. In most people's minds Ironman was far greater. No amount of explanation would get athletes or lay people to understand that cycling the Tour was like racing in 21 Ironman races on consecutive days. Okay, I may exaggerate a little here for dramatic effect, but it really was like racing in 21 Ironman events over consecutive days.

Those people who organise the event and those immense talents that I rode alongside, they knew exactly what it was that we were seeking to achieve. We had a bond built on endurance and achievement where every road led to Paris. We had to tackle one more mountainous stage before a procession into the capital. It turned out to be a whopper.

Stage 20 ran from Albertville to a summit at the ski resort of Val Thorens. It was only 131km long but the climbing started from the word go (well why wouldn't it?) and according to my Garmin we surmounted over 6,209m. We encountered three big climbs, plenty of motorbikes and even more cyclists preparing for L'Étape du Tour.

L'Étape du Tour is a one-day event where riders cycle one epic stage of that year's Tour. Just the one. For 2019 they would be covering stage 20 and it was taking place on 21 July, the day after we had ridden the same route, and one week before the finish of the Tour in Paris. As a result, a good number of the 15,000 L'Étape entrants were out scouting the course for the race the next day, which meant we had company at times. I am not sure if that was good or bad.

From the start, the route ran on a false flat to the foot of the Col de Méraillet. Once we reached the top it would continue on to the Cormet de Roselend combining for a grand total of 20km at an Alpine average slope of 6 per cent. We were warned about the descent from the Roselend because it was steep, fast and very technical in parts. To be frank it was eyes-popping-out-of-my-head, balls-jumping-back-inside hairy. I would reach my top speed of the Tour on this section on the sexy new Pinarello Dogma F10.

We would have a chance to calm our nerves on a flat section for ten kilometres before attacking the second climb of the day. The Côte de Longefoy was a healthy seven kilometres at roughly 7 per cent, a mere blip by the standards of the previous two days. That would change when we finished the stage, and in effect the Tour, with a 33km ascent to the summit of Val Thorens. I was trembling in my bib-shorts, agog in anticipation.

For one final time I got off to a poor start. Three weeks of riding will do that to you; there was something lacking in my legs. For once I had the good sense to not force the issue, desperate to pace myself and save something for the final climb. I had the sense that most riders were thinking and feeling similar things. I got a rhythm going but it wasn't pretty.

Yet another interminable false flat. I can't stand them. You feel like you are riding on level ground and you feel like you should be in a bigger gear and moving a lot faster. You feel like you should be travelling much better than you are and not experiencing the common feeling of traipsing in treacle.

I had decided that I was going to leave absolutely everything out on the road on this stage. I was going to drain every last drop of energy out of my legs, my heart and soul. All of my remaining matches would be well and truly burned to a cinder. The Tour had rewarded me with so much, I owed it my ultimate performance at the very least. Even if I would be moving at half the pace of the professional peloton. This was not a promising start. The problem with false flats is that they suit riders with power. I do not possess natural power and that meant a slow start to the day, a dreary and interminable stoic battle before an epic one.

I had lost all of my usual riding buddies over the previous few stages as we battled with our own fluctuating levels of strength and performance. I drifted in between some faster groups and some of those in the middle. I was mostly on my own, but I was happy with that on this stage because this was my ultimate time trial. Thunder Calves Richard was already a blip fading from view in the distance, his impressive form highlighting many of my frailties.

We had been offered yet another shortcut at the beginning of the stage to miss out the first hill. What were they thinking? No chance. Not for me. I wouldn't be able to live with myself. I do not judge those who took advantage of the shortcuts because we all came to Le Loop with differing journeys, varying stories and different ambitions. Ultimately, we were there to raise funds for the WWMT and I was there to cycle every single, glorious inch of the Tour. Winning mindset switched on. Time to go smash a great stage.

I tried to hold the wheels of some of the quicker riders but I felt myself going into the red. It wasn't worth it so early in the stage. No point burning matches just yet. I was passed by my friend who hadn't allowed me to ride with a strong peloton earlier in the Tour. I tried to cling on and work with his group again but they took one look at me, picked up the watts and dropped me like I wasn't there. It was like swatting flies. Maybe they were right? I probably wasn't strong enough to ride with them. I saved my matches and cruised to the foot of the Roselend.

I liked the Roselend. Not everyone did. For the first half we were mostly shrouded in the deep green cloak of trees. We were sheltered but it was steep and unforgiving. Usual routine, I dropped into the small ring and a granny gear, saving a couple back for more difficult periods ahead. I span it out and found a tempo I was comfortable with. Then I overdid it.

There were quite a few riders on the road ahead of me, the powerful ones who thrive on the false flats and into the wind and they were starting to come within sight. I can't help it. I chased them down. *I see you Trek bike. I've got you in my sights. See that cord? No? I do. It's bringing us closer together. I've got you. I'm coming for you. You are dust. Smashing it.*

'Alright mate. How are you? You're looking strong, keep it up.' I was a mass of competitive and schizophrenic contradictions.

'Good work Ceri, looking strong, buddy.' Always nice to hear that.

I had caught seven or eight quite easily when the road cleared and transformed from a closeted dark and dreary assault to an open and panoramic challenge. At the halfway stage we cleared the trees and glided to the most dramatic, eye-catching lake you could find halfway up an Alpine col. It came as a very pleasant and heart-warming surprise. A vast expanse of turquoise, crystal-clear water framed with a craggy mountain terrain and overlooking it the most enchanting café you could wish to lay eyes on. I was tempted.

The idyll was destroyed by the sound of motorbike engines roaring up the mountain on a Saturday morning time trial. Plenty of Loopers stopped for a coffee and ice cream and took in the view. I should have. I should have taken time out to appreciate where I was, the setting I was in and the life I was so fortunate to be living. My mind was focused on one thing only. Getting to the summit of Val Thorens as quickly as possible. I was an ignorant fool. By forsaking the café, I did overtake another dozen Loopers who were wise enough to stop and smell the roses, but I missed out on appreciating a last idyllic moment of my journey. I made up some time.

We made our way around the lake on a relatively flat section and you know what that does to the average gradient. Oh yes. Things got steeper and the motorbikes got louder. They didn't seem too happy to be sharing the roads with a bunch of skinny, malnourished folks in Lycra. We were an unnecessary intrusion into their race. Thankfully we parted ways at the summit. On reaching the top, they took their photos, sweating underneath their leather façade, turned around and sped back down. We savoured a perfect setting for a feed stop, filled up on cakes and bananas and tackled a tricky descent.

I am not sure if I can ever recall feeling so frightened or ever travelling so fast on two wheels. A gentle breeze drifted down the mountain, gushing its encouragement for me to soar like a pro. I didn't take much of the downhill pass or Alpine vistas in. It was steep, technical and my eyes never left the road. I was clinging on for dear life and carelessly learned an important lesson to ease off.

At one stage I hit speeds in excess of 85km per hour. My Garmin claims I surpassed 116kph, but I suspect that was an error. A positive blip on the screen. Either way I was entering territory that I was unfamiliar with. I was about to attack a hair-raising stretch of the Tour and I was petrified.

The corners were more than just tight bends. They were almost full 180-degree turns with huge drops off the side if you misjudged them and, as I frequently lament, I happen to be a scaredy-cat going downhill. I have never been proficient travelling at high speed, which is not conducive to being competitive in races. My handling skills are okay but I just don't have the confidence in my own abilities to push the envelope traversing the wrong way down a 16 per cent slope.

As my speed picks up and I see the road sliding beneath me I can see the pitfalls and can experience the torture of being detached from my bike. I have had enough crashes to know what the feeling of skin scraping on tarmac and bones bashing on to a rock-hard surface is like. I don't care for it. I also have too much time in my own head, wrestling with my internal dialogue to be able to let myself go and enjoy the wind sailing through my helmet.

Instead of keeping my eyes on the approach to a corner and picking the perfect line, I foresee every little disaster ahead. I see the gravel that can take my front wheel from underneath me; I spot where the gusts of wind will knock me sideways; I see the driving mistakes motorists won't make and I second guess every single handling error I could make. I riddle myself with anxiety and talk myself into overcaution.

My first-ever accident was as a ten-year-old. We used to have races around an old school playground near my home with a lot of the local village kids. We'd sail around in an anti-clockwise circle on old, heavy single-gear bikes, competing for the honours of impressing the three sisters from down the lane. One hot summer's day I lost concentration and almost smashed my bike in two.

I was heading down the home straight, inching past one of my school friends, when I felt a wasp land on my shoulder. At top speed I swatted it, but it wouldn't budge. I could feel it tickling my shoulder blade so I glanced to my left and swatted again only to miss the wasp completely but make direct contact with a very solid obstacle. I had overshot the corner and ridden straight on into a wall at the end of the playground. I was in bits; my bike was in pieces and my confidence on two wheels was shattered.

Kids are resilient and I was back on my bike, both figuratively and literally, within hours. It took a long time to regain my confidence though, and the daredevil streak of my youth has always come with a caveat ever since. That little voice was in my ear heading down the other side of the Roselend.

Some of the stretches were long, straight and steep, with sudden switchbacks at the bottom. There was 19km of this for me to survive and I was on a nervous high. I attacked the downhill with gusto, aiming for my most impressive ride of the Tour, and quickly learned my limitations.

Approaching one of the early hairpins I had just hit my top speed of the whole 21 days of riding, my hands boring fist-shaped holes into the handlebars, my fingers never far from the brakes. I was urging my nerves to quieten and allow me to hit the speeds of my new-found heroes, who were flying ahead of me. The wind was gentle and I could feel every bump in the road. Each one a reminder of my childhood lapse of concentration.

I was concentrating too hard, trying desperately to relax, and my brain went into overdrive.

What the hell are you doing? Do you want to live?

I blocked those thoughts, tucked my head into the breeze and turned the pedals to gain more speed. A left-hand switchback approached and a little gust of wind came from the right. I wobbled. It was nothing. But it sent a shiver through my spine and as I over corrected I took my eyes off the road.

Looking up I saw a very tight turn and I was heading into it on the wrong line. Fear gripped me and I pulled back hard on both brakes. Thank heavens for disc brakes, because I eased up sharply, wobbled as I lost balance a little and then leaned hard to the left, forcing the bike into a dramatic change of direction. Turning and braking at the same time is not a wise idea. My rear wheel slid out a little as a bottomless precipice loomed and I had visions of falling off into an interminable void.

The brakes took hold, the wheel gripped and I came to a standstill after creeping round the corner. I had narrowly missed a calamitous end to my Tour on the last full day of testing terrain. I was also very grateful that no one had been witness to my sloppiness. I was mentally winded.

I eased on to the next stretch vowing to be more sensible as the inner voice took hold.

Come on Ceri. What the hell are you doing and who are you trying to impress? The idea is to get to Paris, not fall off a cliff. One accident is enough, thank you. Take it easy on the descents and attack the uphill sections. And stop shaking will you. Stupid Welsh idiot.

I picked up speed gradually and very deliberately braked early on every corner and over-cautiously took the widest line on each. A nervous restraint overrode my childhood daredevil as I focused on smashing this stage without incident.

A couple of Loopers passed me on the next fast stretch.

'Whoa Ceri. That was a close one. Are you alright?' Once again, I was grateful for the support and encouragement of our team. I was equally embarrassed that my carelessness had been witnessed. They didn't judge me. They were too busy haring off into the distance, reminding me of my lack of descending skills. The Alps had once again taught me that I would never make it as a downhill skier. I was grateful the roads were relatively quiet on this side of the mountain.

We were lucky. There were roughly 100 Loopers on the route. The following day the roads would be heaving with over 15,000 cyclists. That was an accident waiting to happen. Not for me anymore.

I eased down to the lunch stop at the base of the second hill with my ego securely reprimanded and my handling skills in need of considerable practice. By some stroke of fortune, I was dining with some of the faster riders. I hadn't been at these dizzy heights all Tour. I'd caught up with both Richards and Handsome Nick and the people that they were used to hanging out with. That gave me a lift.

My body suffered on the second hill. Maybe I had eaten too much. I wanted the fuel to survive the rest of the day and I was bloated. Maybe my nervous energy made me push too hard at the start of the climb or maybe I was tired after all that had preceded this stage. Either way I hit another gloomy mental spot. Handsome Nick was my saviour. He slowed down and nursed me to the top of the climb. There was nothing spectacular about it, by now a hill was a hill, and this was a seven-kilometre prelude before the main attraction came on the big screen. I was in a dark place as I approached the final feed stop of the day. Coke and crisps time.

This time it was Coffee Ian's turn to be harassed by the locals. He had pitched up by the side of a park and erected the tent and refreshments just inside its boundary. As is so often the case, one local busybody had complained, just like home. The local gendarmerie came to move him on. They seemed tired and frustrated at having to deal with a petty crime of celebrating their national sport and feeding some hungry cyclists.

Ian handled it brilliantly. He smiled, put on a blank expression and explained that he couldn't speak a word of French. I didn't hang around to see the outcome. I was on a mission. Some caffeine, coke and a bar of chocolate and I was away. Time to tackle Val Thorens.

I hit the base of the climb in a group of four. Three strong riders and me. The two very strong Richards and Welsh Rhys. I had barely seen Rhys all Tour, apart from waking him up when I thought I was sharing a room with him. To look at him you wouldn't think he was much of an athlete, but when he sat on a bike he was like a whippet on amphetamines. He could fly. Two Welshmen and two Englishmen. That made things a little interesting.

'Wales versus England then boys,' said Rich number one. I pointed out that wasn't fair because Rhys had me as a team-mate. No one disagreed. They could have at least pretended.

We rode together in a nice tempo. The slopes were steady enough to spin out a nice gear, just above the granny spot. This was a battle of endurance over brute force and I was in good company to be helped up the climb. The traffic was busy, ridiculously so at times, and there were plenty of L'Étape du Tour riders who tried to keep pace with us. By now we knew our bodies and knew how to get the best out of the mountain pass.

For five or six kilometres we were great company. The banter was puerile and very funny and I didn't notice the tarmac passing under foot. I was having the time of my life. Then I started to fade. I had probably been trying too hard to keep pace with these titans and I was burning matches. I dropped off the back.

Rhys very generously said that he was feeling the pace and slid back and rode with me for a few kilometres. We were letting our country down and it was England 2, Wales 0.

We let the English Richards go and Rhys nursed me along. Steep walls of rocky outface to our left, sharp drops into a wooded abyss to our right. 'Keep your eyes on the road Ceri. Traffic backing us up.'

At one point two cars struggled to pass each other and the traffic crawled to a standstill. Reluctant to let us pass, we were brought to a halt. It only lasted a minute or so and was no fault of our own, but I couldn't get going again.

Recommencing on a 7 per cent slope I struggled to clip into both pedals. I was okay starting off but getting my second foot clipped in seemed impossible. After half a dozen aborted attempts and forcing the wheel round with only one foot, I eventually managed it. Not as impressive as Steve had been two days before, where he rode with one leg. Rhys had floated off into the distance. I was on my own again but there was a long way to go.

I found my rhythm and either the espresso or the sugar kicked in. It could have been adrenaline or my sheer brilliance, but most likely the cola. I kicked it up a gear and found a strong, almost powerful, cadence. Before long I saw

Thunder Calves Richard at the side of the road. This time it was a puncture; he wasn't having much luck.

There was nothing I could do so I wished him well and trundled along pretty confident that he would ride back up to my wheel and I would have someone to work with. I wouldn't see him again until dinner that evening. He said that Rhys was flying ahead.

Once again, I was riding on my own with no one to share the workload. I became lost in my thoughts and was prone to the vagaries of my internal dialogue. This time I was in a form of cycling utopia, riding the time trial of my dreams. If only the road wasn't so steep or so long. It was the longest climb of my life.

I started talking to myself, telling my legs to get a move on. I pictured our finish line in Paris and the joy it would bring. I imagined returning home to a hero's welcome and being feted with champagne on the streets of Tenby. Anything to boost my morale.

When my mood dipped, I tapped into small amounts of rage. Anything to force me through some bleak periods. I hadn't forgotten being rejected by faster riders during the Tour or sharing a room with Buddy, who nabbed the double bed. I could hate them momentarily. I was able pick up my adrenaline and find my tempo. For the most part I was in a very happy place.

I dropped a couple of L'Étape riders and in turn was passed by a handful of local club riders who cycled the hill every weekend. I foolishly tried to hold their wheels and held brief conversations with some of them. They looked at me with pity in their eyes and left me behind like a Porsche racing a Fiat Uno. No matter, I was about to experience redemption.

Just over halfway up the mountain, before we reached a few of the resort villages, I spotted two riders in the distance. They were in unison and looking strong. Perfect unison. It couldn't be? Oh yes it was.

Four or five hundred metres ahead of me were an unlikely duo, which included my chum who had deemed me to be an odd number and wouldn't let me ride with his elite group. In all fairness he was a more accomplished and stronger cyclist than me. Until stage 20. The tortoise was catching up with the hares. That gave me a massive lift. I locked in on them with a tunnel-like vision, refusing to let them out of my sight. I was determined to reel them in. *I've got you. This is Ceri, I'm coming for you. Think you're too good for me, well the road will see about that. I'm not going anywhere so try as you might, I'm after you.*

I tapped back into a little rage and used it to my advantage. I was now racing for real, not just trying to keep up with the stronger Rhys and two Richards. It didn't take long. They were spent and I was flying in the midst of one of the most exhilarating rides of my life. I caught up with them and decided not to hang around.

'Hiya folks. Looking good. Keep it up.' I savoured the look of shock on their faces when they saw a lesser rider passing them. That raised my spirits. I needed every resource and ounce of motivation I could get to help me reach the top without cracking.

A couple of kilometres later I saw the other Richard in the distance; he was riding with Wim, another top cyclist who I hadn't been strong enough to cycle with. They were coming out of a public toilet and were roughly 400m ahead. They were unaware of my presence. I hunted them down.

Rather, I tried; they were strong and working together. They were too strong. The gap never closed but to my relief it never increased either. I was stuck on the end of a piece of string and they were pulling me along. Three, four, maybe five kilometres and they took me up a good chunk of the hill. No rage to motivate me here; a respectful desire to share the road with a couple of top athletes. Then it happened.

Through no skill of my own I overtook them. Quite easily. They had stopped for an ice cream break in a café.

'Bloody hell Ceri, where did you come from?' I heard one of them shout. 'Come and have a coffee.' That was very gracious but I was on a mission. I was flying by my standards and I wanted to make the most of it. Never mess with a purple patch and never stop on a hill. Didn't people know that by now?

With ten or so kilometres to go I was running drastically low on water when the road provided once again. In actual fact it was Kate from Le Loop who provided, dishing out water from a fountain to Loopers who were in dire need. You've got to love France and its public amenities. I stopped only to fill my bidons and thank Kate for her timely intervention. She took great delight in handing out Le Loop flyers to L'Étape riders in between filling up water bottles. Ingenious.

I had caught up with and left behind Rhys at the feed stop. He had bonked. The hunger knock had taken everything out of him. I suggested he ride with me and we make it to the top together. He politely declined, opting instead to grab a snack and a drink to try and recover a little. I also passed a couple of riders who had taken the shortcut on offer. They had skipped the first 40km of the day and I was passing them. I was on fire. There were a few of them ahead of me and I now had carrots dangling in front of my bike to chase down.

With all Alpine passes, the higher you get the steeper the road becomes. We were into the thin air, above 2,000m and it was starting to cool in the mid-afternoon. My legs were plenty warm enough and my heart surged with delight at the ease with which I passed those ahead of me. I had found my niche. I had found my real strength on a bike and I finally believed that I belonged with half-decent riders up in the steep hills of France. It had been a very long time coming. I was ecstatic and that carried me up into the land of the gods, where the air was in short supply and the views bountiful. I wanted it to last forever. I wanted to reach the finish as quickly as possible. I passed Kelly who was singing Eagles songs, followed by nine or ten others and rounded the corner into the resort of Val Thorens: 32km of climbing down, one more to go. Almost there.

Through the town and a left turn into the barriered-off section for the race finish. Another kilometre to go. A tiny drop down. A short flat and then an 800m steep sprint to the line. A Welsh voice in my ear. Was my internal voice being expressed out loud again? Surely not.

'Alright Ceri. I'm wasted mate. I have nothing left.' It was Rhys. He had found his second wind and had buried himself to catch me. He had some fire in his belly that man.

He had been chasing me for almost six kilometres, struggling to reel me in and dropping plenty of others along the way. I was very happy and said it would be good to ride across the finish line with him.

'To hell with it. Let's race,' he said. I cursed vehemently and just as quickly I relented. Game on.

I could see the pain he was in and set off early, leaving him suffering in my wake. A hundred metres up a 10 per cent pass and I thought I had him. But he had the spirit of a lion and the legs of a racehorse. He fought back.

With 600m to go we were at 95 per cent effort, pushing uphill with wheels almost touching. Neither was prepared to give an inch. Neither backing down, but not strong enough to break away. Is this what it felt like for Geraint Thomas the year he won the Tour? It was exhilarating and better than any drug you could ever take. Tourists were walking in groups down the middle of the road, straight towards us.

'Get out of the way!' we screamed. They laughed and pulled to one side, cheering us on as we both refused to give an inch.

Four hundred metres to go. Legs burning, lungs screaming, heart rate up to a dangerous 190. Three hundred metres. Two hundred. The gradient rose and the line was in sight. At 100m I kicked. I pushed hard, with every last drop of energy I had and took a slight lead. I was too far out. Rhys waited until 50m. He went. He went with all his might. He beat me by a wheel.

We had cycled close to 3,500km over 20 stages and a dumb Welsh idiot wanted me to race him at the end of a 33km mountain climb. I have done some foolish things in my life. I have made mistakes, but I have few regrets. Certainly not there and then. That was arguably one of the happiest moments of my life. With only a processional stage into Paris the following day I had cycled the Tour de France. Wales 2, England 0 – albeit because of a puncture and a coffee break. Well done Rhys.

Dinner would be served in a restaurant at the very top of the mountain before we would embark on a five-hour coach transfer to Lyon airport. A brief overnight stop and then another long transfer to Rambouillet on the outskirts of Paris, for the start of our final day in the saddle. It was time to unwind and celebrate a little.

After catching my breath and letting my heart rate settle back to normal, I had an inordinately long hug with Rhys. Top man. He had brought the very best out of me and provided a fantastic conclusion to the Tour. Shortly after we had finished, I settled in for my final massage. As I was being pummelled a friendly hand reached out to say well done. It was my elite chum, the one I had dropped on the hill.

'Great ride Ceri. Well done. We were really impressed with you today.' That pissed on my fire. I was blown away. It was incredibly generous from someone I thought had looked down on me. It was magnanimous and made me feel ten feet tall. I felt like I belonged. It had only taken 20 days and the most fantastic bike ride of my life. I shook his hand and uttered my admiration for his all-round brilliance and joined him for a drink in the restaurant where something magical happened.

As we were eating so other Loopers began to wander in, appearing ghostlike in various states of fatigue and dishevelment. As they did, we rose as one and proffered a standing ovation. It brought a shiver to my spine as we recognised the efforts of every individual who conquered their demons and achieved their goals. Dreams duly fulfilled.

I didn't get a standing ovation. It transpires that I was one of the first dozen or so to finish. Nowhere near the elite guys but surpassing all of my wildest expectations. I had just completed my greatest ride ever.

During the stage I had spoken to quite a few of the people riding L'Étape du Tour the following day. They would all proudly boast that they were riding stage 20 of the Tour de France. We had the perfect comeback:

'I've cycled the whole of the Tour.'

Distance covered: 131km
Time: 8hrs 11 mins
Elevation gain: 6,209m
Calories burned: 6,926
Highest speed: 85kph

SOMEBODY BEING BETTER THAN YOU ISN'T FAILURE. NOT TAKING A CHANCE AND NOT GIVING SOMETHING A REAL GO IS FAILURE. SUCCESS IS IN THE TRYING – Dame Kelly Holmes

THE JOURNEY IS THE DESTINATION – Anon

REMEMBER TO CELEBRATE MILESTONES AS YOU PREPARE FOR THE ROAD AHEAD – Nelson Mandela

Chapter 22

21 July 2019, Paris
Celebrate

A YEAR before, I had set myself a challenge. As it transpired it would become dual challenges, combining two of the biggest passions of my life. I promised myself that I would cycle the entire route of the Tour de France in 2019 and that I would write a book telling my story.

As I laid out the book, I started to focus not on how I would write but more on how I would cycle the Tour. This in itself automatically led to the format of the book. I have some experience with success and related theories but I needed more help and I needed to simplify my jumbled thoughts. I did a lot of research online and spoke to a lot of people that I look up to and who have been successful in their own right. As this organically came to fruition my focus drifted away from writing a book and I concentrated on one goal at a time. My priority was to complete Le Loop and fulfil a lifelong dream.

I ploughed all of my energies into being successful in just the one challenge, sometimes at a cost (or benefit) to my career. One year on, I was leaving Rambouillet on the final processional leg that took us on to the Champs-Élysées in Paris. It happened to be my birthday.

Getting to Rambouillet was long and arduous and well worth it. I had my first real drink in nigh on two months on top of Val Thorens and I would have been happy staying there long into the night. But France is a big country and we had nine hours of transfer to get through. Uncomfortable sleep on a coach, two to three hours kip in an airport hotel with a large pancake-fuelled breakfast, before a further five hours to get us to the beginning of the stage. By the time we departed I had no idea what time of day it was and I was in a little bit of a daze.

Emily gave her final briefing as we lined up with our slightly frayed Le Loop kit. Each jersey and bib shorts combination told its own story of epic mountain climbs, fast sprints, long days in the saddle and the odd little accident.

The uniforms held firm to amble the final 78km over a rolling, gentle terrain into the heart of the capital city.

My Garmin notes would show that it was very much a stop-start slow ride to complete the adventure. Perhaps we were fatigued or maybe we were savouring the last chance to ride alongside some awesome new friends. I knew I was taking in every single moment and I didn't want it to end. Emily was on high alert and warned us against stupidity or loss of concentration.

It turns out that historically the last day of Le Loop had proven to be the most dangerous stage of all. Riders are exhausted and their bodies are shutting down, in the knowledge that one relatively easy stretch (in comparison to what had gone on before) was all that stood between them and reaching their goal. Minds tend to wander and bodies tend to switch off, causing puerile little incidents and final-hurdle mishaps. Not on Emily's watch.

Her last order before we set off was to award her final prized arrows to Eric and Benoit, our two French riders and fully deserving of the honour. Mine was safely packed away in my holdall and ready to be framed and hung on my glory wall at home. I had another reward in mind for completing my journey. Given that Trigger was broken and not suitable for her intended use, I planned on painting her yellow and hanging her on the wall in my office. But first a celebratory trundle into the city was on the cards.

I was pleased to be the one who started the celebrations. We only had the one feed stop and I had paid for freshly baked chocolate eclairs for everyone, including riders and support crew. Sarah had done an excellent job in sourcing them for me. Why should I be surprised? Le Loop had a bottle of champagne for me and the peloton was informed that it was my birthday.

I couldn't think of a better way to celebrate it, riding into Paris with an inspirational group of people for a brilliant cause. Eric also got one final ice cream in before the day was out. It was nice for me to be able to give back a little with the cakes.

Cycling through Paris wasn't a great deal of fun. It was stifling hot and impossible to get a rhythm. Being a Sunday, the traffic wasn't too bad but the lights were interminable. Every 100m or so we would pull to a halt and unclip from our pedals. The lack of sleep and tiny hangover affected my patience and I didn't enjoy the nervous trek through the suburbs and into the built-up urban parade of a capital city.

For us Loopers, the roads were not closed so we finished the Tour with a truncated version of the final stage. Unable to do multiple laps of the city centre we headed straight to the Eiffel Tower for champagne and photos. It was quite bizarre. One minute the tower was a target looming in the distance, a focus of our dreams for three event-filled weeks, and the next we were in her shadow being congratulated on a humongous achievement.

I was trying to take everything in. In that moment, I was in a daze. I was floating around, unsure what to do with myself. Family and friends had gathered in anticipation of our arrival and our numbers multiplied. There were tears, screeches and the popping of champagne corks as the realisation of what we had completed sunk in. Not for me.

I was lost and a little bitter that my team celebration was being ruined. I hadn't invited any family to be there. It was selfish, but it was my goal and my journey and I wanted to savour it with my team-mates. One minute I was cycling through the city streets with Carmen, Kelly, Nick, Eric and a few others, chatting away and discussing what we would do post Tour. The next we had turned a corner and they would no longer be a part of my life.

The Eiffel Tower suddenly emerged into view. We pulled to a halt, Stuart's family were playing bagpipes and everyone was engulfed by family members. My journey with these awesome people had abruptly come to an end. I didn't want their families to be a part of this. I wanted to celebrate with my team-mates before we let them in. I didn't know what to do with myself.

A guardian angel came to my rescue in the form of Kate from the Le Loop team. I was wandering around like a lost child, not sure what to do with myself. Carmen was kissing her husband and Kelly the same with his wife. In a matter of seconds, I didn't exist to them. Kate gave me a sense of order and took some photos of me, ensuring that my black eye was prominent in front of the monument.

She organised all of the team for a large group photo and I restored my equilibrium. I pulled myself together and managed to grab some pics with a few of my friends, but nowhere near enough. This was a defining moment in my life and it was almost time to party like it was a new millennium. It was a bit of an anticlimax. I didn't want it to end. I had said as much when Katy the physio had interviewed me for a quick video before the stage start.

'Right then Ceri, what are your thoughts on the last day into Paris?'

'Mixed emotions. Deliriously happy. Terribly sad. I could ride for another week and, big secret, given that it's my birthday today this will probably be the greatest birthday of my life.'

'Oh. My. God.' Katy was incredibly generous and ran off to return with a banana with 'Happy Birthday' written on it. Like the whole of the team, she was something special and it reinforced the knowledge that I would have achieved nothing without them. I'll never forget that little gesture.

I genuinely didn't want Le Loop to end. I would have thought after all of those miles that I would be sick of my bike, but if I had the choice, in that moment I would have set off to do it all over again. I had to settle for losing another sprint, this time on the Champs-Élysées.

The final moment of our Tour was to make it on to the famous tree-lined street that leads to the imposing Arc de Triomphe, to do battle with the scatter-gun traffic and that one last effort. The road was uneven, with gentle cobbles. Have I mentioned that I hate cobbles? These weren't too bad but neither did they make the ride comfortable.

I had set off with a fast group of guys, finally confident in my abilities as a rider and, in no time at all, we were racing for the ultimate time. I was left in their wake. I had nothing left to give and I couldn't compete. I was empty. Physically and emotionally. I couldn't have cared less because I had cycled the whole of the Tour de France. Maybe I wouldn't have been able to do another three weeks after all. My saddle sores would have objected at least. That was the final moment of our Tour in reality, apart from a short whip through the city streets to the hotel. This time I was able to take it all in.

I made sure I had plenty of photos under the Arc de Triomphe. In the middle of the thousands of cars that pass around it I recognised the brilliance of Carmen, Eric, Stuart and so many others and my bitterness subsided. I was no longer jealous of their normal lives and their own everyday realities. I was caught up in the moment of one epic adventure.

A year before I had finally set out to emulate a hero in Geraint Thomas. I had embarked on a journey to cycle the Tour de France and fulfil a dream. Not only that, I wanted to ride it entirely substance free and be able to say 'up yours Lance', proving that cycling is and can be a clean sport. In taking on a seemingly impossible task I wanted to inspire others by proving that we can do whatever we want in life and our only limitations are our imaginations. My goal was small in comparison to those of other greater people, but it was important to me. Cycling Le Loop would go on to change my life.

In that year leading up to Le Loop, I laid out my own personal plan for success. I utilised most of my tools and theories to help me achieve the first part of my dream.

My theories are fluid and continually evolve as I try and grow as a human being. Experience has taught me that my seven (and a bit) rungs on my personal ladder help me achieve success. I would like to think they may work for you as well.

A day after our Tour was completed, I sat outside a bar near the Sacre Coeur, a refreshing beer in hand satiating a thirst that had built over 21 days of hard slog around France. The artists were engrossed in painting their portraits;

caricatures of tourists and copies of the masters. I had a small hangover from the night before. I reflected on my progress so far.

How had I fared? Did my theories really hold up?

1. Dream Big and Commit

This was the easy part. Anyone can have a dream. Putting together a plan and maintaining a process to see it through to realisation is the difficult part. Nevertheless, I think my dream was pretty epic and I think I committed to it.

I set myself the goal of cycling the entire route of the 2019 version of the Tour de France. I followed that up with a twin goal of documenting my experience and writing a wildly successful book. I couldn't fulfil the second part of my dream without the first, so I booked Le Loop and committed myself to one life-changing journey. That set a deadline and provided a definite focus for 12 months of my life.

As it turned out it provided a focus for over two years of my life. I didn't maintain epic writing habits during Le Loop. I failed to keep a journal or write a blog. I only managed to make a few brief notes on my Garmin at the end of each day and I updated social media just four times. That was with the sole aim of generating sponsorship rather than storing memories or preparing for a prize-winning tome.

Seven months after my Tour finished, I was out of work and ready to write my story when two things happened. Firstly, I was offered another job I just couldn't refuse and, secondly, coronavirus swept the world. The new career allowed me to work from home and my hours were reduced so I quickly made the decision to stick to my success matrix. I committed to writing the book and devoted three hours every day for four months so that I could realise my entire dream.

I followed my rules. I committed myself to my twin dreams and I set myself a deadline for completion.

I succeeded in cycling the Tour de France and that memory will last forever.

I finished writing my book. Whether it is any good is up to you to decide. At the very least I have a permanent reminder of the greatest time of my life and proof that my theories for success have worked for me.

2. Preparation. Preparation. Preparation

My preparation was slow to get off the ground. The beginning of 2019 was a tumultuous period for me, both professionally and with my training.

I was able to push through because I had clear goals and a solid plan. I maintained my epic habits and drew on the experience from many years of working life and sporting efforts. I may not have reached levels of superstardom in my life but I believed that it had prepared me to deliver in following in the footsteps of Geraint and beyond.

I had a superb bank of training from my triathlon and marathon-running experience which will always stand me in good stead. I also had a more varied professional experience than most, which allowed me to remain level-headed and determined throughout the whole thing.

I never got too excited when I achieved small victories and I did not become too despondent when I suffered setbacks. Emotionally my professional experiences were a drain on my energies, but that is part and parcel of life's great tapestry and the greater the effort the sweeter the victory. As the year progressed, I was able to get some great mileage under my belt and some quality tempo and cross-training sessions.

As July neared, I had prepared as well as I could have and this stood me in great stead. At no stage during the Tour did I have any doubts about cycling the entire distance. That was because I had planned to succeed and had put the work in beforehand. I had many doubts over my abilities as a rider and whether or not I was worthy of cycling with everyone on the Tour. Ultimately, I knew I would prevail.

3. Live and Love

I can state, without any shadow of doubt, that I lived for the Tour and I loved every moment of it.

I loved the process of training. I loved lying in bed until the early hours dreaming of scaling those Alpine peaks. I loved waking in the middle of the night worrying about my sentence structure or factual accuracies of the Tour once I had started writing. Every waking moment for the whole of the year was focused on completing a goal and fitting it in around my life. Cycling Le Loop took over my life and became my *raison d'être*. I loved every second of it.

Even when I hit the tarmac. It was all part of the rich experience of being a Tour de France cyclist.

In the end, cycling Le Loop was not something I dreamed of. It was the dream that kept me awake at night.

4. Hard Work and Resilience

Did I work hard? I think cycling up to ten hours a day for three weeks and then spending time being professional by cleaning my bike, stretching regularly and fuelling correctly answers that. I believe training for 15 to 20 hours a week on top of working a 60-hour week is testament to the fact that this goal was achieved with a little bit of effort. As for resilience? I have experience with that.

I believe that my experiences in both Ironman Nice and especially Ironman Tallinn provided superb preparation for some of the mishaps that would come my way in France. On reflection, failing my first year at college as a juvenile may not be the cataclysmic disaster I have frequently punished myself for. I had to rebuild my life, and pretty quickly, and I learned to focus on new goals and make a success of them. The proof would always be in the pudding.

I didn't want stage 16 and the crash to define my Tour. I don't think it did. When I look back on my experience the first thoughts that come to mind are: powering up La Planche des Belles Filles, battling every other climb that took us above the clouds and even doing my best to stay upright on the cobblestones. I have an overwhelming sense of warmth and happiness when I remember the camaraderie and the discussions and laughter around the dinner table each night. The support and inspiration from my team-mates and the staff of Le Loop brings great satisfaction to my heart and I am privileged to have been part of this adventure.

The fact remains that I did crash. It was a hefty one. The accident has impacted my life a little. I have been laid up with back problems in the year since my Tour finished and I know I had suffered a delayed concussion. Nothing bad enough to stop me riding my bike or going to work, but severe enough to make me take it easy for long periods.

I keep going and I keep turning the pedals, one revolution after another. I guess that is resilience.

I demonstrated that by finishing stage 16 and the rest of the Tour.

5. Motivation

I listed three elements that are key to my motivation and they all worked for me in abundance. Even in overcoming obstacles and maintaining resilience.

Throughout Le Loop I held a vision of me cycling on the Champs-Élysées, of having my photo taken with my bike in front of the Eiffel Tower and of celebrating hard on a boat on the river Seine. I even had post-event dreams of framing a few pictures and painting Trigger and hanging her on my wall. These images stayed with me throughout and provided light in times of darkness and a focus which I would not let go of.

I believe in focusing on success and being able to see yourself celebrating that success. It may not be for everyone but it works for me. It provides clarity to a dream and a very positive reason to just keep going. It worked during the Tour. Right now, I am dreaming of being interviewed on *BBC Breakfast* by Dan Walker and Naga Munchetty, celebrating the launch of this book. Naga is impervious to my flirting but she loves the book. Susanna Reid is cross that I didn't do her show first.

I also believe that Love and Rage are the two greatest motivators on this planet. They can be intertwined at times but we need to be able to tap into these emotions to allow us to prevail.

I easily tapped into rage as I approached the base of Prat d'Albis and it fuelled my desire to complete the stage. There was no doubt in my mind, but I exaggerated a flimsy feeling and used its energy to climb mountains. Literally. I am not comfortable with rage because I hold no hatred in my bones, but learning to tap into rage and then just as easily release it is a great skill to develop. Love is a stronger emotion and provides greater long-lasting power.

Throughout my experience I was riding for love in many forms. I was riding for the sheer love of being in a happy place on my bike. I was riding for my own ego, which is a powerful force in my life. I love myself and I wanted to be able to boast about my achievements. Funnily enough I don't need to now because I am very comfortable in my skin and I know what I have done. Plus, very few people understand exactly what it is I achieved and that includes people within the sporting and cycling communities. But those who rode Le Loop know and that satisfies my ego.

Oh, who am I kidding? I cycled the Tour de bloody France and I am going to brag about it until the day I die. There is an old triathlon joke: how can you spot an Ironman at a party? Don't worry they will tell you all about it by the end of the night. I fear a Tour de France finisher may be a little worse.

Above all I was riding to make my niece and nephews proud of me and to inspire them to be the very best version of themselves. Which conveniently leads on to …

6. Include and Inspire

Inspiring those nearest and dearest to me has made me a better man and more importantly helped me succeed.

Not having children of my own means that my niece and nephews are constantly at the forefront of my mind and in everything I do. I want the world to be a better place for them. I want them to grow up as confident, diligent, hard-working, honest and successful human beings. The only way I know how to help them best is by setting a good example. I also want them to love me as I do them. Inspiring those munchkins has changed my life for the better.

I also talk about including and being included because no man is an island. I played my best-ever level of football 30 years ago with the best team that I was in. I have achieved my greatest successes at work when I have been a part of a great team. Even in my solo events like triathlon I have been supported and aided by great people around me: mechanics who have looked after my bikes; family who blindly support me no matter what; my brother who relents and comes out for long bike rides; and friends who just listen to my crap.

In this challenge I was supported by the greatest team imaginable. I could not have cycled the Tour without the amazing event that is Le Loop. The organising team are second to none. The cyclists I got to share the road with were inspirational. For three weeks all of them were family. I included them in my goal and we all succeeded. I especially benefited from their support and immense generosity and I like to think I gave back on occasion as well. Without the group of people that I rode with I am not sure if I would have achieved everything that I had dreamed of. Thank you to Carmen, Eric, Stuart, Andy, Rich, Rich, Kenny, Kelly, Nick D, Handsome Nick, the Canadians and their funny accents, Deano, Rhys, Jackie, Wim and so many others.

For three weeks they were family and I am a better man for knowing them all.

Above all I felt included and a part of something bigger than my dream. I was a part of the William Wates Memorial Trust and we were changing lives for the better. With all of this behind me, how could I fail?

7. Celebrate Hard

I have everlasting memories of my adventure. I have a bike hanging on the wall in my home office. I have a framed photo of myself in front of the Eiffel Tower in the glory corner of my living room. I have a brilliant poster from the *English Cyclist* which shows the profile of our entire journey around France. Above all I partied into the early hours in Paris with superb company to celebrate our success.

After the euphoria died down, I would go on to suffer a big exhaustion in the weeks that followed. I wasn't helped by not having an everyday road bike to ride, given that mine was being inspected by my insurance company. I was lost without the daily focus and the exercise.

I knew earlier in the year that I had outgrown my job and succeeding in this one goal gave me the courage to embark on a new career and to finally start writing another book.

As I started focusing on Le Loop, it came to take over my life. It filled me with a desire that my career had long since lost. It made me question what was important in my life and what I wanted out of it.

I know that I am capable of great things. But I struggle to decide on what I really want out of life and what I want to do. Once I commit to something, I have learned to channel my energies and I usually succeed these days.

My lack of passion for my career meant that I was in danger of failing. That job eventually reached a natural denouement as a result of setting my sights on cycling into Paris. Looking at a balance sheet and dealing with the day-to-day routines of my team became mundane and bland compared to the greatness I had experienced. It no longer provided the thrill that kept me awake at night. It became difficult to maintain my hunger and hold my attention. I gradually developed a new challenge in itself. I had to decide what I was going to do when I grew up.

By the end of the year, I would finish with the company, satisfied at a job well done. I think we parted on good terms. I had made them a lot of money and they had provided me with a good living in return. I was very nervous about what 2020 would hold. Little did I know at the time quite how dramatic that year would become. It was quite the contrast to my year of adventure and personal growth.

I took on a six-month contract that led up to the summer months, which was incredibly rewarding. The effects of the Tour were still lingering. I was lost at sea having discovered a newer and better version of myself and for a while I believed that if I could cycle Le Loop I could do anything I put my mind to. Maybe I can, but I accept that is a mindset which needs to be channelled correctly.

At the time of writing, my struggle is centred on how to focus my abilities and desires. It's time for a new career. I have no idea in what field and with another lockdown looming I will no doubt have some time on my hands to discover a new professional goal. I signed up for another Ironman race and I am still frustrated that even though cycling the Tour is arguably my greatest achievement, it is never recognised as such. Joe Public is far more impressed with finishing a triathlon in one day compared to cycling over 21 stages of the toughest race on earth. I am comfortable with that, to a degree.

These days I nod politely and say, 'Yes, L'Étape du Tour,' when people do not understand what I undertook. I know what I did and so too do the 50-odd Loopers who I had the pleasure of riding with for three weeks. We have a bond that is unspoken and cannot be broken. The roads of France will do that to you and the road never lies.

On reflection I loved France. I have visited a few times before and had the pleasure of working in Paris for a couple of months in the mid-nineties, but Le Loop showed me aspects of the country that are not available to the naked eye.

I loved the quality of the roads. I loved riding in a country that celebrates cycling rather than seeing us as a nuisance or hindrance to their journey. It was an incredible pleasure to have juggernauts patiently waiting for a gap to pass a peloton, without so much as a harsh word or hand gesture. Just a friendly wave and the occasional 'vive le Tour'.

I marvelled at the variety of the breathtaking scenery and it was a delight to be introduced to villages, towns and cities that would never have been on my radar. Too many to mention but the warmth and hospitality was second to none. I wished that I had taken more of the country in rather than focusing on the road. But I was lost in a bubble which became an addiction.

I had come to fall in love with the country and the country seemed to appreciate my humour. My shirt with the words 'Pain is just a French word for bread' was well received. Many a time on an uphill struggle a car would slow down and shout, 'Great jersey. Bonne chance.' I will certainly head back to France sometime soon and quite likely with Le Loop in the near future.

I cannot recommend Le Loop enough. Everything about the event is superb and of the highest order. The charity, the organisation, the tiny details, the support, the signs, the food, the lead rider, the physios and so much more. I talk of including and inspiring as a means of motivation, but being included and inspired by Sarah, Kate, Emily, Rick and the rest of their team meant that I succeeded.

Because of the Le Loop team I was able to ride in the footsteps of giants for three weeks and I was able to feel what it is like to be a grand tour cyclist. Few other sports can provide that experience for a mere fan. That is the beauty of cycling. Every day we can race on the same roads as heroes.

I know that I will never be as talented as a Geraint Thomas and I am as likely to cycle in the real Tour as I am to play for Swansea City. They still keep telling me to stop calling. I was 52 when I rode into Paris and I will never get any quicker. For three epic weeks I got to experience the thrill of cycling the Tour de France. I got to experience what those titans go through on a daily basis and I got to ride with the gods, as a god, for a brief period in my life.

I may not have stood on a podium but cresting the Galibier, La Planche des Belles Filles, the Izoard, Iseran, Peyresourde, the Tourmalet and Val Thoren, gave me an insight into their lives and I envied them their glorious torture. For three brief weeks I lived the dream. And I did it clean. Despite a bad crash, some resulting headaches and constant sore muscles, fatigue and laziness I took no more than a vitamin tablet. No EPO. No Tramadol. No steroids. Not even an ibuprofen or paracetamol. Solely *pain y agua* (bread and water). We proved that the Tour can be ridden clean and I proved I could succeed without taking any shortcuts.

Maybe, just maybe, the 18-year-old me can now forgive himself for mistakes he made during one failed year of computer science. I think it could be time to let that go and use it as fuel for another challenge.

It may also be time to forgive Lance Armstrong and his cheating cohorts. I have proven that the Tour can be cycled without performance-enhancing medication and by rights I should be entitled to scream, 'Up yours Lance.' When it comes down to it, I don't have the stomach to kick those guys while they are down. Their legacies and footnotes in history will do that for them.

I have made mistakes and I have cheated in the distant past. I have learned to forgive myself and more importantly learned the lessons from those errors. I also had friends and family who stood by me in my darkest hours, so perhaps I should pay some of that same forgiveness forward. If I can move on then maybe I should stop using the drugs cheats as a form of motivation and instead thank them for the inadvertent inspiration.

I reinforced the message that hard work and honesty does pay the rent. For that I am grateful to the Le Loop team. If you get the opportunity to ride a leg of this magnificent event, snap it up. It will change your life. I owe a huge debt of gratitude to Le Loop and I will never forget what they did for us. I hope I won't because I plan on going back to ride with them again sometime soon. They were, and are, epic. They were, and are, personal heroes and they have inspired me to be the best I can be. My hope is that I may have inspired one or two others to reach for the stars and take on their own monstrous challenge.

I was delighted that on my first visit to my sister's house after finishing the whole thing, my niece and nephew were riding their bikes. They wanted to emulate their uncle in the same way that he had wanted to emulate Geraint Thomas, Julian Alaphillipe, Bernard Hinault and Greg LeMond. That warmed the cockles of my soul. It provided me with a small measure of achievement, knowing the little things we do make a difference.

With my relative fulfilment in mind this begs the question that if you have made it this far through my journey, what is it that you want to do?

What is it that you are passionate about? Will you decide on what you really want to do? If so, set yourself a deadline and then work out a plan for how you will achieve your goal. If I can do this, then so can you. And when you get there don't forget to reward yourself and celebrate.

The way I see it, if you are not living life on the edge then you are taking up too much space. There is no time like the present to be the person that you were meant to be. Maybe you should spend ten minutes filling out my Success Matrix at the back of this book. You never know, you may just surprise yourself with what you can do. I know I did.

And I earned my reward of a great big birthday party blow-out in Paris. We celebrated hard that night on the river Seine.

I have promised myself that I will buy a new bike if this book is ever published, but if it isn't, I will still be left with a fantastic memory. Ideally, I am dreaming of the same bike that I finished the Tour with. I think I deserve a little treat.

Even though cycling the entire Tour (without any performance-enhancers, Lance) doesn't get the reaction I would have hoped for, I am still very happy in myself. I know what I have achieved. Those that rode with me know what we accomplished. We became members of an exclusive club and I couldn't have asked for much more. I achieved almost everything I ever dreamed of. Happy birthday to me.

Stages:	21
Kilometres:	3,516
Total elevation:	55,717m (that is six times the height of Mount Everest)
Steepest gradient:	La Planche des Belles Filles – 25%
Longest stage:	244km
Total riding time:	174hrs (twice as long as Geraint)
Saddle sores:	5 minor ones
Calories burned:	139,457
Crashes:	1
Loan bikes used:	2
Punctures:	3
Croissants consumed:	123 approximately
Total funds raised:	£350k for the William Wates Memorial Trust

1 EPIC ADVENTURE

SUNTANS FADE, MEMORIES LAST FOREVER

Epilogue

'HOLD THE lift!' came the shout.

The Tour was over. Our epic adventure had come to its conclusion. Apart from a huge celebration whilst floating down the river Seine that night, I was now lost. I didn't know what I should do, both with myself and to a degree with my life. I had fulfilled a lifelong dream and there were no arrows pointing me in the direction of what to do next.

Where would Sarah be when I needed to decide on my next career move? She had controlled everything marvellously over the past three weeks. I may not have shown my appreciation, being wrapped up in my own narcissistic little quest, but she was superb and she had been our rock. Help me please Sarah. What do I do now? Where are the arrows for me to follow?

I had cycled my final kilometre. Not just in France but as it would transpire for the rest of the year. It took my specialist bike insurers more than five months to replace the broken frame on Trigger. I had to adapt from cycling at least five times a week for the best part of a year to barely at all in the following six months. That was quite the come-down. I needed Sarah and her arrows to help with that. Emily came into my head. Turn the pedals one at a time. As it is on a bike, so it is in life. I held the lift. My heart sank.

I moved aside and pressed up against my holdall and carry-on bags. No souvenirs to bloat them just yet. It was tight. Enough room for two skinny cyclists but not enough for all their equipment as well. Did I need to have packed all those energy bars and spare shirts? I made room for one more and he squeezed into the snug gap. Sardines would have complained that it was snugger than a tight embrace, or tighter than a tin of, well, sardines. It was cramped and we were up close and personal.

'Cheers mate.' It was Buddy. The last person I wanted to see. I was euphoric. I was exhausted. I was emotionally lost and I was in dire need of a hot shower. I didn't have the patience for fatigued and pointless small talk.

'I'm spent Ceri. I left everything out on the road this year.'

I looked right through him. Incredulity writ large in my eyes. *The hell you have. You only rode half the Tour and if we were racing you would have been out of the whole thing by stage four. You're full of it.* It was what I thought in that instant. I fear my eyes may have given my true feelings away. I looked to the floor, sheepish and ashamed at my own selfish musings. I blamed the fatigue.

I considered what we had achieved. I had cycled over 3,500km and ascended more than 55,000m around France. This guy had his struggles. Maybe he wasn't as well-prepared as I was. Maybe he was a little complacent. Maybe he was fighting a battle I knew nothing about. Who was I to judge him?

He found it tough going, but he kept on fighting. That was worthy of recognition in itself, even if we didn't always see eye to eye. He hadn't cycled quite as far as me, yet he had still covered more than 3,200km and he had raised more than £5k for a brilliant and worthy cause. The William Wates Memorial Trust were very grateful for his efforts. That was still a heroic achievement.

I had no right to judge him and I had no idea what struggles he had to face along the way. He certainly didn't need my criticism and I should be better than that. All roads did indeed lead to Paris, no matter which route we took. I took a slow and deep breath and looked him in the eye.

'Well done mate. That was some journey, eh?' and I smiled.

It was indeed one hell of a journey. It had been epic in so many ways. I had cycled every single inch of it. I didn't need to belittle someone else's personal voyage or growth. We were all riding different races in life. I was able to be very comfortable in my skin. Sorry pop psychologists, I like myself even more than I did at the start of this adventure.

I had completed everything I had set out to achieve 12 short months beforehand. An amateur counsellor might call that personal development.

I had cycled the entire route of the 2019 Tour de France.

I hope that might be called a success.

Acknowledgements

SUCCESS IS a team effort and I am indebted to the help and support of so many in my journey. If I have failed to include you, I apologise. There isn't room for everyone by name but don't let that detract from the gratitude I feel for your efforts and unequivocal backing. Here are some key players:

Taela, Kaster and Oliver for being my inspiration. You have made me a better man. Go live your dreams.

Mum, Dad, brother and sister for your unflinching support and for rescuing me whenever I am stranded in the Preseli mountains with yet another mechanical.

Everyone at Le Loop and WWMT for making dreams come true. You change lives for the better.

Tim Rees for being a good friend and telling me that my baby is ugly. I didn't like it. I took on board every word and am very grateful.

Carol Cole and her magic ironing board.

Steve Whiff Richards. I told you I cycled the Tour.

Everyone involved with the British Educational Suppliers Association for your generosity and support.

Elaine, Bev, Doug, Rich, Sheila and Ali whose hard work and professionalism allowed me to take a three-week holiday at a very busy time of year. The business doesn't know how lucky they are to have you.

Every one of the titans who I had the immense pleasure of sharing the road with for three weeks. You have enriched my life in so many ways.

Everyone who donated their hard-earned cash to the WWMT. You have made a massive difference to some vulnerable youngsters.

Finally, to the event known as Le Loop. I urge everyone to get on their bikes and ride and where better to end up than as part of the greatest race on earth:

www.rideleloop.org

Matrix for a Dream

Name: . . . .

Date: . . . .

Passion
What do you want from your life?

What are you passionate about?

1. . . . .
. . . .

What are your values?

2. . . . .
. . . .

If money was no object, what would you set
your heart on?

3. . . . .
. . . .

What do you really want from your goals? Success?
Wealth? Happiness?

4. . . . .
. . . .

What impact will your goal have on yourself and others?

5. . . . .
. . . .

Will it do good in the world? How?

6. . . . .

. . . .

What do you enjoy learning about?

7. . . . .

Commitment

I . . . .
set myself the following goal(s) in life:

8. . . . .

. . . .

9. . . . .

. . . .

I will achieve this dream by the following date:

. . . .

What is your plan?

Write down your plan

10. . . . .

Break it down into small manageable chunks

11. . . . .

. . . .

Sign at the bottom of the next page and make a
commitment to keep it

Visualise your success

Spend ten minutes in a quiet space and picture yourself
achieving your goal

What does it sound like?

12. . . . .

What does it look like?

13. . . . .

How do you feel about it? What are the
  emotions involved?
14. . . . .
  . . . .

What can you hear?
15. . . . .
  . . . .

Who does it affect?
16. . . . .
  . . . .

Other key emotions or feelings.
17. . . . .

Who inspires you?

Can you work with them or seek advice from them?
18. . . . .
  . . . .

How can you emulate them?
19. . . . .

How can you get help from them?
20. . . . .

Who do/will you inspire?

What are their names?
21. . . . .
  . . . .

How will you inspire them?
22. . . . .

How will that make you feel?
23. . . . .

How will they help you in your quest?

24.. . . . .

Who do you love most in the world?

25.. . . . .

What motivates you?

What makes you happy?

26. . . . .

What makes you angry?

27. . . . .

What is the one thing you want from your goal?

28. . . . .

What one image of success will you hold on to?

29.. . . . .

How will you keep going in difficult times?

30.. . . . .

What do you love most in the world?

31. . . . .

What do you dislike most in the world?

32.. . . . .

Celebration

How will you celebrate small victories?

33.. . . . .
. . . .

What are those smaller goals on the road to
overall victory?

34. . . . .

How will you reward yourself for overall success?

35.. . . . .

How does that make you feel?

36. . . . .

What does it look like?

37. . . . .

. . . .

Who will you include?

38.. . . . .

I make this contract with myself to fulfil my goal as outlined above and promise to follow my steps on a pathway to success.

I am awesome. I am capable of achieving anything I set my mind to. I will prove to be brilliant.

Signed: . . . .

Date: . . . .